D1505404

Gift Of Life

by Henri Landwirth

with J.P. Hendricks

Foreword by Walter Cronkite
Afterword by Senator John Glenn

DEDICATION

This book is for my three children - Gary, Greg and Lisa, that they might know me a little better and understand how much I love them, and how important each of them is to my life. It is also for Give Kids the World. Revenues the sale of this book may generate over the years will go to the Give Kids the World Foundation, to help ensure that the children and families who need us will always be served. And finally, dear reader, this book is for you. Thank you for reading it and sharing my life's journey with me. And most of all, thank you for supporting the miracle of Give Kids the World. Without you, the miracles would not be possible.

Foreword

by Walter Cronkite

The modern day is plagued with crimes against humanity, from the more obvious terrorism which has crossed both international boundaries and moral ones, to the offenses against civility which touch our lives at every turn of daily existence. In this mode, we hear much of "values." Politicians in recent years have debased the term by using it to identify whatever sins they wish to accuse the opposition of committing. But "values" still have value as we consider the human condition, and, although unfortunately more often in the breach than the performance, we still honor courage and industriousness and fealty and charity.

And we appreciate the more cosmetic virtues on which we judge our fellow humans–personality and humor.

If these are to be the criteria when we reach the Pearly Gates, I can envision the following scenario when the author of this volume reaches that heavenly portal.

St. Peter: Your name?

Henri Landwirth: Henri Landwirth

St Peter punches up "Landwirth, Henri" on the computer (instructions to producer – we do not know whether this is IBM or Apple compatible.) St. Peter frowns as he ponders the computer read out. He brushes his robe back from his sleeves and attacks the computer keyboard again. This performance will be familiar to any air traveler who has been stricken with fear as the ticket clerk checks his/her reservations.)

St. Peter: How do you spell that name again?

Landwirth: L-a-n-d-w-i-r-t-h, sir.

St. Peter: Well, there seems to be some mistake. This says you were supposed to have been here a long time ago...back in World War II. But we had a lot of people coming in about that time and there could have been a mistake. This record goes on to indicate you were down on Earth a long time after that. And, wait a minute, this goes on another page.

Glory be, Henri – if I may call you that – there seems to be another mistake. You were supposed to have made Saint back in 1986 when you founded Give Kids the World. And all these other good marks. My, my. Wait right here, Saint Henri – I'll send for your escort and you're entitled to a fanfare. I'll send for the trumpeters.

Landwirth: If this is a joke, Peter, I'll get back.

That's the way I think it will be.

I have had the privilege of knowing Henri for a good forty-one years at this writing – and I mean "good." Henri in this volume tells of his business philosophy for pleasing his hotel customers, but that philosophy is also part of his character. In his heart, he wants to serve and this has become the personality that envelopes you when first you meet him. As I shook his hand for the first time in the lobby of his new hotel in Cocoa Beach, I felt a warmth that has blessed our relationship for all these decades.

And that part of my scenario in which Henri threatens to "get back" at the august figure he now familiarly calls "Peter" also is taken from real life. As you'll read here, he and the astronauts and other of his close friends played practical jokes with almost juvenile fervor, and when Henri was the goat, he always promised to "get back". And he usually did.

I thought my then five-year-old son, Chip, should share in the history that was being made with almost every launch from Cape Canaveral and I took him to Cocoa Beach for a couple of the launches. Henri and his staff virtually adopted him and he them to the point that I was beginning to suffer the pangs of irrational jealousy. They gave him the run of the place and surfeited him with cookies, popcorn and other forbidden delights. Henri maintained that they never had a problem finding him – they just followed the trail of crumbs along its circuitous course through the lobby, past the pool, back to the lobby and back to the pool.

It was a number of years later before I had another opportunity to visit a Landwirth hostelry in company with my son, by now, of course, considerably beyond the toddling stage. We checked in, the clerk told us Mr. Landwirth was not immediately available but would join us shortly, and sent us around to our room. It was a far smaller room than we had expected. In fact it seemed barely larger than a broom closet – and a broom closet it closely resembled for stacked in one corner was a large collection of various-sized brooms, mops, pails, sponges, cleaning rags.

Timed perfectly for the call of complaint he expected from me, Henri walked into the room, beaming his cheery welcome.

"I thought we would need these with Chip here," he said. "My, how he's grown."

And then he opened a door which connected with an elaborate suite, decorated with balloons and streamer, food and drink heaped on every horizontal surface, and a large sign:

"Welcome home, Chip."

Henri gives unstintingly of himself in whatever task he undertakes. And he goes far beyond the extra mile when a friend is in need. Since he seems to have embraced the whole human race, this largesse is beyond our ability to count, particularly since so much of his help goes unremarked by him.

Except for Give Kids the World!

He shouts its virtues from the rooftops, uses every means of public communication to advertise its existence and thus build ever greater support for it. With that devotion to this country that he discovered as a poor and wounded immigrant, he has tapped the spirit of volunteerism that he found here and touched the heart of corporate America with a cause that represents the grandest proof of the values that Henri Landwirth encompasses.

–Walter Cronkite
October, 1996

INTRODUCTION

The modern world is filled with miraculous happenings. Unfortunately, today's world is also a very busy place filled with many distractions. Most of us race through life so quickly that we fail to recognize the miracles that guide each and every life on this planet.

I am writing this book for my three wonderful children: Gary, Greg and Lisa. It is my hope that they will read it and learn things about me which I have not been able to put into words to them before. It is partly because of my total love for my parents and the devastation that consumed me when I lost them, that I may have become a more distant parent to my own children than I ever wished to be. To depend on anyone as much as I had depended on my parents, to love anyone with that depth of soul and heart, was too much vulnerability. Not for the person being loved, but for the person giving the love. I realize now that I may have quietly encouraged emotional distance from my children to protect them from the pain I experienced, first by losing my father, and then, by my mother's senselessly tragic death. I am proud of my three children beyond all expectation, and love them with the deepest love that can ever live within a father's heart.

I am also writing this book to help fund a modern day miracle called Give Kids the World, an organization devoted to terminally ill children and their families. I will tell you wonderful stories of how over 100 American businesses and corporations donated services and goods to build a village for these special children unlike any other in the world. How these same companies continue to participate in Give Kids the World without the support of lengthy legal contracts. This miraculous place was built on a handshake and a prayer and continues to operate on this most special of business arrangements.

I remember in moments, and that is the way I have written this book. Many of the stories, particularly from my childhood, I have never told before.

My life began in Europe, and I will tell you of the horrible pain I suffered in the labor and concentration camps of Nazi Germany, of the almost unbearable agony of losing both parents to the Holocaust, and of the year following the war when I sought nothing but vengeance in an effort to soothe my hate-filled heart. These stories are painful for me to write and they will be painful for you to read, but I ask you to read each and every word, because even amidst this despair, I witnessed many miracles, and I will share many of them with you.

After the war, I came to America as an uneducated immigrant who could not even speak English. I will tell you the story of my life as I struggled to earn a living and become a part of this wonderful country. Like millions of others, my first image of America was the Statue of Liberty and the promise of her words:

Give me your tired, your poor,
Your huddled masses, yearning to breathe free.

In America, I found truth to those words. Opportunities unavailable anywhere else on earth were open to every person, regardless of where a person was born, or to which social class his family belonged. In America, there was no class system that prevented me from aspiring to my dreams. There were no closed borders where uniformed guards could demand to see my papers and detain me at their whim. There was only opportunity, real opportunity, which allowed anyone who was willing to start at the bottom and work hard to make a success of their life. When I was a busboy and a night clerk, I did not dream of someday owning hotels, but in America, this miracle happened.

Because of the pain of my early life, I have a measure by which to compare the joys available in this country. I wish each American could have such a means of comparison that would never again allow a single person to take what we have in America for granted. I find it difficult to put into words what this great country means to me. Where else but America could a person like me have an opportunity to meet heads of state, to become lifetime friends and business partners with America's first astronauts, and most of all to build a dream called Give Kids the World? Where else but America?

I will also detail my experiences with the Mercury astronauts and those exciting early days at Cape Canaveral. And then I will tell you, dear reader, the story of Give Kids the World, the reason for this book. The place that proves to me each and every day that miracles really happen and are happening even now.

Thank you for reading this book and for helping Give Kids the World. Proceeds from the sale of this book are being donated to Give Kids the World. By purchasing this book, you help the dreams of terminally ill children come true.

My prayer for each of you is that your eyes will be open to the wondrous happenings of your own life, and that you, too, come to believe in miracles.

With Margot, my twin sister, 1931

PART I

The Holocaust

Those who cannot remember the past are condemned to repeat it.
—Santayana [1896]

Part I: From the Ashes

He looks around in despair,
Barbed-wire madness everywhere.
He turns his gaze to the air,
No escape is waiting there.
If there's God, does He care?
Is there peace anywhere?

Too sad to cry, beyond all pain
Hunger and thirst drive him insane.
He looks within, finds nothing there
Soul-filled smoke fills the air.
His parents gone, his sister lost;
What else can this madness cost?

Control is gone, souls are bound
Into an endless night without sound–
His time to join the ceaseless caravan
Comes without purpose to any man.
The gun is raised at forest's edge,
Instead of death comes a single pledge...

And run he does, and disappears
Still held captive to his fears.
The war around him rages on;
He sits and waits to be set upon–
His fingers trace the mud-filled ground;
In a world at war, can peace be found?

Part II: Revenge and Resurrection

The wheel has turned, the child sees,
And points to the creators of his miseries.
Their hatred cannot touch him now;
The guilty swear they don't know how
Such horrors could have happened anyway...
His ears do not hear a single word they say

"An eye for an eye," the Bible said,
But he has no joy with vengeance fed,
Only the memories of his lost and dead.
His parents voices whisper still within his head.
He finds no comfort in the softest bed;
No bandage to heal a heart so bled.

Finally the child lays down his cross.
Night has come, he is still lost.
Mama and Papa, victims of the Holocaust,
Cannot be found now at any cost...
But rumor says his mirrored twin
May be a search that he can win.

If it is true, she is alive,
May slumbering God open his eyes.
The journey moves from town to town;
There is no army that can stop him now.
His sibling is lost, she must be found–
He listens and hears a whistling sound...

A child's game and the twins unite
A drop of sun into darkest night
They mourn together, vow to take flight
They cannot stay where wrong was right.
America beckons with Lady Liberty's light–
Return of control is finally in sight.

CHAPTER 1

We are healed of suffering only by experiencing it to the fullest.
–Marcel Proust [1913]

There is a picture at the Holocaust museum in South Florida that has a child, a boy of six or so, standing in front of a soldier with a rifle pointed at him. He is dressed in a pitiful beret, and he is wearing a coat which ends just above his bare knees. He looks as if he just came from school.

The child has his hands raised above his head. His mother is next to him. She has one hand raised, and one is reaching out for the boy. The child has tears on both cheeks; the mother's eyes are filled with something much worse than tears. The soldier is smiling, as if posing for the picture. The single word below the picture tells the story: *Arrest.*

****

Tattooed in faded blue ink, on the inside of my left forearm is the number B4343. It is a permanent reminder of the many horrors perpetrated by Nazi Germany against humanity, and a personal reminder that I live on borrowed time. For the last 52 years of my life, most of it is borrowed. I never thought that I would live through the time when I was a teenager. From age thirteen to eighteen my life was not my own. The experience of those terrible years in the camps has shaped all that has come after.

I see life differently from someone who has not seen life's dark side. Moments are precious, every moment, and because of what I have experienced, I know and appreciate this.

I was born in Antwerp, Belgium on March 7, 1927. My family moved to Poland in 1930, before my third birthday. My father was born there, and he believed the family would have more opportunity for success in Poland than in Belgium. The Nazi party was founded in 1930, but Europe's political climate had yet to turn extreme, and there seemed no more risk to our family in Poland than we faced anywhere else. This would change dramatically in the years that followed.

For my first thirteen years, I was Henri, the son of Max and Fanny Landwirth, when B4343 became my identity.

In the five years that followed, I was shuffled from labor camps to concentration camps, one after the other, from Plaszow, to Ostrowitz, to Auschwitz-Birkenau, to Matthausen, to Gusen, to an underground place without a name. I saw, heard and experienced man's inhumanity to man firsthand. The scope of the devastation witnessed from one day to the next was beyond a normal person's imagination, certainly beyond the understanding of a child.

I begin the story of my life here for two primary reasons. First, because it was in the camps that I temporarily lost all feelings of love, hope and compassion, replacing those life-sustaining emotions with life-draining hatred, a quest for vengeance, and a deep seated numbness. And second, and most importantly, because it was in the adverse soil of the concentration camps that a miraculous seed of faith and love was planted and took root, although I was unaware of this then.

My experiences in the camps left me blinded by my hatred, by a need to take some action, any action, against those who had caused so much pain to so many innocent human beings. I was filled with a child's need to hurt others as I had been hurt, thinking this would help fill the empty places for all that I had lost.

For awhile, these thoughts were all consuming, and although they didn't last long, I didn't know that they would ever end. I was too young; my body too broken; my spirit too shattered; my grief too overwhelming, to think this change of heart and soul could ever be anything but permanent.

The Holocaust took everything I had believed in and turned it upside down in an instant. In a world gone mad, there was no longer a reasonable set of expectations upon which a child could base any kind of belief that the world offered hope or promise. The anchors of family and the belief in social institutions disappeared. Overnight, it was no longer possible for me to find peace or hope inside myself. There was only pain and suffering and torment. In the blinking of an eye, my life and the lives of everyone I loved stopped having any value.

I begin the story of my life's journey in the camps, because it is important that each person who reads this book realize that this is an eyewitness account of actual events. This is not fiction. It is not remembrances related to me by others, or things I read in books. The events that follow were witnessed and experienced by me. The few instances in which events are related which I did not actually see have been painstakingly documented through eyewitness testimony of other survivors. It is important to state this to discredit those few people who would distort history and dismiss the Holocaust as a media fabrication. It is imperative that our children's children, and their children after them, and future generations in turn, remember what happened in Nazi Germany. Each and every horror.

Remembering a painful past is one of the most difficult things a person can do, and I am no different. Most of the events detailed here, I have never before discussed with anyone, not even my twin sister, Margot, herself a survivor of the Holocaust.

My sister and I survived the death camps where millions of our fellow human beings, including our parents, were murdered. It has taken me a lifetime, more than fifty years, to tell this story. I've searched deep within my own being to answer why I did not speak of these events earlier in my life. While there are many reasons, self-preservation and protection of my sanity are two of the primary ones. The odyssey of my life has now brought me to a place in time when the reasons for silence are no longer compelling enough to remain quiet.

* * * *

I have had six lives.

My first life lasted thirteen years, beginning in Belgium, where I was born and spent my first few years with my parents and sister living a relatively normal life, and concluding in Poland, where the horror of the war caught my family fully in its grasp.

I lived in a very strict home. My mother was the disciplinarian of the family. She was very much the boss of the house. My father was a soft spoken, kind, very gentle man. I remember him traveling a lot. He did not spend that much time at home because of his job.

My mother had a small club that she was in charge of where people would play cards almost every evening. Both of my parents loved life. When my father was home, they would often go out together. They seemed perfectly suited to each other.

One of my fondest memories of my mother and father was their love of dancing. When they had the chance, they would go out, laughing and smiling, and dance until late evening. When they came home, they would come into our room and kiss us goodnight and make sure we were in good shape. When I remember Max and Fanny now, I see them as they were then, filled with a love for each other, for my sister and me, and for life itself. Our household was strict, but there was also a lot of love.

My earliest memories are filled with joy and sense of family, of being permanently connected to something larger than myself. One of the most enduring and painful effects of Nazi Germany's madness was to rip families apart, to take away the value of each individual family member, thereby undermining the institution of the family. For centuries, the thread of Jewish life which held all else together was rooted in family and religious traditions. The Holocaust tore at the very heart of this fabric.

We had a woman who took care of us, a young Polish woman, who prepared most of our meals. My parents were very busy trying to make a life for us and I don't remember them being home that often for dinner, except special occasions and holidays. My mother was an excellent cook, a great baker. When she prepared a meal, if we didn't feel like eating it, we had to eat it the next day. She was very strict and there was absolutely no question that we would ever waste food.

My mother was considered an extremely bright lady. She was very pretty and commanded respect wherever she went. People would stand

My mother, Fanny Landwirth

up when she entered a room. My father was a great dresser. He always looked like a million bucks. That was his business, selling clothing, men's clothing, and he dressed very well. They were a very attractive couple.

My parents had a good marriage. They were married very young. My mother was seventeen and my father two years older. They tried to have children right away, but they couldn't. After ten years, they had twins, my sister Margot and me. We were born in the house, not the hospital. I was born about five minutes before my sister.

Margot and I have always been very close. She was a beautiful little girl. She was the family favorite and she could get away with many more things than I could. I always felt she was getting much more than I was getting. It got to the point where my mother would ask me first if I wanted what she was holding in the left hand or the right hand, because if she didn't, I would complain that Margot was getting more candies or cookies.

16

With my mother and sister, 1927

Margot was taller and bigger than I was, and I could never win in fighting her. She has always been a fighter, and I'm sure her toughness is one reason she survived the camps.

She was playing downstairs the first time the Germans came. I was upstairs. It was 1939 and I saw everything. They went through the house looking for valuables. I stood beside my father when a German soldier put a gun to his head. The soldier held the barrel of his pistol against my father's temple and demanded to know where we kept our jewelry, furs, anything of value, or he would kill him on the spot. I will never forget that moment. I thought my father was going to be killed. My father said, "I told you everything. There is no more!" *That* soldier didn't pull *that* trigger *that* day, but his action foretold my father's eventual fate.

Later that same year, in November of 1939, my father was taken to a prison called Radom and incarcerated there without a trial. He had committed no crime. He was an honorable man, a successful traveling salesman, who had broken no laws. My mother, Fanny, took the arrest of my father very hard and fought vigorously to have him released. She did this at great personal risk to herself and her children. Every day she would try to talk her way in to see my father, and every day she was unsuccessful. My parents loved each other very much, to be separated compounded their suffering greatly.

From the second my father was arrested, everything changed. My mother spent all of her time and every penny we had left trying unsuccessfully to get him out.

Imagine that one day you are asleep in your bed. Your father is asleep in his bed. Your mother is asleep in her bed. Your sister is asleep in her bed. Everything is okay. You can sit up in bed and feel safe. Your family is there around you. Together, you protect each other. If you want, you can walk around the house and look at everybody sleeping. Then one morning you wake up and everything has changed. There are no more beds, no more house. There is no more father asleep nearby watching over you. Where there was once peace and quiet and safety, there is now danger, noise and constant

17

threats. Imagine how you would see this if you were a child. Imagine how frightened you would be.

Although I was not aware of it, amidst this loneliness and despair, I began to learn how to survive; my child's suffering spirit began to grow. It was a cruel thing to take parents from their children and children from their parents, a very sad and terrible thing.

But because it was so bad, I became stronger inside.

My father's imprisonment is the beginning of my second and saddest life.

* * * *

Like most of those who would eventually find themselves imprisoned in death or labor camps, my journey began in a walled-in ghetto in Krakow, Poland. Those targeted to be exterminated were singled out for their Jewishness, or their ethnicity, or some other excuse. Of course, we did not know the reasons then. We only knew that our lives were dramatically changing, getting worse by the day.

We were herded like animals into the poorest and dirtiest sections of the city. In Krakow, the Germans built a ten foot wall around the part of the city they had designated as the ghetto. Housing was totally inadequate. It was not unusual for a dozen people to share a single room. We had less food than we were used to, but at least we had enough. The constant battle with starvation and hunger that would follow later in the concentration camps was still far from my experience and imagination. Few agonies in life measure anywhere close to the pain of real hunger and thirst. I will tell you more of these twin demons later.

Isolating Jews in the ghettos was the first tactical decision in Adolf Hitler's strategic plan to exterminate the Jewish race. The ghettos were little more than holding areas, points of concentration, where large groups of Jews could be assembled for eventual deportation to concentration camps. We did not know this at the time. We were too busy trying to survive to contemplate anything larger than where our next piece of bread was coming from. Hitler's grand strategies were far from our simple thoughts.

My father had been arrested prior to our time in the Krakow ghetto. It was very frightening to be experiencing these terrible things without him to protect us. A child thinks their father can ward off any evil. It was in the ghetto that I first realized what being Jewish meant. That here in this time and in this place it could mean death. After my father's arrest, as I was approaching my thirteenth birthday in 1940, my mother insisted that a bar mitzvah be held for me. I was taken into a cellar with ten men who would help complete the ceremony, two men stood nearby watching for Germans. If we were caught, we could be shot and killed on the spot. That did not matter as much as denying my heritage. My mother gave me a great gift that day, although I remember being scared as I said those sacred words that made me a man and acknowledged that I was a Jew.

It was in Krakow ghetto that many horrible things first happened to my family. The harsh realities we were facing every day would pale with the horrors that followed, but we did not imagine this then.

Before his arrest, my father was alarmed by the changing political climate and the increasingly open hatred and hostility towards Jews in Poland. He decided it was time for us to get out of Europe. He made plans to get

My father, Max Landwirth

us out through Russia and into China, but my mother would not go. She said as long as we were together, we would be okay. I'll never forget her exact words, "As long as I have my bed and my family is together, we will stay!"

My memories from the Holocaust are remarkably clear. The day of my father's arrest is vivid, painted on my memory like a photograph. It was this single event, more than any other, which changed my perspective of what was happening around me. To lose our home, our possessions, all connection to material things, was terrible, but it was bearable. These were, afterall, only things. But to lose each other, to have the foundation of our family shattered simply because we had been born as Jews was an unbelievable sadness that words cannot convey.

My father never returned to our home in the ghetto. I found out later that Max Landwirth, my dear father, was marched to a mass grave near Radom and made to stand in a hole with several other men. A German soldier stood behind each man. A rifle was pointed at the back of my father's head, and the trigger was pulled. This time, unlike the earlier incident in our home, he was not spared. He was murdered without cause and buried in an unmarked grave filled with other victims.

When I remember these events now, I have no doubt that my father's last thoughts were of my mother and of me and my sister. Max loved us all without question, and since the day he died, there has a been a void within my soul that no amount of success or love has been able to lessen. This emptiness was compounded a hundred times when I heard of my mother's murder years later. Margot and I were among millions of children who were left orphans by the Nazis.

Life in the ghettos was designed to be worse from one day to the next. The evil minds at work plotted to follow the horrible by the terrible, the unthinkable by the unimaginable. The arrest of my father marked a worsening of the conditions in which the rest of the family struggled to exist. The already meager rations were cut even further. It was in this period, from late 1940 to early 1942, that the true purpose of the ghettos began to come into focus. The ghettos were really little more than way stations to gather Jews and other "undesirables" together to be transported to worse, less public places, to places were crematoriums burned around the clock, to places where a slumbering God could not see.

****

The Germans prohibited all Jews from practicing our religion or to pursue any educational or cultural activities, yet many of the adults organized groups to educate the children and to conduct religious services. If they were caught, they could be deported or killed on the spot.

From this denial of our basic human rights, and our access to material goods and simple sustenance, an inspiring kindness grew among many of the imprisoned. Much has been written about Jews who turned their back on their fellow Jews and helped the Nazis. Not enough has been written about Jews who found strength and depth of character amidst these trials that rivals any great heroic story of history. I witnessed starving people sharing their crumbs of food; dehydrated bodies offering their drops of water to the lips of a child; and many other selfless acts.

In my ghetto, there lived a beautiful young woman with short black hair and bright, brown eyes – I never knew her name – who bravely stood up against a Nazi SS officer. "You cannot treat human beings this way!" she said, rushing towards him. The soldier pushed her away from him easily, withdrew his pistol and shot her in the forehead. She fell dead in the street. The murderer holstered his weapon and stepped over the woman like a man stepping over a mud puddle. Her life's essence as meaningless to this killer as a drop of rain. This victim was one of thousands, tens of thousands.

You cannot imagine how it was. The soldiers had complete control and they used it. Our lives had no meaning to them. We were like ants...like bugs. To step on us made no difference. Most human beings would not treat the lowest animal like we were treated, but Hitler found many who would treat Jews this way. There was no shortage of willing participants. When I remember the first days in the ghetto and later in the camps, the disbelief that such things could happen, that all control could be snatched away in an instant, seems like a bad dream. And it was more than just control that was lost. It was any feeling of safety, or well being, or peace of mind. It does not seem possible that people could do such evil to other people.

We were always looking to escape, to find some small way to fight back, but the magnitude, the sheer size of what we were up against was intimidating. The Nazi's war machine seemed so massive, so brutal and unstoppable, that even in our imagination, we could not picture an outcome where we would emerge victorious.

****

The Warsaw Ghetto Revolt is the most famous symbol of Jewish resistance. It was here that the Jewish Fighting Organization led an unsuccessful attack against the far larger and better equipped German forces guarding the ghetto. I was not in the Warsaw ghetto, but witnessed many similar acts of courage by individuals in the Krakow ghetto and small groups who were not afraid. Most of those who resisted were singled out for immediate deportation and execution. Nevertheless, many Jews demonstrated amazing courage and faith.

Deportation is a civilized word for what came next. To rid the Jews from all European society, the Nazi German government devised a secret plan to segregate us and then transport us to secret camps where they could exterminate us. It was in the ghettos that the first selections were made. The term "selection" refers to a forced assembly of Jews for the purpose of choosing those individuals who were to be sent to the labor camps and eventually gas ovens and crematoriums. Mothers and children were forever separated; husbands and wives torn apart; brothers and sisters pushed to different fates; one towards certain death, the other toward another day of misery in the camps.

A woman in the Krakow ghetto named Dasha Rittenberg is a survivor of several concentration camps and remembers a day in August 1942 when

21

she witnessed her first selection and saw firsthand what was happening to the Jewish race in general and her family in particular. Thousands of people were marched into a sports arena. Those selected would be loaded onto cattle cars and transported the next morning to labor or death camps. On this day, Dasha lost her mother and sister-in-law, who was nursing a child. Her brother moved into their single room with the five other children and the nursing child. Word spread throughout the ghetto that an infant child needed milk. An unrelated young mother, who's child had been torn from her arms and tossed to his death from a third story window the day before, came to nurse the infant. As the baby suckled the mourning mother's milk, tears fell from the woman's eyes and ran down her breast to her nipple, mingling with the life-giving milk, feeding the child an equal measure of tears and sustenance.

This is one of a thousand, a million, sixteen million tragic stories. No one who was imprisoned was immune. To be there was itself a tragedy. To survive, we began to steel ourselves against the horrors around us. The more the Germans wanted to kill us, the more we wanted to live. Even in a place without hope, in surroundings which promised that death would be a release, not a torment, we wanted to live. I wanted to live.

Hitler designated the transportation of the Jews to the labor and death camps as a top priority. Rail transportation, already in short supply, was diverted from transporting supplies to the German troops on the Eastern front, to deporting Jews instead. This totally irrational action was an important factor in Germany's inability to gain a rapid victory in the battle for the Eastern Front.

The Germans went about the business of genocide in systematic and methodical fashion. First, they conducted a detailed, country-by-country census of all Jews in Europe. This number totaled more than 11 million people. Reichsmarschall Hermann Göring, after extensive consultations with Adolf Hitler, ordered SS Reinhard Heydrich to implement plans to murder each and every one of the 11 million Jews in Europe.

Heydrich was not daunted by the scope of such a request. To kill 11 million human beings was not going to be easy, but it was possible. What was required to assure success was an efficient means by which to kill the victims. Heydrich likened the extermination of the Jewish people to a scientist who had to kill 11 million rats for the betterment of mankind.

The first phase of the Final Solution was the organization of a group of 3,000 men into mobile killing units called *Einsatzgruppen*. In a period of five months, this 3,000 man army managed to shoot and kill over 1.5 million Jewish people. That means that on average each man shot and killed more than 500 people in a span of 150 days!

A civilian engineer named Herman Graebe witnessed one such mass execution and described it this way:

"The SS man at the pit shouted something to his comrade. The latter counted off about twenty persons and instructed them to go behind an earth mound, where they were confronted by a tremendous grave. Some of the people who had been shot were still moving. Some lifted their arms and turned their heads to show that they were alive. The pit was already two-thirds full. I estimated that it held a thousand people. I looked for the man who did the shooting. He was an SS officer who sat at the edge of the narrow end of the pit, his feet dangling into it. Already the next batch of victims was approaching. They went down in the pit, lined themselves up against the previous victims and were shot."

Heinrich Himmler, the head of the SS, was outraged that so many bullets were being used to kill Jews. He ordered more efficient methods of execution to be developed. "It is like a business," Himmler said. "Cheaper and more efficient means greater success."

From Himmler's demand came the introduction of mobile gas vans. The Nazis had experimented with gassing people in enclosed areas as early as 1939. Himmler ordered the data from these "experiments" and studied it closely. Under the euthanasia program of 1939, mental patients, paraplegics and retarded children were gassed to death en masse. From these tragic crimes came the idea for gassing vans and trucks which could kill up to 150 people at a time. Jews would be loaded into the trucks and vans and killed by the introduction of carbon monoxide or poison gas into the vehicles.

Himmler was still not satisfied. He required a method by which he could kill, not hundreds or thousands, but hundreds of thousands and millions. This ever growing need for bigger and more efficient killing machines led to the creation of the death camps. The Germans called the annihilation camps *Vernichtungslager*, a euphemism for annihilation.

The camps were designed to use cyanide gas, known at that time by its registered German name of Zyklon B, to kill as many people as possible, while expending less money per death than the cost of a bullet.

The procedure to gas innocent victims was deceptively simple. Groups of Jews would be told to strip and led into a shower room. The room looked ordinary. What the victims could not know is the windows and doors were sealed. Special piping had been installed that resembled normal water pipes, but was designed to carry the deadly gas instead. The prisoners were told they were going to take showers, or be deloused. The doctor or soldier on duty would then order the door locked, and the victims would be gassed to death.

The standard operating procedure at the death camps was to cram victims into the "shower rooms" one person per square foot. The room would then be sealed, and the gas administered. The gassing would take as long as thirty minutes. The dead would not even have room to fall. They stood erect, naked and lifeless.

One guard, who herded thousands of people into the gas chambers of Auschwitz, remembers that the dead "stood like pillars of salt...their eyes wide and disbelieving."

The first camp constructed solely for the annihilation of human beings was built near Chelmo, Poland in late 1941. Within the months that followed, Belzec, Sobidor, Treblinka and Auschwitz were renovated to include giant crematoriums. Each of these labor camps was converted into a death camp and began its evil business in earnest by June of 1942. By the end of the war, more than 70% of Poland's Jewish population was murdered!

My sister and I were two of the very small percentage who survived.

Common questions many people ask are these: Why did we willingly go along with such events? Why would anyone knowingly get on a train that was taking him or her to a death camp? Why didn't we forcefully resist? The truthful answer is we didn't know where the trains were going. We were told we would be re-settled in labor camps in Eastern Europe. To further this lie, Jews who were selected for deportation were told they had to pay for the one-way train fare. Our German tormentors also told the Jews being transported they would be allowed to bring only one bag of their prized belongings. By doing this, they could more easily plunder the wealth of the people being deported.

My first experience on a deportation train is burned into my memory as if the experience happened yesterday instead of more than 50 years ago. I don't remember the exact date I was sent from the ghetto to a labor camp, but it was very cold. I will never forget the horrible, dehumanizing conditions inside the box car that, in a more sane world, was designed to transport cattle. Passengers were separated by sex, all the men being sent to the left, the women to the right. We were then herded into these cattle cars. I'm not sure how many people were packed into a single car, perhaps as many as one hundred, but there was only room to stand. There was no food or water or bathroom facilities.

This nightmare went on for days. There was no room and little air. Many people were sick with diseases and could not survive such deprived conditions. As the trains slowly traveled towards their destinations, many people died. For the survivors, the experience was particularly gruesome.

To be treated in a manner which is beneath that of an animal is at once both confusing and frightening. What words can convey the total lack of dignity that takes over a person's soul when such unimaginable events suddenly become the only reality?

I often wonder how such transports through thousands of miles of countryside could be allowed to happen? The common answer is that the German camouflage worked because the normal imagination of a human being was not dark enough to imagine such hellish actions from fellow human beings; but to me, that answer is not enough. I don't know why the Jewish people allowed ourselves to experience such tortures; or why the masses of Germans stood by and watched.

Perhaps acceptance was rooted in the Jewish traditions, the belief that God's eye was always on His chosen people. Perhaps we subconsciously delayed our comprehension of the truth because such total destruction, such genocide, would require the participation and knowledge of a far greater force than Nazi Germany could muster.

* * * *

Questions of God and man's relationship to Him have filled the consciousness of almost every human being. One of the many ideas that man uses to help understand God is the concept of universal suffering. There is a tradition among the Jewish people, a long history taught in the Talmud, which says, God loves the persecuted and hates the persecutors.

Many European Jews did not fight back. Choosing instead to rely on the teachings of the Talmud. Great emphasis was placed on the virtues of self-discipline and endurance. Nonviolent means of resistance became an important method to lessen the impact of the Holocaust. To react violently, to many, was a sign that God had indeed abandoned them. To be powerless became a positive Jewish value within the religious traditions.

Roman Catholics believe that there is a place called purgatory, which exists between heaven and hell. It is a place of atonement, a point of reckoning, where a soul can temporarily suffer and experience great misery to atone for past sins. In Roman Catholic doctrine, souls of those who die in God's grace, may make satisfaction for past sins, and by doing so, become fit for heaven.

In Judaism, the concept of suffering is also a basic tenet of religion. Many Jews believe that suffering is our inheritance, but unlike the Catholic concept of purgatory, Jews believe suffering is for the here and now. Suffering is a recurrent theme of the Holocaust.

In the camps, there was suffering and there was fear, and there was a combination of the two which was very difficult to endure. There was no longer normal human law to follow, and no reason to expect anything but ever-escalating madness from those in power. Our lives had lost their value and we knew it. When we looked to heaven, we saw only an empty sky. Certainly there was no heavenly power which sought to intervene and protect the innocent. There was only chaos and darkness. Endless night where the meanest, cruelest beast ruled over all others.

At such times of personal despair and crisis, people are forced to evaluate what they truly believe. Gone are the easy answers and optimistic expectations. The frills and trappings are stripped away, leaving only the foundation of one's personal belief system.

Terrible things can move a person towards faith or away from faith. It depends on the individual.

I was young and strong and able to work, so I was separated from my sister and my mother. I feared for their safety, and for the first time in my young life, I felt truly apart, disconnected and alone.

I wondered why a loving God would allow the Holocaust to happen? Where was God when we needed Him? I certainly didn't feel God's presence during my first experience with deportation. In fact I was feeling something quite different, a kind of nervous fear that found its way permanently into my heart. Maybe we really were alone. What if it did not matter how loud our screams echoed? What if the number of dead grew to the thousands? The tens of thousands? God forbid, the millions?

What if the world knew what was happening and did not care? What if sane men and women around the world knew what Hitler was trying to accomplish and shrugged their shoulders over steaming dinners and thought such death and destruction of the Jews may not be such a terrible thing?

Worst of all, what if God did not exist?

Where does a heart truly broken, a spirit hopelessly abandoned, find hope? What exists within a human being that allows for survival amidst such devastation? It must be God. We might not know it, or believe it, when we are in the middle of the fire, but it must be God. Who else could it be?

CHAPTER 2

A hungry stomach cannot hear.
– Jean de La Fontaine [1678]

In times of crisis, one can always look to history. In 1820, the German poet Heinrich Heine wrote, "Where books are burnt, human-beings will be burnt in the end." The poet was right. But he could not have imagined the horrors inflicted against the unfortunate people who found themselves imprisoned in the concentration camps of Nazi Germany more than a century later.

Modern medicine has thoroughly documented the total systems breakdown that occurs when the human body is starved. The systems of the body are inter-connected and the failure of one system often leads to the failure of another. The systematic destruction of the Jewish people began with depriving them of basic sustenance. Food and water were rationed to the barest minimums required to sustain life.

In the Spring of 1942, in the camp of Auschwitz-Birkenau, rations were cut in half, a decision made following an inspection of the concentration camp by Heinreich Himmler. He complained too many people arrived at the camp so it was no longer necessary to keep alive those who were already there. He also urged camp commandants to withhold all but the most necessary water from prisoners. "If they are totally dehydrated their corpses will burn more quickly."

Were the Germans unique, or given the same set of circumstances, would other cultures demonstrate similar behavior? When German soldiers used whips to drive naked victims into trucks bound for the gas chambers, did their consciences whisper to them? Did they experience remorse or guilt? Did they fear that their immortal souls would one day burn in hell for all of eternity?

The list of moral questions is endless.

****

To be hungry, really, deathly hungry, to ache for food is the worst torture anyone can imagine. It has a way of focusing all of a person's energy into himself. It's hard to think of your neighbor's pain when it feels as though a wild animal inside your stomach is eating you from the inside out.

29

To be thirsty is even worse. I was hungry and thirsty for more than five years. Starvation and thirst led to hundreds of thousands of deaths in the concentration camps.

A normal daily ration of bread was less than two ounces. If it was a good day, inhabitants of the camps also received three or four ounces of watery soup. In a sane world, such soup would be considered too rancid to eat. In the camps, the soup was good fortune of extraordinary measure.

There is little dignity in being hungry. Real hunger and thirst reduces man to the level of animals. We had no meat on our bones. I could look at myself and see all the bones in my body. I remember one day standing in line. We were naked and I looked at the back of the man in front of me. I was shocked by how clearly I could see his skeleton through his skin. I remember how his backbone was divided into inch long little circles stacked on top of each other. And from his spine, how his ribs turned downward in both directions. His rib bones reminded me of a barrel without a lid. On his shoulders, his blades stood out. The real shock came when I realized the man behind me, the man looking at my back, was seeing the same thing.

My body changed my mind. The hungrier I got, the less I thought about bigger issues and the more I focused on my personal suffering. I thought about food constantly. All kinds of food. Banquets of food and pitchers of ice cold water and juice. I thought so much of food that the thoughts themselves became an evil torment. I felt the lack of food in my head, my stomach and my soul.

With hunger comes craziness. It is impossible to think clearly or to focus on any bigger thought than when the next meager ration will be distributed. To be without food and water is to understand how small man really is. When reduced to the most basic elements, we become creatures of instinct. We fight to survive. Or we don't.

* * * *

The Germans designed a food rationing system that would reduce a person to near death conditions in four to six months. They even utilized caloric charts that allowed for lesser portions to be calculated, a how-to guide to starvation.

The starved would then be marched off to the gas chambers, crematoriums and mass graves where they would be systematically murdered. Those who were older, sick or less capable of work, were branded as undesirable and sent directly to the gas chambers. Each murder was duly recorded as a piece of historical data Hitler demanded of all field commanders. Each unfortunate statistic was replaced by a new victim. The trains moved people in and out of the camps constantly. Each day, thousands of human beings were killed and each day thousands more arrived. The killing represented madness on a scale never before witnessed in the history of our planet.

One of many miracles saved me from being labeled as an "undesirable." I had psoriasis, a skin disease with visible symptoms. The condition was permanent and I had learned to live with the visible marks on my face and neck. The amazing part was when the Germans came, I didn't have any patches, not even the slightest blemish on my skin from that psoriasis. If my skin would have been peeling, or if I had any spots at all, I would have been killed. The Germans did not spend time trying to figure out how to make someone better. A visible disease of any sort was a death sentence.

For those of us healthy enough to pass the first inspection, we were thrown into a nightmare where the goal was to starve us as quickly as possible, while still getting several month's forced labor out of each prisoner before he or she died.

I think it would be a good idea if each and every American could understand, really understand what it is to be hungry. I think every person should go on a personal fast, a hunger strike for a couple of days, to understand firsthand what really being hungry is like. Hunger and thirst are feelings that must be felt to be understood.

I remember my life as a child. Before the camps, I had never known hunger. There was always plenty of food, and as I mentioned earlier, my mother did not tolerate waste. I often thought about this in the camps. When I had nothing, when the moldiest black bread was a gift, I thought about my mother putting the same food on the table the next day.

There is a terrible memory–a painful memory–that I have of my mother. We had been separated for many months and when I finally got the chance to see her, I was shocked at how ravaged her body had become. She was starving. We were all starving, but it was particularly painful to see my mother in such a condition. She smiled at me and said, "You wouldn't have an extra piece of bread, son, would you?"

I did not. I had nothing.

It was so painful for me to see the people I loved the most in this world so devastated by hunger. I could see myself by looking at them.

31

We looked the same; bones poking through our skin, eyes deep within our faces, as if we were being swallowed from the inside.

Those who were hungry were together in our misery; and after awhile, to each other, we didn't look so bad. I know to normal people that we were frightening to look at. I sometimes look down at my arm and see it, not as it is now, covered with healthy flesh, but as it was then, a bone-stick covered with tightly drawn skin. It was a difficult thing to be so hungry and to look so bad and to hurt so much and yet continue to live.

* * * *

Individual journeys to the camps had many common elements, from the ghettos, to the cattle cars, to the eventual starvation and the inevitable ovens. What was not common were the individual trail of tears each and every solitary journey to the camps created. When history examines the Holocaust now, it is with the dispassionate eye of time and distance. The concentration camps are pictures in books, much like today's starving children in Africa seem slightly unreal because we view them through the dispassion of the television screen.

My path through the fires of the camps is not altogether unlike a million others. My memories are made up, not so much of the massive horror of it all, but of smaller, individual moments.

* * * *

The Holocaust became one of the great lies of all time. Many of us who survived go back to this basic premise again and again.

They were all liars. They lied to get us on the trains to take us to the ovens. "We are re-settling you to another place," they said. "You will be re-united with your family and loved ones there," they said. It was all lies. If a Nazi told me the sun was going to rise in the East, I would turn my back and look to the West. From the day they tattooed us, it was nothing but lies.

Maurice Bauman and I were together when we arrived in Auschwitz. We had been sent to Auschwitz from a forced labor camp called Ostrowitz. Maurice had been the messenger that carried the unbearably sad news of the murder of my father.

He didn't want to tell me. I was just a boy and Maurice was perhaps ten years older than I. He had been asked by a cousin to help me. He didn't know me but he found me in Ostrowitz. He told me every Jew in Radom had been taken to the cemetery and shot.

I can't ever remember feeling such sadness. I shook my head and slumped to the ground. In a normal world, the most terrible thing to happen is when a child loses his parents. In this world, it was the common thread that connected and covered all of us in a blanket of sadness.

There was a long line that we waited in to receive our tattoo, our number. I did not want to be tattooed. I walked to the back of the line. Got pushed forward, slid to the back again. I wanted no part of that tattoo. It did me no good really. I was tattooed anyway.

I remember in moments. Sometimes a moment can seem as endless as time itself, like the day Maurice was put between two electric wire fences, which were about two feet apart, maybe 20 inches. He had to stand between the fences for 24 hours. If he would have moved backward of forward, he would have been electrocuted. I don't know how many amps of electricity were charging those fences, but I had seen others killed on the wire in seconds. Maurice's brother was with us, and we spent as much time as we could urging Maurice to stay awake and to be strong. He survived by spending the hours digging a hole in the ground with his feet to steady himself. Those 24 hours seemed endless.

Other moments.

Like the Polish dentist, whose name I can't remember, who was such a sweet human being. He was kind to many of us, sharing what he had. Helping us.

Or the adults who risked their lives to educate the children to keep the Jewish traditions alive. Or the hundreds of small words of encouragement we offered each other every day. Or the prisoners who risked their lives to sneak me medicine when I got typhus.

Many, many moments.

CHAPTER 3

*And I looked, and behold a pale horse: and his name that sat on him
was Death, and Hell followed with him.*
The Holy Bible: Revelation 6:8

There is a haunting picture in the Holocaust museum at Dachau, a
concentration camp near Munich, Germany. Its caption reads:
A family on their way to the gas chamber.

In the picture is a young woman with a black kerchief tied around her
head. She is wearing a torn print jacket and a long black skirt. Her body
is very thin. It is cold. There is vapor, the woman's breath, visible in the
picture near her head. The woman is bent over with one arm wrapped
tightly around two children. A third child is just out of reach of her
extended hand, but the boy has his hand hooked to his smaller sister's
hand. A fourth child, an infant, is being crushed to the woman's chest
with her other arm. Behind this young mother, a small girl, perhaps five
or six years old, walks with her head down. She wears only a coat. Her
hands are tucked deeply into the pockets. Her feet are wrapped in rags.

A family on their way to the gas chamber.

* * * *

Songs of mourning were the anthems of the camps. Mothers for their
children...husbands for their wives...sons for their mothers...daughters for
their fathers...siblings for each other. The list is endless.

My sister and I learned firsthand what it was like to lose our family
members to cruel and unnecessary deaths. Gone were our aunts and uncles,
our cousins, our nieces and nephews; gone forever were our dear parents.

By destroying the Jewish family, Hitler sought to accomplish something
which went beyond the death of an individual life. By treating a mother's
treasure, her children, as valueless, by sending one parent to the ovens
and the other to forced labor, he turned all normal expectations inside out.
If a person survived today's selection, so what? Tomorrow would bring
another selection and another the day after that.

The fabric of every society is woven through the family unit.
Throughout history, societies who have held the family in slight regard
have fallen, while those cultures who revered the family have prospered.

The Jewish family, by tradition, has one of the proudest and most supportive family structures of any culture. This is no doubt one of the primary reasons that Hitler took such measured aim at the destruction of the Jewish family.

For so many of us, seeing those we loved in such pain was among the worst miseries we had to bear. The sight of those we loved most, suffering in such an evil place as the camps, hurt so deeply it was as if our very souls were bleeding.

The smell of burning bodies always hung in the air. The smoke of the dead was so thick it filled my throat. I thought I would go crazy. I wanted to tear my heart out and stop living that very second. I felt powerless to help myself and worse, powerless to help those I loved.

I sometimes looked to God for a miracle, but I saw no sign that miracles existed in Auschwitz, only nightmares come awake. At least that's what I thought before my eyes learned to see that there were miracles happening all around me.

* * * *

Often, as family members from one family were lost, orphaned children were brought into the family of someone who had known that child's loved ones. There was a vast network of people helping each other, sharing food and trying to keep in some small way the traditions of the Jewish family alive. These people, thousands of them, reached out to the children of the lost and offered help, love and support.

There was goodness. On the darkest moment of the darkest day there was kindness and goodness among the victims. Were it not for such kindness, I would not have survived.

I must also point out that many Jewish prisoners were almost as bad as the Germans. For them to be able to get more bread, more food to eat, they had to watch us. After years and years of being there, they knew their way around and they were actually, in some cases, worse than the Germans. They treated us the same. For them to survive, they beat us. These Jews were constantly abusing us.

"I must tell one story about Jews who were not Jews," said Sarah Grobman, a fellow survivor of Matthausen. "I was in a work camp, not a death camp, when a fellow Jew came up to me and told me to work faster. I had only been there from the day before. I told him to mind his own work. He had a wooden handle and he hit me with it right between the eyes. I saw double for more than a year. To this day, I still suffer seizures and dizziness. It was the worst injury I received in four years of moving from one camp to another and it was inflicted on me by a Jew who was not a Jew."

A sad fact of life is many Jews became worse than the Germans. Some men will do great evil not to be on the receiving end of a punch.

Personal suffering can bring out the best or the worst in a person. It goes to our individual character. What values our mothers and fathers have taught us. As the son of Max and Fanny Landwirth, I had certain values that would not let me do certain things. Those Jews who lost their values are to be pitied, not hated.

* * * *

Auschwitz was my first realization that the camps were for our extermination. I never expected to get out of there. I knew that in a matter of time it would be my turn and I would be murdered liked the rest.

There is a night I remember in Auschwitz. I was watching the crematoriums. You could smell the human skin burning and the stench was terrible. A sick smell worse than any words can describe. It was a putrid, hellish smell. The people were lining up to go to their deaths. I couldn't take my eyes from this scene. It was so crazy it didn't seem like it could actually be taking place. I saw a woman, I think by her look that she was a French woman, grab a gun from an SS man. She was so brave. She tried to kill him. But he grabbed the gun away from her and shot her in the heart. She died on the spot. I remember the guards picking the woman up and carrying her over to the crematoriums like she was a piece of wood for a fire.

I pity those Jews who helped the Germans kill us. They are truly the loneliest people on this earth.

But for every person who helped the Germans, there was a hundred of us who did not. We were kind and encouraging to each other. "The Americans are going to be here and liberate us. The Russians are going to come. It's going to happen. This madness will end." I don't think we believed this, but it helped to support each other.

There is something that exists within the human soul that awakens when suffering is great and death is imminent. It is like a mechanism that comes awake and helps us fight to stay alive. There is something inside of us that hangs on to life, that refuses to let it go.

I saw firsthand time and again that many of those who were dying during work or in their sleep were those who had given up completely and who could simply not go on any longer. I never experienced this personally until very late in the war, almost a month before the war ended. Up until then, there was a voice inside me that urged me to keep living, keep trying. It seemed to me then that the life in the camps was going to continue. I could not even imagine having another life, much less surviving this one.

* * * *

There are many kinds of family. A family, to most people, is a mother, a father, children, grandparents, some aunts and uncles. In the camps, our families were those who shared our suffering. We were brothers and sisters of torment; mothers and fathers of pain; children of mourning. This was our family. This is our family still today.

In the camps it was difficult to have hope that things were going to change. Each day the horrors were worse than the day before. Life had no value. Those the world should treasure, the very young and the very old, were killed immediately. Infant children were of no use to the Germans. They were ripped from their mother's arms and tossed out of high windows or their heads smashed on the stones. It was the same with the elderly and the sick. They had no chance. Their lives had no value to our tormentors. When they took away our families, they took everything.

One of the few reasons that I fought to survive was the hope that my twin sister might still be alive, and if so, would need me if the madness of the death camps ever came to an end.

I always believed Margot was alive. Always. I think I would have somehow known if she did not survive. As long as there was a chance that she was alive, I wanted to stay alive, too, to help her, to be her family. We were twins and we were very close. We depended on each other.

* * * *

To be in pain is a terrible thing. To watch those you love in pain is unbearable. Most people find it very difficult to watch their loved ones suffer. In the camps, parents of suffering children prayed that God spare their children and give them the burden to carry instead. "Please God...let it be me, not my children!"

But burdens do not fall only to those strong enough to bear them. Suffering touches every life, the innocent and unscrupulous alike. Many of the most impassioned writings from the Holocaust quote members of families as they relate the personal agonies that happened, not to them as individuals, but to their loved ones.

"I was a child of 10," one anonymous survivor writes, "when my mother and I were sent to Auschwitz. For awhile, my mother and I worked together gathering shoes from the piles of clothes of those people who had been sent to the ovens. We would carry the shoes several hundred meters to a warehouse where they were saved. The most vivid memory I have is of my mother, her shaved head bleeding from open sores, sitting on top of this huge pile of shoes. She had used a ladder to get to the top of the pile. The shoes reached to the ceiling in a warehouse as big as a barn. My mother was sitting on these shoes and she was looking at her own feet. I think she knew her shoes would soon be added to the pile."

Such experiences were not uncommon. Tens of thousands of children were ripped from their families and sent to labor and death camps. Imagine the horror that must have gripped each and every child's heart when such unimaginable events suddenly became their reality.

It was hard to believe that there was any power in the world that could come into our houses and take us out and throw us into prison, or kill us, or do whatever the Germans felt like doing to us. Many families had the means to get out of Europe before the killing started. My family was one of them. What we did not have was the imagination to believe that we would be killed one after the other until all Jews were dead. No one believed such a thing as Auschwitz could exist.

* * * *

By definition, genocide is the deliberate and systematic destruction of an entire group of people. Hitler's plan to eradicate Jews in Europe put special emphasis on the destruction of Jewish children. One of over 100,000 German memoranda marked SECRET URGENT confiscated after the war reflects this with a brutal harshness:

Sub: Transfer of Jews to Auschwitz, deportation of Jewish children
The Jewish children held in the camps of Pithiviers and Beaune-La Rolande will be immediately transported by rail to Auschwitz for extermination. There will be no exceptions from this policy.

The Germans had only our destruction on their mind. Everything else took second fiddle to that. I saw many children killed. First because they were Jews, and second because they were children. Genocide eliminates the entire tree, from the seed, to the branches, to the roots.

Hitler claims he got the idea for the concentration camps and the annihilation of the Jewish people from his study of English and American history. In the first instance, he expressed admiration for England's cruel treatment of the Boer prisoners in the makeshift camps of South Africa; and from America, Hitler claims he got the inspiration for his systematic annihilation of all Jewish people. He pointed to the extermination of the American Indian through starvation and one-sided wars and told his generals that the world would allow the destruction of the Jews. "They are less than Indians," Hitler reasoned.

The idea to focus, first on the destruction of the Jewish family and then on the destruction of all Jewish children, is documented in many thousands of official government documents.

As I mentioned earlier, the last time I saw my mother was in Auschwitz. It is one of my most painful memories, and I cannot allow myself to think of it too often or I would not be able to bear it.

It was winter in 1943, I went to the place where the women were. We were separated by wire fences. The women and girls on one side of the camp, the men and boys on the other. Somebody told me my mother was there. I hoped with my whole heart that this was not true. We were not allowed to go to that side of the camp. We could be shot or hanged for being there. But I didn't care. I had to see my mother. Before that day, my last memory of her was the day I did not have bread to feed her hungry stomach and I wanted to see her again, to replace that memory with a different one. I went to a place where I could see the woman's side. I saw my mother. I didn't say anything. I would have put her in danger to call out to her. Besides what was there to say?

A son, seeing his mother suffering, and having not the smallest comfort. What torment!

She looked very, very bad. She looked so pitifully small and broken. It was so painful to see her that way. That was the very last time I saw her. As I looked across at her, I tried to remember happier times, but no good thoughts came.

40

After I saw my mother for the last time in Auschwitz, I was sent to a series of other camps, and I did not quit fighting. Not at Schwientochlowitz, or Matthausen or Gusen or an unnamed underground camp where I would almost die. The possibility that my mother and sister might survive, however remote, was enough to make me continue the struggle to survive.

Imagine as a child having to face such brutal atrocities one atop the other? Your father shot; your mother starving; your family devastated. What primal survival mechanisms activate themselves and keep the human heart and the indomitable human spirit from giving up? What exists within the human soul, that in the midst of such devastation, hope can still be found?

For me, it was not hope or faith. Not at first. In the beginning, my hatred kept me going. There was nothing else to lean on.

****

One day in Schwientochlowitz there was a Polish or German woman who worked in the place where they marched us each day to work. She brought me a piece of bread. I put the crust of bread in a piece of cloth and tied it around my waist to save it. Later when we were marching back to the camp, we had to go through a gate, and I was caught with that piece of bread. I was taken to a room and they beat me with a leather truncheon, a big one, with little raised knobs on the end. They probably hit me with a leather whip about 25 times. They made me take off my pants and they beat me so badly and it was so painful that I fainted completely. I couldn't sit for weeks and weeks and weeks. My skin was so raw I did not think I could survive.

From Schwientochlowitz, Maurice and I were loaded onto cattle cars and transported three days and three nights to Matthausen. This was one of the worst experiences I have ever lived through. It was absolutely less than human. There was no place to sit...no place to go the bathroom. Finally, at the beginning of the second day, I managed to sit down, and from there, I squeezed myself into a cramped laying position.

Before we were forced to board the cattle cars, we were given one piece of bread. The Germans said the trip would only take a day, but I knew better. I knew how they lied. My body was screaming to eat the bread, but I would not let myself. I could not face the possibility of being on that train without bread. I simply could not. I put my piece of bread under my head and fell asleep. When I woke up, the bread was gone. One of my fellow unfortunates had stolen it from me. I was totally without food or water for three days. I wept when I lost my bread.

When the train finally stopped it was bitter cold. Many people did not survive that terrible train ride. As we marched to the camp, I felt the cold inside myself in a way I had never felt anything before. I knew I was dying. I stared at the ground and wondered which step would be my last. My mind was very clear. Death was near and I knew it and welcomed it and had no fear of anything that came with it. How could it be worse than this life?

I don't know how I survived. We arrived at Matthausen dressed only in rags. There, they took all our clothes from us. Everything. They stripped us naked and left us in the freezing weather for more than a day. This was a death camp. A terrible place. The Germans wanted as many to die by the weather as possible. And many did die. More than I can count or remember. There was so little regard for the life of human beings. A person mattered less than a piece of dust.

After Matthausen, Maurice and I were separated.

From there, I was sent for a brief time to a camp called Gusen, which was located just northeast of Matthausen, and then on to an underground camp. I don't know what the name of it was, but if it is possible, this camp was a worse nightmare than Matthausen and Gusen combined.

I lived without seeing the sun for more than a year.

I slept on a spring without any mattress. My only pillow was my shoes. We didn't get to shower very often, and when we did it was with cold water. I became infested with fleas. Every night I would kill fleas until I finally fell into a fitful sleep.

In this camp we had to deal with a massive outbreak of typhus. Guards and prisoners alike died one after the other. As prisoners got sick and inched closer to death, they could no longer eat. We would eat what they had left, knowing we would soon be sick and dying ourselves, but we were unable to let a crust of diseased bread go uneaten.

My job was in a tremendously big factory which made anti-aircraft guns. I worked on huge guns designed to shoot down Allied planes. I was very skinny. I had lost so much of my body weight that I was constantly cold. It was very cold in this place and we did not have warm clothing.

They were trying to kill us, to work us to death in the cold. I did not think I would ever come out of that camp.

It was in this underground camp that I was contacted by other prisoners who worked with the Resistance. They asked me to misuse a tool, a very precise instrument used to measure the diameter of the gun barrels of the anti-aircraft weapons. If I was off by so much as a fraction, the barrels would be unusable. When the Germans went to fire them, the ammunition shell would not have room to escape the barrel. The gun would explode on those using it.

It did not take much convincing to win my cooperation. One of the men said to me, "Henri, you help us and we will help you when you get sick." You see, in this place, it was not a matter of *if* you got sick, here everyone got sick eventually; it was only a matter of when. Once you got typhus, you usually died. There was no medicine available to us to help fight the disease. I was tired. My will to survive, even for the sake of my mother and sister, was growing weaker. I was happy to mess up the guns. The thought that these guns would be useless made me feel good. The fact that those firing them might be blown up as a result of my deliberate mistake made me feel better still.

One day, a fellow prisoner came down with typhus. He wasn't yet dying, but we all believed that to fight against the illness you couldn't eat. He offered me his soup, and although I knew I would catch the disease, I ate it anyway.

I was eventually sent to the camp infirmary, a holding area where the typhus-infected patients were put to await death. My fever was very high and I think I was again close to death.

There were over 25 men dying in that room. The smell of death was in the air. I was put in a corner. The man next to me was dead. The room was filled with the groans of dying people. It was in this death-filled room that another miracle took place. In the middle of the night, I was nearly out of my head with fever, when a man came to me. He probably stepped over dead men to reach me, but I couldn't see because it was dark. The man said my name. "Landwirth?" I managed to nod my head. He bent over me and lifted my head and put a pill into my mouth and gave me a sip of water. It was like being visited by an angel.

When I awakened the next morning, almost every man in the room was dead. I sat against the wall looking at the room filled with corpses and a few men still fighting death.

The only thought I had was why was I left alive? Why me?

When they were carrying the dead from the room, a guard noticed I was still alive. He looked at me like I was a ghost and told me to go back with the others, with the living.

I left the infirmary with a strange sense of power.

What else could anyone possibly do to me? I began to go a little bit crazy. I told anyone who would listen that we should just start running. What did it matter if they shot us in the back? Better a bullet than the slow death that would come anyway.

Running seemed to me to be a great idea. It was this idea that took the last of my fear away.

CHAPTER 4

Me miserable! which way shall I fly
Infinite wrath, and infinite despair?
Which way I fly is hell; myself am hell;
And in the lowest deep a lower deep
Still threat'ning to devour me opens wide,
To which the hell I suffer seems a heav'n.

John Milton – Paradise Lost [1667]

In late 1944, the Germans were losing a great deal of ground to the advancing Russian and American troops. I was working in the German munitions factory and it had become an important Allied target. The Allies could not be concerned that the Germans were using innocent civilians as slave laborers.

When the Americans started shelling the camp where the munitions factory was, there were about 2,000 people there. This number included about 1,500 prisoners and 500 guards. The shelling was relentless. Most of the 2,000 people were killed. When the total number of survivors was less than 300, the Germans decided to evacuate us. We marched for two days and nights with only very short periods of rest. I was still a little crazy and I kept saying to my fellow prisoners, "Let's run! Let's run into the woods! We can escape! The hell with them! Let's run!"

Unfortunately, I was overheard by a nearby German soldier. The soldier walked over to me, and holding the barrel of his rifle like a sledge hammer, swung the rifle in a full circle, smashing my skull.

I saw the soldier swing the rifle, and I knew he was going to hurt me, maybe kill me, but for some reason I didn't move. I stood there and he smashed my head with the butt of his rifle. I fell to the ground covered with blood. The soldier turned his attention back to the others. Just before I lost consciousness, I managed to crawl a few inches and burrow into a small pile of straw. When I came to, it was dark and I was alone. The Germans must have thought I was dead and left me there.

The soldier who hit me may have ended up saving my life. I learned later that most of the other prisoners I was with were executed and buried in a mass grave the way my father was.

47

My head ached, my skull was fractured and the wound was bleeding. I felt dizzy and sick. I got to my feet, walked a short distance and sat down. Within a very short time, I was recaptured by different German soldiers and taken to still another prison.

As I was marched towards my newest torment, my mind turned once again to escape. This time I knew the soldiers would easily shoot me in the back and my life would be over. Just as I was making the decision to run, one of the soldiers took hold of my arm and led me into the town jail.

He pushed me down a flight of stone steps into a dungeon, a basement with stone walls. Water ran down the walls. There were rats and mice and other rodents screeching in the blackness. There was absolutely no light. The wounds on my head were festering and I became afraid in that place. After all I had been through, this dark place with its bugs and rats and vermin was scaring me. I began to cry. I just couldn't take any more. I had reached my limit of endurance.

Three days later, a soldier opened the door to the cellar and called for me to come out. By this time, I felt giddy, numb and no longer afraid of the rats, the bugs or even the Germans. The fear had been replaced with something quite different. I was going slightly mad.

When I heard a soldier calling me to come out of the basement, I knew he was going to shoot me. I could hear it in his voice, and when I could look into his eyes, I saw it in his face. He told me to kneel and kiss his hand and beg for mercy. I did these things. And while I was doing them, I felt apart from myself, totally numb, as if I was a person watching from a distance. These things were happening to me, but at the same time they weren't. While I kissed the guard's hand, I thought, if you want to shoot, go ahead and shoot me.

There is a funny thing about that soldier. I remember his face more clearly than almost any other face of the war, that well-fed soldier who took such delight in humiliating a starving boy. If I was an artist, I could draw his face perfectly from memory. He told me to run like a dog and I did.

Soon I was recaptured by different soldiers and taken to a room outside of town with two other prisoners. I was fluent in several languages, including German, and I had no trouble understanding that the guards were ordered to take me and the other two Jewish prisoners into the forest and shoot us.

I thought this would really be the end. We were going to be marched to the woods and shot. I would be my father's son and die as he had died with a senseless bullet to the head. I really believed death was moments away and I was surprised at the depth to which I did not care. I thought of praying, but found no prayers in my heart. Perhaps because I had lost all control, it was easy to simply accept my fate. For whatever reason, I was very calm as the Germans marched us into the forest.

One of the great miracles of my life took place at this forest's edge on the way to my execution. One of the soldiers looked troubled by the fact that he was going to have to shoot one of us. The soldier turned to his comrades and said, "The war is almost over. I don't want to kill these people." The other soldiers shrugged their shoulders. They didn't seem to want to kill us either. The soldier turned to us and said, "Line up over there facing the trees. I'm not going to shoot you. When I raise my gun, run into the woods."

I still thought he would kill us, but I walked with the two other men to the edge of the forest, looking over my shoulder as the soldier raised his rifle and then lowered it. The three of us set off running in different directions. As we disappeared into the trees, I found myself believing a little more strongly in miracles.

* * * *

With the war raging on all sides, I ran a half mile or so into the woods. The other two prisoners were nowhere in sight.

As soon as I felt sure I was alone and safe, I stopped running. I had to. I was in terrible physical shape. The wound to my head had become badly infected. The odor from the rotting flesh was very bad to smell. I also had bad wounds to my legs. My left leg was particularly sick. There were large holes all the way down to the bone. Inside these open wounds a wild red meat was growing.

During this time, I had no real contact with other people. As I continued walking, the wounds on my legs became infected with gangrene. The pain I was experiencing was very severe.

I had to find a doctor, but I was convinced that if I showed myself I would be either recaptured by the Germans or shot or hanged. Any alternative was better than being back in their hands again, so I kept walking, getting sicker with every step.

I wondered if my sister was still alive? Could that be possible?

* * * *

As I moved from village to village, from small town to small town, I tried my best to keep myself hidden. I estimate I wandered for several hundred miles. Sometimes I followed roads, sometimes not. I traveled around for a few weeks, stealing food when I could. I did it without guilt. Besides, after almost five years of the camps, I did not require much in the way of sustenance in order to keep going. My body was little more than a rotting, flesh covered skeleton. My leg wounds were getting worse by the day.

The infected red meat that was growing in the holes in my legs began to run with an ugly, stinking green pus. The pain was very intense with each step I took. It was like walking on shards of broken glass. At this point, I was really crazy. I yelled at the sky and made no sense. I wandered the countryside as a madman. A mad boy, really. I was only 17. I slept on a sack of straw I carried on my back. That was my bed.

I thought about many things as I walked the countryside. First of all, I was very angry inside my soul, and as I walked, these feelings of rage got worse. It was very hard to close my eyes without seeing the crematoriums and the suffering. Very, very hard. It was like music playing constantly inside my head, I couldn't get it to stop.

When I could bear the pain in my legs no longer, I found an empty house on the outskirts of a small village. I went inside and fell asleep on my sack of straw. I did not know this then, but I was in the city of Dvûr Králové, near Prague. I had walked from one country to the other. I was in Czechoslovakia.

I remember going to sleep in that house and feeling very content. If it was time to die, that would have been okay with me. I fell asleep, for the first time in a long time not worried about anything.

* * * *

I was awakened by an old woman who found me sleeping in the empty house. After so many weeks without human contact, I was frightened by her, not by what she might do to me, but by what she must think of my shattered body.

The woman told me I was in Czechoslovakia and the war was over. It had ended three days earlier. She said I didn't have to run away anymore. I remember shaking my head. I couldn't accept that. The old woman must be mistaken.

She kept urging me to go across the street to her house. She had a radio. She told me she would turn it on and I could hear for myself that the war was over. I limped over to the woman's window. She went inside the house and turned the radio on. When I heard the truth, and believed it, I slumped to the ground and began to cry.

The woman's husband's came outside and asked if he could carry me inside and give me a bath. I had not bathed in many months and my body was covered with festering wounds. He picked me up and carried me like a child. The man washed my body and cleaned my sores as best he could. He did not see me as I saw myself. He and the old woman were filled with kindness towards me. I cannot describe what this meant to me, to be touched in a kind way by any human hand felt like the most wonderful thing in the world. It was as if the man was saying, I will replace your bad memories with this gentle one.

The couple brought two doctors to see me. They confirmed that the wounds on my left leg were infected with gangrene. They excised the wounds as deeply as they could. The possibility of amputation if they did not go deep enough was very real.

It was an awful pain when the physicians worked on my leg. One of the worst physical pains I have ever experienced. They had to burn into my leg all the way to the bone. They removed a great deal of infected flesh. I remember one doctor telling me how lucky I was that not another hour had passed. He said I was absolutely at the last minute that they could treat my legs instead of amputating them. They saved my legs and I will always be grateful for that. They also drained an infection from my fractured skull which made me feel much better.

It was about this time I first saw myself in the mirror. In the camps we didn't really realize how horrible we looked. The only mirror we saw was reflected through the eyes of people who looked the same as we did, and as bad as it was, our misery was shared and our broken bodies the norm, not the exception. As strange as it sounds, I think we all got used to our appearance.

When I looked into that mirror it was almost beyond my comprehension. Yet it was an experience all who survived shared. We looked the same. I wanted to see myself, but at the same time, I wanted to look away, but I could not. My eyes kept staring into that glass. Where my face should be, I saw little more than skin covered bones.

That picture of a face and eyes I knew, but didn't know, travels with me still.

* * * *

After several weeks of recovering in this kind family's home, I felt ready to try to find my own family, my twin sister and any other member of the Landwirth family who might have survived. The radio had announced that there was a Missing Persons Center in Krakow where survivors, the homeless and those who no longer had a country, could come for information on their loved ones.

The old couple had treated me with incredible kindness. They fed and cared for me. Without them, I would have lost both my legs and maybe even my life. I thanked them but I had nothing to give in return. They wanted nothing from me, they helped me because I was a human being in need of help. This was an important lesson I learned from them. I will never forget that couple's kindness to me, although I am embarrassed to say I do not remember their names.

It was hard to leave the comfort and security of that place. But I felt in my heart that my sister was still alive. Although I did not believe my mother survived, I was still hopeful. If my heart was right, it was time to go and look for them. If I had to, I would have walked across Europe to find them.

CHAPTER 5

I have been a stranger in a strange land.
−The Holy Bible: Exodus 2.22

When I left Czechoslovakia, I was still angry, still kind of crazy. Little thoughts bothered me. I thought of the Germans who didn't actually participate in the camps but who let them happen by their silence. I felt a tremendous hatred for all Nazis.

Now that the war was over, they were on the bottom of the stick instead of holding it against us. As I wandered, I picked fights with former Nazis and Nazi supporters. I beat them up because of who they were. This hatred grew as the months passed, and became the foundation of my third life, my life of vengeance.

Walking along a river between towns, I came upon a German boy dressed in the uniform of the Hitler Jugen, Hitler's organization for children. He wore black leather pants and shirt. He was proud of himself, I could tell that. I blocked his way. It was just him and me.

I asked the boy if he was a good Hitler Jugen and I could see in his eyes that he was scared. I told the boy to take off his uniform. I wanted to hurt him in some way. I told him to strip naked or I was going to kill him. Those were my words: "Take off your clothes or I'm going to kill you!" He realized that I was serious. I was so angry, I think if he had refused I would have actually killed him with my bare hands. He took off everything but his underwear. I told him to take them off, too. I took all his clothes and I threw them into the river. Then I held him by the neck, and a strange thing happened, I stopped wanting to hurt him. I told him to run. I started to yell at him in German. He was very afraid. And he ran.

I watched the Hitler Jugen run away until he was out of sight. I watched him but thought about myself. What I had done to him hadn't made me feel better, it made me feel ashamed. I did not want to become what I despised. Any fate was better than turning into one of them.

"Cruelty has a human heart," wrote poet William Blake. But the opposite is also true. Where else but the human heart and soul can true values exist? What other of God's creatures can aspire to the noble and selfless pursuit of that which is good and kind and benevolent? Who but man knows the soaring power of love?

* * * *

I made my way to Krakow, mostly on foot, and found a job working for a dentist. The dentist also let me sleep on a couch in his office. Each day around one o'clock, I took the trolley to the Missing Persons Center to see if there was any news about my relatives, particularly my mother and sister. I feared the worst about my mother, but at this time still did not know her fate. During this time, I met many people at the center who were also awaiting news on lost loved ones.

The Missing Persons Center was a very sad place filled with people hoping for a happy ending. Not many of us were fortunate enough to find one.

One day on the trolley car, I saw a woman who looked vaguely familiar. I wasn't sure who she was, but something about her face, the line of her neck and her eyes seemed like I should know her. The trolley car stopped and she got off. I followed her, walking a few feet behind her, not sure what to say.

Finally I said, "Please stop." The woman turned around and I asked her name.

My attention disturbed and frightened her. She told me to leave her alone at once or she would call a policeman. The woman turned around and began to walk quickly away.

I don't know why, but I shouted my mother's name. "Fanny! Fanny Landwirth!"

The woman stopped as if she had run into a wall. "How do you know that name?" she asked.

"She is my mother."

"Oh God!" the woman answered. "I am Mrs. Zawuska, your mother was my best friend before the Germans came to Poland."

We talked for a long time. I gave her my address at the dentist's office and finally, we shook hands and parted.

Walking back to the dentist's office I had real feelings of hope. If I could find this woman whom I hardly knew, I could find those I had loved the most.

* * * *

Finding Mrs. Zawuska on a trolley car in Krakow made me aware of miracles. Finding this woman led to many other important events in my life. This chance happening was a doorway to many key things that would quickly follow.

The day after I met her, Mrs. Zawuska sent a chauffeured limousine to the dentist's office to pick me up. I hadn't known she was wealthy. The driver told me to bring my things because I would be living at Mrs. Zawuska's house. I told him I didn't have any things and went with him.

I was still very sick and weak. I was emaciated and couldn't seem to recover from my physical injuries. But where I was sickest was inside my head.

Mr. Zawuska was a very kind man. I remember dinner the first night in their home. I had forgotten how to use a fork and a knife. I ate with my hands. His voice was very soft and kind when he asked me if he could teach me how to use utensils.

Mrs. Zawuska paid to have the best doctors available to tend to my condition. They told her that I was suffering from a nervous breakdown and needed total isolation from other people. The Zawuska family gave up their home for almost a month. They went to the country and let me stay in their house. The only people I saw during this time were the doctors and a woman who brought me food. The doctors gave me some reading material and let me listen to soft music.

In the weeks following, I began to slowly regain my strength.

About this time I found out about my mother's death. This was the worst news I had ever received. She had died near the end of the war. Maybe just weeks away. I don't know for sure. My mother had managed to survive that long, almost to the end of the war. The Germans took more than a thousand female prisoners, women and girls who had managed to survive, and they put them onto a large, rusted hulk of a ship. The ship was moved out onto the ocean. The crew fled the ship by life boat, but before they did, they rigged the boat to explode. The ship exploded and sank miles off shore. My mother was killed. I know this because the sole survivor of the explosion was an Olympic swimmer, a Polish girl, I think, whose name I cannot remember. She told me that my mother had been on the ship. She told me that my mother had died senselessly in the cold waters of the Atlantic Ocean. She had survived because she was a swimmer. My mother could not swim.

Three weeks after I found out about my mother's death, still in a stupor of grief, I received a small ray of hopeful news.

The doctors and Mrs. Zawuska did not want me to continue going to the Missing Persons Center, but I could not stay away. I heard from a woman who had seen Margot that my sister was alive and living with a group of other women who had survived. The women lived in a small town in the center of Germany. This town was about five hundred miles from Krakow.

Mrs. Zawuska and her husband were very opposed to me trying to find  Margot. They wanted me to continue to recuperate. We had a very heated conversation and Mr. Zawuska told me he was not going to give me any money to travel. I told him I did not want money. I wanted Margot. I set out walking the very next day. Mrs. Zawuska gave me a small amount of money and a bunch of candies which I ate during the trip.

With Margot

I got a few rides, but mostly I walked. It took me more than six weeks before I arrived at the town where the woman at the Missing Persons Center said my sister might be living.

The whole time I was walking to this place, I was focused only on the journey to get there. Now, as I walked into this town, my heart was beating very fast. I did not want to discover more tragic news or disappointment. I had come all this way and now stood in the very place I set out to find, and I wondered what to do. I felt afraid of what I might find out. For a while, I just stood there listening to my heart.

Finally, I stopped the first person I saw and asked him if he knew where any survivors were living. I went from house to house. I asked every stranger I ran into. Up one side of the street and down the other.

Just as I began to feel this might not be the right town, a stranger told me he didn't know Margot, but several young women and girls who had survived the camps were living on the other side of town. I ran to the street he described and found the house he was talking about.

I was out of breath. There was a man outside the house working in the yard. I asked him if he knew Margot Landwirth? The man shook his head and told me there was no Margot Landwirth there. It was like being punched in the stomach. I then asked him if this was the house where the survivors lived? The man told me it was.

I walked up to the end of the walkway, still trying to catch my breath. I needed my breath in order to whistle.

Margot and I had a secret way to whistle when we were children, a whistle only we knew. It was a secret way to call each other. As I was catching my breath from running, I remembered that, along with our whistles, Margot and I had secret names for each other. I called her Doda and she called me Didek. I turned around and asked this man if there was a girl named Doda, and I knew before he answered that I had found her. I began to whistle and a moment later I heard Doda's answer to my whistle!

I did not know there was such joy left in the world. How my heart leaped when I knew it was Margot! Finding my twin sister amid the ruins, finding love and hope, hearing her whistle, knowing she had survived! It was a great gift, a miracle.

On our eighteenth birthday, Margot and I promised each other we would never be apart again. She gave me a gold ring which I have never taken off.

****

Where does a human being begin the search for peace after surviving an apocalypse? Are there any answers to the unanswerable questions survivors of the Holocaust endlessly ask themselves? Is there a theologian alive who can adequately respond to a survivor's heartfelt doubts about God and the broken covenant with the Jews?

From Bach and Beethoven to Hitler and Eichmann. What a strange journey from creative excellence to demonic destruction. The decay was born with hatred for the Jews, but the most dangerous enemy was not God; it was the German bystander. Neutrality always helps the aggressor, it never helps the victim.

Survivors remember those who committed the crimes. Their faces are never too far away. If I want to, I can close my eyes and picture their faces. Most of us can. Not enough night exists to banish them from our memory, not enough time has passed to allow them to slip away.

I'm sure many of the executioners were sadists who enjoyed what they were doing. Others did it to survive themselves. Still others used the excuse that they had to follow their orders or be thrown into the ovens. When I think of all the people who committed these crimes, I do not feel hatred anymore. There isn't forgiveness, but there is no longer hatred. Those who were the torturers and the murderers and the liars will pay the price for it. No man can escape that.

Survivors are people like other people, yet we are different, too. We have experienced firsthand and seen the worst man can inflict on his fellow man with our own eyes. We've heard the anguished screams of our families as they were separated from us and some even tortured and killed. Our bodies have felt the piercing sting of countless unanswered blows. We know what it is like to be so hungry the thought of a piece of bread is worth killing another human being, or so thirsty that a single drop of water would be worth a hundred sacks of gold.

With this perspective, we are different. We are human beings, and in that sense we are part of the broader family of man. But we are also survivors, and by this experience our lives have been changed forever. Our perspectives, for good or bad, have been shaped in a way that a normal person, God willing, will never experience. Pain and suffering become like mortar to those who have endured it together, we are held together by it, joined in a common way, one to the other, by the burden of having shared the same pain. If we are in a cell together, you and I, and we are hungry and thirsty together, and we are being deprived of our freedom together, we are sharing nothing but misery, yet we are sharing an experience at the very depth of who we are as human beings. After this, when we are free, when we have food and water, we value these things in a way that others who have not been without can ever understand. We have become brothers by our shared suffering. Maurice Bauman was my brother because of the pain we shared in the camps.

Each of us who was there is family to the others, whether we survived or perished. Family.

For each and every atrocity committed in the Holocaust, there was a human being, an individual at both ends of the equation. Tormentor and tormented, pain-giver and pain-receiver. Sir Isaac Newton determined that in nature, for each and every action there is an equal and opposite reaction. Perhaps this basic law of physics best demonstrates who I really am.

I am here now. There is too little time to spend it wondering why I survived and others did not. I realize as I get closer to the end of my life that we really have such little time to accomplish what is important.

In the early part of life, we try to find our way, to be a success. In the middle part, we have our family and we work harder trying to have more success so the family is comfortable. And then at the end, when all of that is passed, there is time to do other things, to get on with our most important work.

When I think of my life in the camps, it is difficult to imagine a person moving from that life to this life I live today. I sometimes wonder where my life would have led had the Holocaust never happened? But that is not a good way to spend time, either. We live, not in the past and not in tomorrow, we live in today. Today is the day we must choose to make a difference.

* * * *

As my experiences began to block out my memories, God became a distant entity. If He existed, so what? Why worship a God who would allow such suffering to be perpetrated against the innocent? God is supposed to be all powerful. We are taught as children that God has perfect wisdom and goodness, and that God is all powerful. If this is true, then what was happening could not be.

In the camps, it was very hard to believe in anything good when everything around me was so bad. I felt very dead inside. If there was a God, where was He? How could He turn away from all those little babies that didn't do anything? How could He let such terrible things happen to fathers and mothers who had done nothing wrong?

I think Elie Wiesel has explained it best. Wiesel challenges God, yet does not abandon Him. He writes that the relationship between God and man is a two-way communication. Just as man can be judged by God for failure to live up to God's law, so too, can God be judged by man for His failure to enforce the very laws He gave us.

While most of us in the camps still believed in God, it was a conflicted faith. When a human being has religious faith, that person is expressing many things. First, there is a belief and trust in God. Second, there is a loyalty to God, which is not based on proof. Faith is an expression of love through trust. It requires a certain amount of obedience on the part of its possessor; and most of all, faith remains constant in times of joy and in times of sorrow alike.

Faith is a word, that in practice, is much more difficult than in its definition. Faith can be lost over and over again, only to be found in the most unlikely of circumstances. Take this story from a 76-year old survivor of Treblinka:

"I bowed my head to pray. My infant daughter was lying dead inside a suitcase that stood alone in a boxcar without space. I asked Almighty God to take my life, to let me be with my child. Soon after I started to pray, I heard the anguished cry of another mother...she was cradling her dead child, just weeks old, in her arms. I moved to her and took the child

61

and put him with my daughter in the tiny coffin of the suitcase. We sang kaddish for our children and many others joined us. We were a train of dying children and mourning mothers. I do not think any of us cared too much at that minute to be Jewish. Had I been able to save my child, I would have renounced my Jewishness in a second. But then, what mother wouldn't?"

The poet Jacob Glatstein said, "God gave the Torah at Sinai and took it back during the Holocaust." He was right. In these few words both God's power and God's failure to the Jews is acknowledged.

God and man...man and God.

The spiritual and the physical. Does my belief in God allow me to come to grips with what I saw happening all around me?

It is easy to blame God for the Holocaust. It is harder to look at a society like Germany, a culture at the forefront of the arts and cultural expression, and understand how an entire people could turn so rapidly from the pursuit of excellence and beauty to an acceptance of racial genocide.

I believe a man's spiritual condition, his values and belief system, are the key to his success or failure as a human being. This belief, coupled with the fact that I am a survivor of the Holocaust, suggests there is an important lesson to learn by examining the roots of my six lives, which were planted in the soil of love and trust, but fertilized with the misery of captivity and human suffering.

Values are everything. Caring, trying to give of yourself, love. That is what is important. I will not let myself hate any more. Hate is too consuming of an emotion. Hate feeds on itself. It consumes you. People who hate hurt themselves more than they could ever hope to injure those they are hating.

To try to be a caring person takes too much positive energy to waste time with hatred and vengeance. I try to live my life in the present. I worry about things I must do today, and I think about the plans for tomorrow. But I try not to live too much in the past. When I think of my parents, I try to remember them dancing and filled with life. I try not to think of my father standing in a mass grave waiting to be shot or my mother lost in the Atlantic Ocean.

What good can come of it? I leave my hatred to the past. There is no room in my life for it. I pray every day to focus on the living, to give to others today. I want to have peace in my life. To help others and be peaceful.

If I can achieve this, that is enough for any man.

I often tell people I live on borrowed time. This is very true. If God did not have a plan for me, there was a hundred times along my life's journey that He could have left me in the dust. But here I am. And for today, my goal is to give something to someone in need, to reach out to someone who needs a hand up. For today, I will try to be a better man.

German society did not exist within a vacuum during the Holocaust. Outside of the barbed wire fences of the death camps, life went on in a relatively normal fashion. German church-goers attended services and prayed to the same God as those who were being incinerated a few miles away.

Such a paradox can never be totally explained or understood. History must examine why the German people and the world did not raise up their voices and demand that the systematic destruction of European Jews stop.

In western Europe, where there was less support for Hitler's Final Solution, the death rate among Jews was dramatically lower. The refusal, by some non-Jewish people, to blindly follow Germany's anti-Semitic rhetoric did make a difference.

Resistance to evil is certainly no guarantee that evil will not prosper. However, refusing to go along with events that one knows are wrong, even if such refusal is at great personal risk, is the most basic first line defense against evil. It is also the fundamental obligation of each human being.

* * * * *

"In spite of everything, I still believe that people are really good at heart," fourteen year-old Anne Frank wrote from her attic prison. To her child's eyes, the world was not an evil place; sometimes a person just had to look harder to find the good in people.

For us, too, in spite of everything, we wanted to live. There is a certain strength that takes over that helps you stay alive. Some voice inside says, "You are going to live!" The only time you die is when you give up completely and you cannot go on any longer, when your spirit cannot fight any more.

I remember a time about a month before the war was finished, a voice inside me was constantly telling me to keep on living, to keep on fighting to stay alive. I didn't know that the war was going to be over soon. I thought life in the camps was going to continue forever. But there was something inside me that was always saying: "Keep living...keep trying!"

In the camps, my spirit was the first thing taken away from me. I was humiliated every single day, and as hard as it may seem to believe, I got to used to that, too. My will to live was always there. There is a resolve that exists inside a man who is facing crisis that is difficult to describe, but very real. Maybe that is what helped people like me live when the suffering was so great, and the choice not to continue living seemed to be the easier choice.

From the darkness of the concentration camps, grew many compassionate, courageous and generous souls. From the almost unspeakable pain and suffering, came countless acts of genuine selflessness.

Each and every child on this earth is an innocent being. And it is for the innocent, that the moral questions of the Holocaust must be asked, and our answers to those questions, studied.

Is a man who steals bread from a starving man more guilty than one who makes a tick mark on a pad as people are loaded onto cattle cars for transportation to the death camps? Is the concentration camp guard, who marches victims daily to the gas chambers, more or less morally accountable than the German bystander who sees his Jewish neighbors being murdered and does not take a stand against it?

Is a German soldier who fires his rifle at a cringing child any different than the officer who gave him the order? Do the prayers of a German bystander, who walks to church each morning within sight of the smoke-filled sky of the crematoriums, carry the same meaning as those prayers offered up by a Jew awaiting the moment his body will be turned into that smoke?

The moral questions are never-ending, and yet, they are in many ways the same question. To answer any of them, one must assign guilt and innocence; one must create an equation of values where each action can be weighed in relation to the circumstances surrounding it.

Where do we begin to look for answers to these most fundamental questions? Perhaps the best starting place is with the people who performed the deeds, those who ran the death camps. Much study has been undertaken in the last 50 years trying to determine some cause and effect between the camps and those who presided over them.

From the first day, the commandants of the death camps were fully aware of their mission. Their loyalty was to their Führer and the SS, and most served without being overcome by revulsion. When family members of two camp officials were contacted for comment for this book, both denied their fathers had participated in any way. When told that the historical record was beyond challenge, they held to the assertion that history was confusing their fathers with others of the same name.

I have spent a lifetime wondering why the Nazis did what they did. I don't think it so important anymore to understand why the Nazis wanted to kill all Jews. It is more important to realize that such hatred exists; it doesn't go away. It is still out there.

The lesson all men must learn from the Holocaust is that evil is real. It has existed since the inception of man, and it will continue until mankind is extinct. Our protection from future Holocausts starts by acknowledging the existence of evil. As we struggle in search for answers to the moral questions of the Holocaust, all other possible explanations must be stacked on the unshakable foundation of this premise.

The Holocaust can happen again. I believe there is enough hatred and ignorance in this world that death camps could one day happen again. That is why we must talk about what happened in the concentration camps; why we must teach our children where unchecked hatred can lead.

CHAPTER 6

Vengeance is mine; I will repay, saith the Lord.
 −The Holy Bible: Romans 12:19

Perhaps no year was as important to my return to normalcy than the year following the war. In 1946, I was a 19-year old boy in need of revenge. I wanted the Germans to suffer as they had made us suffer. I had no sympathy for them at all. If I could have wiped them all from the face of the earth, I would have done it.

During this period, Allied troops were rounding up Nazi soldiers, collaborators and sympathizers. The Allies gave the Jews who survived the camps a great deal of latitude.

American and Russian soldiers told us to take whatever we wanted. We went from having no bread to taking over the best house on the street, if that's what we wanted to do. Funny, but very few of us cared about that. We were wild children who had been let out of a cage after a long captivity. The normal rules of society did not apply to us.

During this very strange year in my life, Margot met a man and decided to get married. I warned her this was not a good marriage, but she wouldn't listen. I begged her not to marry him, but she was young and in love.

Our time in the camps had affected us. Margot was doing what I was doing, but in a different way. For her, there was only today. If she was in love, she should get married; it was that simple. For me, I became a part of a gang, a band of survivors. We did crazy things. To us there was no law. Nothing mattered.

In the months that followed, we formed an alliance with the Russians to help smuggle Jews across borders. Many of those who were imprisoned in Auschwitz now ranked high in the new scheme of things.

Saccharin was in very short supply in Poland but was in abundance in Germany. My gang decided we should start a business and move saccharin across the border into Poland. This was illegal, but we didn't care about that. After the death camps, smuggling saccharin seemed like a very small indiscretion. We donned the uniforms of Polish soldiers and crossed back and forth between the two countries.

The saccharin business was successful beyond our wildest dreams. We made tremendous amounts of money, whole suitcases of it and we didn't know what to do with it. We went from not having the smallest crumb in the camps to all this money.

After one particularly lucrative trip into Poland, I returned to Germany with two others. We had seven suitcases filled with money. We literally had so much money it was difficult to transport it. Our normal arrangement at the border did not work, and the border guards confiscated the money.

They took every single penny. Tens of thousands of dollars, probably. And the funny thing is we didn't even care. After what we had been through, money was meaningless. We did these crazy things not to get rich but because we had to stay in motion. Constant activity delayed thoughtful introspection.

During this same period, I volunteered to work with the Russians and the American CIA to identify and evict Nazi sympathizers. I spoke German, Polish and Russian and I would do anything, absolutely anything to try to get back at the Germans. One of the jobs I had was to evict people in the middle of the night. American families and Russian families would then go and occupy the houses. We were kicking out the Germans, the Nazis.

I remember their hypocrisy very well. In almost every house, there was a picture of Joseph Stalin and a picture of Franklin Roosevelt hung side by side on the wall. The pictures of their Führer had been destroyed. I believed the Germans were a false people and this seemed to prove it to me. Those pictures really made me hate them more.

In nine out of ten eviction cases, when I walked in, one German would fall all over himself giving me the name of another German. He would say, "Maybe I was a Nazi, but the guy down the street was a *real* Nazi. I was a little guy, he was a leader, a big Nazi." Whenever they did this, it made it very easy to do my work.

I realize now that this aggression was my way of getting over the war. I felt nothing but hatred for the Germans and this small action against them allowed me to settle that hate. If a German didn't leave, I threw him out onto the street. I told him his house wasn't his anymore. And I meant it. When they begged me for mercy, I did not hear them. I thought of my mother and father and I didn't hear them at all.

* * * *

Next, I went to Berlin, to a Jewish refugee camp set up to house Jews awaiting return to Belgium. At this time, my brother-in-law, Adam, and I started to work with the Jewish Underground. Adam was a survivor of Buchenwald. The Underground organization was still critically important to the survival of many Jews. Polish Jews, for example, were being detained in Germany by the Russians until they could be sent back to Poland. The Underground worked to smuggle as many of these people out of Germany into Italy, and from there on to Israel, as we could.

We helped save hundreds of people. We had survivors who had learned a great deal in the camps. Between us, we were able to provide perfect papers for the people we were trying to help. Our goal was to get Jewish families out of Europe to Israel. I worked primarily with getting Polish Jews out of Germany. These Jews were put into retention camps by the Russians who wouldn't let them leave. We started a movement and it gained momentum very quickly. Many people were saved that otherwise might have spent their lives as Russian prisoners or worse.

One experience I remember did not turn out so well. We negotiated with the Russians to allow us to come in and remove a whole camp of Polish Jews who were being detained. We returned to the camp with six large covered trucks to remove the prisoners, but the camp was empty. The Russians had moved them before we could get them out. It was just one more lie.

During my work with the Underground, I had my first experiences with helping those really in need. One mission the group adopted was to get pregnant Jewish mothers to hospitals. After the near genocide of the Jewish people, every baby was important.

I loved helping the new mothers. This was the first time in my life that I had really experienced the pleasure of helping. We became quite well known in the retention camp in Berlin. People who needed help to get their relatives out of Poland sought us out, and most of the time, we helped them.

I worked as an operative of the Allies for thirteen months. By the time I was ready to leave and pursue another path, the worst of my hatred was gone and my anger had started to subside.

During this time, I got so many bad things out of my soul. I was very lucky to have this way to come back to a normal life. So many survivors never had a chance to take any action against our tormentors. For them, it is harder to get on with life. They are still filled with that feeling of powerlessness. Only by taking power, was I able to rid myself of that feeling of having no control. What people should realize is that most of us would have done anything for vengeance. We would have killed. If I had seen the men from the death camps, it would not have taken me a second. I would have tortured them and killed them. This is not a good thing to know about yourself.

But facing the truth is important. This period helped me get rid of all the anger and bad thoughts that had consumed me. I found some peace with myself and the world around me.

There is no life-affirming value when a person keeps hatred and anger in his heart. Only bad things can come from such thoughts. It is possible to take that hate and anger, every drop of it, and change it into love and caring. Once a survivor can reach this point, he will be on the way to a better, more fulfilling life. No matter how cruel the past has been to you, today can be a happy time. Just for today, let yourself enjoy life. Instead of hating, reach out to your brother or sister and help them. Kindness makes all the difference, both to the person receiving it and the person giving it.

I still have certain strong feelings, they are not hate, but feelings with conviction against the terrible things which took place in Germany. I will never go back to Germany, but I don't hate Germans, this new generation.

* * * *

In 1947, I returned to Belgium. Margot was seven months pregnant and did not want to have her baby in Germany. Travel papers were pending and would not be ready in time for her to leave before the baby came. I went to Belgium in an attempt to make arrangements to smuggle Margot, her husband and father-in-law out of Germany.

In Belgium, I was arrested and thrown in jail. I had been traveling with two other people, a man and a woman. The man had papers and we did not. Belgian authorities put me in a town jail with Nazis. I went crazy and began screaming and fighting. After a week, they found out I was born in Belgium and they contacted my Uncle Herman.

Herman was a well known and respected diamond broker, a wealthy man whose main business was importing rock diamonds from England. He got my friend and me out of jail.

I still had to arrange for Margot and her family to get to Belgium. I contacted some Belgian soldiers and told them what I needed. They agreed to smuggle her in the back of an army supply truck. By this time, Margot was eight months pregnant. The soldiers put a cot in the back of their truck and blocked it in with supplies. Looking at the truck from the outside, it looked like it was filled with boxes. Margot and her family made it to Belgium in time for her to have her son there.

With this job behind me, I went to live with my uncle and his wife.

Herman and I didn't get along very well. He was rich and he was very focused on the material world. I liked my aunt, who had my mother's name, Fanny, but my uncle was a hard man to like.

I didn't have a profession and was trying to decide what to do with my life, and how I was going to make a living. I asked my uncle to help me and he arranged for me to go to a factory to learn how to be a diamond cutter.

Each morning, I went to the factory and spent my day learning the art of how to cut diamonds. All around me, the people I worked with, were people who had cheered on the Nazis and who hated Jews. They weren't open about it now that the war was over but it was still very clear to me how they felt.

I got a little angrier each day working side-by-side with the same people who had done nothing while so many innocent men, women and children were killed in the concentration camps in their backyards. My rage from the war was still very close to the surface, and I could not get along with some of these people. Herman was involved in everything in this factory and he thought I was the one making trouble. I wasn't the bad guy, but I told my uncle that I would make peace and learn how to be a diamond cutter.

In spite of our differences, in the following months my Uncle Herman became attached to me. While I was learning how to cut diamonds, and there is an art to cutting stones, my uncle was planning something else. Herman never had any sons and he came up to me and said, "I want you to be my son." It was hard to imagine what being Herman's son would be like, but at first I didn't say no.

Herman took me to his safe and opened it and pulled out three long boxes filled with diamonds. The boxes were about six inches wide and three feet long. They were filled with thousands and thousands of diamonds. It didn't phase me. The diamonds didn't mean anything to me. The boxes could have been filled with sand. Riches of any kind didn't matter to me at all. Just as when we made suitcases of money smuggling saccharin, money was unimportant.

After Herman showed me his wealth, he repeated that he wanted me to become his son. He ran a large and successful business and he wanted me to take over for him one day.

Adoption in Belgium is quite different than in the United States. The person who wants to adopt and the child being adopted go to the police station and fill out papers. We went to the police station and right in the middle of filling out papers, I stopped.

I couldn't go through with it. I didn't really love Herman, and I didn't respect him. Max Landwirth was my father. His being dead didn't change that. Other than the financial security Herman offered, I didn't know why I should become his son, or why he should become my father. When I told him this, he became angry, hurt and embarrassed. We left the police station. Herman did not want to have much to do with me after that.

I moved out of Herman's house and decided to move in with my sister, Margot. She had just had her baby, and was on her own. We both needed to be together as a family. We moved into a small apartment together.

I began feeling restless and thought constantly about starting a new life in a new country. For hundreds of thousands of Europeans, America loomed across the Atlantic Ocean as a potential refuge from Hitler's insanity. While Germany had expelled all non-Aryans as undesirable, America held opened her arms with the invitation that in America, we were all immigrants. America offered opportunity for every man or woman willing to work hard.

I wanted to go to America and see these things for myself. If the stories were true, anything was possible. I could start over and become anything I dared to dream.

* * * * *

In 1946 and 1947, I became very close with my cousin Kitty Birnbaum. She was important to me after the war. We were great friends. I told her I had decided to leave Belgium and make a life in the United States. I had no money, no possessions. I couldn't ask Herman for money now.

I went down to the dock in Antwerp hoping to find a boat that was going to America that needed a crew member willing to work for passage. I went back to the dock every day for a couple of weeks. I became a familiar face there, and one day a dock worker pointed me to a ship that needed crew members. As fate would have it, the boat was bound for the United States. I signed on to work my way to America.

The day I left Belgium for the United States, I had few clothes, and no money. Kitty came to see me off and gave me $20 dollars, which at that moment was more valuable to me than all of Herman's diamonds. That was just like Kitty, she always gave everything. She held nothing back. It was a very kind and touching good-bye.

I was very sad inside. I was breaking the promise Margot and I had made on our eighteenth birthday never to separate.

I don't remember the name of the ship, but it was a large cargo boat. Other than the few clothes I owned, I had very little in the way of possessions to take to America. I did have something very special to bring with me, though, one of the most special possessions I've ever had. In a small suitcase I had an old Torah that was discovered after the war. Polish Jews had buried the Torah deep in the ground to keep the Nazis from burning it. After the war, the survivors dug up the sacred book and Pinkus Steinbach, Margot's father-in-law, gave it to me to bring to America. The Torah is hundreds of years old, and to those who value history, probably priceless as well.

With the Torah, and Kitty's $20 bill, I boarded this old run down ship and worked my way to America as a deck laborer. After five weeks at sea, the ship sailed into New York Harbor.

It is difficult to express my feelings as I arrived in America. I felt so many emotions all at once – joy, fear, happiness, melancholy. I missed my parents very much, as only a child who has lost his parents to violence can. But at the same time, I was very excited to be arriving in America. I had dreamed about it for so long.

In the months immediately after the war, when I was trying to find myself and to create a life that had meaning, I had faced one defeat after another. These setbacks didn't bother me as they might have bothered someone who had not survived all I had. My idea of real suffering was on a totally different plane than life's normal disappointments.

As I looked at the Statue of Liberty, I did not think of the bad things, only the possibilities opening up to me. The same voice that kept me going during the war, now urged me to do my best once my feet touched American soil.

Part II of the book will tell you about my experiences as an immigrant who could not speak English. I will tell you about one of the most exciting times in my life, in America's life, with the story of the Project Mercury astronauts. Part III of my life story will take you inside Give Kids the World.

Thank you for sharing my pain in Part I. I hope in parts II and III you will share my joy and love as well, as I tell you the story of one man's journey to this extraordinary country of America, the only place in the world that allows each and every person an opportunity to plant their dreams and watch them grow.

The Project Mercury astronauts: (seated) Senator John Glenn and Betty Grissom, for late husband Gus Grissom, (from left) Gordon Cooper, Scott Carpenter, Alan Shepard, Wally Schirra, Deke Slayton

The Mercury Years

When it is dark enough, men see the stars.
—Ralph Waldo Emerson [1840]

Part III: Reaching for the Stars

Seven men come to Cocoa Beach
To test the limits man could reach.
An innkeeper watches them, one by one,
Ride their rockets towards the sun.
First Shepard breaks the earthly plane,
Orbits the world, and back he came.

Grissom and Glenn, in their turns,
Circle the earth in rockets that burn
With America's hopes and dreams.
Watching, as they shed their earthly seams,
Is the awed, up-turned eyes of an immigrant,
Who sees the future in that instant.

From the barbed wire of the devil's gate,
He frees himself, lets go of hate.
For Max and Fanny, he pushes on and on,
For he is here, and they are gone.
He finds the spirit of God, which lives in man,
That conquers the past as no man can.

From the fires of Hitler's hell,
To the dreams of The Starlight Motel.
Who could have foretold such a journey?
From riding atop death's gurney,
To a limousine in a hero's motorcade.
What a remarkable journey made!

Part IV: America...America...America

A young President challenges us to be great,
To overcome man's prejudice and hate;
To the adventurers, he points to space;
To the earthbound, he opens his arms to embrace
Every color on God's palette;
In the immigrant's heart, a fire is lit

That burns more brightly with each passing day.
From last to first, he leads the way;
By humble example and selfless toil
 A common man rose to royal
Expectations; But still, there are the children...
Innocence, fighting a race so hard to win.

Embracing America as a native son,
The innkeeper puts himself above no one.
America, where all men are equal to achieve
The grandest magic imagination can weave.
America, where the challenge to be great
Overcomes the madness of any tyrant's hate.

The American Dream, so simple to impart.
For all who seek it, the American Heart.
He adds his love to the country he chose,
Dedicates himself to the memory of those
Who perished...especially the innocent...
Perhaps it was for the children he was sent.

CHAPTER 1

To find your way in this world, listen to your heart.
—PJ Hendricks [1972]

Because of the quota on Belgium immigrants, I needed a sponsor in America, or I would not have been allowed to leave Belgium. My Aunt Selma and Uncle Ernest sponsored me to come to the United States.

Aunt Selma was very good to me and helped me a great deal. I lived with her and Uncle Ernest in Jackson Heights, New York. For a while, I slept on the couch in the living room.

Before the war, Aunt Selma had not been a particularly religious person. However, she made a promise to God during the war that if her family survived, she would turn her life to God. When I saw the depth of her commitment to her faith, I took the Torah that had survived the war and gave it to her as a gift. She in turn, gave the Torah to her synagogue.

The Torah, particularly because of where it had come from, and what those who had saved it had suffered and endured, was a treasure to me and to all Jewish people. The Torah is a symbol of goodness. This one, because of where it had been and what those who saved it had suffered and endured, was particularly special.

America's promise not withstanding, I did not have an easy time of it when I first arrived in the United States. For many of us who came to America after the war, we came with the expectation of a good job and endless opportunity for all. It did not take long for reality to replace the fairy tale expectations. Making a life in a new country, especially in the melting pot of New York City wasn't going to be easy. However, America offered the one thing that did not exist in Nazi Germany: hope.

I was lucky. I had a place to live and a job. Not knowing much English made it very hard and a little frightening for many of us, but Aunt Selma and Uncle Ernest made it a little easier for me.

I had focused on leaving Europe and getting to America for many months. Now that I was here, I had to find a job to support myself. My diamond cutting apprenticeship in Antwerp had readied me for that profession. I became quite adept at cutting stones. So good, that a diamond broker from the United States named Abe Silverstein came to Belgium to

81

see stones I had cut. The diamond broker told me that if I ever came to New York City, to look him up and he would give me a job. The day after I arrived in the city, I did just that.

It so happened that my Uncle Ernest also worked in diamonds. He took me to see Abe Silverstein in the heart of the diamond cutting district of New York City and was instrumental in helping me get a job.

The only problem was the way they cut diamonds in Europe and they way they cut them in America were two different worlds. I would have starved cutting stones the way I was taught to cut in Antwerp. I had to re-train myself completely and cut the diamonds the way they were cutting them in America. In the United States, it was all production, numbers and gross quantity. In Antwerp, cutting diamonds was an art. I had to stop being an artist or I wouldn't earn enough money to feed myself. Uncle Ernest took me under his wing and showed me how to cut diamonds the American way.

In the weeks that followed, I learned more was better. Quicker, more profitable. I was paid for the number of stones I cut, not how well I cut them. Changing what I had learned was hard, but if Mr. Silverstein didn't care how pretty the cuts were, why should I?

New York City troubled me. I wasn't very happy there. I looked around at the city, the size of it, the crowds and the dirt, and I began to have some doubts. Why had I left Belgium? Like many immigrants, I thought New York City was all there is to America, when it really is a city unlike any other place in the world.

During the months that followed, I grew less and less fond of New York City and more and more homesick. I decided to go back to Belgium to attend my cousin Kitty's wedding. On the ship back to Europe, I had a lot of time to think. I didn't feel right about returning, but I didn't yet feel like I belonged in America. I felt like a man between two countries and wondered if I would ever feel at home again anywhere.

No sooner than I had boarded the ship to return to Europe did I realize that I didn't want to go back to Europe any more than I wanted to stay in New York City. What I wanted was to find a place in America more suitable to what I needed. A better place for me to pursue my personal goals and dreams. I realized as we sailed out of New York Harbor, away from the Statue of Liberty, instead of towards her, that I was making a mistake. I would probably be back as soon as this boat landed and I could get on another one heading back to America.

I was still very young and the war was still very much with me. The time on the boat back to Europe helped me get my mind straightened out.

When I got to Europe, I attended Kitty's wedding and spent a short time in Belgium visiting. Within six months, I was once again on a ship working my way back to America. I think I needed that time to find my own heart. When I came back to America, I knew this time things would be better. I would make a success of my life no matter how hard it was to get started.

As I tried to find my way in America, I tried to do everything with tremendous passion. I wanted to prove I could succeed in this great country. I wanted to honor the memory of my mother and father so they would have been proud of me. When I returned to New York, every job I took, I tried to do the best job that I could. I tried to be the best bellhop, or the best floor sweeper. It did not matter what the job was, I tried to do it as if it was the most important job in the world.

Things began to improve almost immediately. I began to feel more a part of things, more confident. Then in January, 1950, I received a telegram from Uncle Sam. I had been drafted into the United States Army!

With my boot camp platoon getting ready to ship out to Korea

I thought someone had played a joke on me. The draft notice was real, though, and I reported to Fort Devens in Ayer, Massachusetts for basic training to learn how to be an infantry soldier. I was on orders to go to Korea when the Korean War was going full force. I had been sent with 500 other soldiers from Fort Devens to Fort Dix to ship out to the war. I still couldn't believe it; but I wanted to live in America. If the price for living in this country was to fight in the Korean War, I would be willing to pay it.

A couple of hours before we shipped out, an officer looked over my record and saw that I had been a diamond cutter. At that time, the Army used field radios which relied on crystals for tuning sensitivity. Crystals had to be cut and placed in the radios to make them work. There was a tremendous shortage of experienced people working with these crystals and the officer thought since I knew how to cut diamonds, I could cut crystals, too.

The two jobs didn't have the slightest thing in common, but I didn't argue the point. Even though I didn't know what the heck a crystal even looked like, I kept my mouth shut. The alternative was to get on the boat and go and fight in the war. I already loved America, but I had had enough of war. If I could avoid it while still doing my duty, that was okay with me.

I got pulled from the ranks of the infantry soldiers and was given amended orders making me a stateside crystal cutter. This led to a job as a telephone installer and repairman.

At Fort Dix I was assigned to the radio shack for the First Army. To learn my job I had to first learn how to climb telephone poles, but every time I tried, I got dizzy. The Master Sergeant in charge of my training thought I was just goofing off, and from those first days I got on his bad list. He assigned me to clean windows as punishment. Finally, I got into the radio shack to learn how to repair telephones. The Master Sergeant told me to take the half ton truck parked outside and go and pick up supplies. I didn't know how to drive, and I told him this, but he thought I was malingering. He said he didn't care if I could drive or not, just get in the truck and get the supplies.

I got in the truck. I had no idea how to drive. I put the truck into gear and it immediately backed into the radio shack. That accident caused a lot of damage. My boss was so angry he put me on KP for six weeks. When I was done pushing pots and pans, I had to go to driver's school to learn how to drive.

My two years of military service concluded and I was honorably discharged from the Army in 1952. Serving in the Army helped me get my bearings on life in America and I began to live my fourth life in earnest. My years in the service passed so quickly. It seemed that one day I was waiting to get on a ship bound for Korea, and the next day I was being discharged. It all seemed to happen almost overnight.

I got out of the Army and went back to New York City. I wanted to work for the telephone company, but at that time there was a strong anti-Semitic bias and I couldn't get hired.

I didn't really want to be in New York City, but it was the only place I knew that a person could work in diamonds, and cutting diamonds was the only trade I knew, other than the skills I had learned in the Army. Once I was back in the city, I decided that if I went back to the diamond business, I would probably never leave New York, and that was not how I saw my future. I decided then and there to take any other job, learn a new trade, and someday relocate to a different city in the United States.

* * * *

In 1952, I was at a crossroads. I had completed my military service, and now I looked at the world around me with a new set of eyes. What did I want to do with my life? I had been pulled out of school and thrown into a concentration camp at the age of 13. My formal education had been interrupted. This logically limited my opportunities, but I did not think about the obstacles that had been placed in front of me. I asked myself this – if I could do anything, work in any business, if education and money weren't considerations, what would I choose?

I didn't have an easy or fast answer to this question.

I moved into a small, closet-like room and started paying five dollars a week rent. The room was so tiny that I had to get undressed in the hall-way. If I was in the room, I was on the bed. It was the only furniture. There wasn't room for anything else. If I had food, I usually ate it on the bed. During this time, I often slept past breakfast because I couldn't afford to buy anything to eat.

The hospitality industry did not require a person to have a college degree, so I decided to give it a chance. This began a series of entry-level jobs in the hotel business. From hopping bells, to working the night desk. At one time or another, I did every job there was to do in a hotel, from changing linen and cleaning bathrooms, to managing the front desk.

My new career began in earnest on November 11, 1952 at The Wellington Hotel on Seventh Avenue and 59th Street in New York City. I worked the night desk and began to learn the hotel business. About this same time, I used my GI Bill benefits to enroll in the New York Hotel Technology School. I quickly learned some fundamental lessons in hotel management.

The hotel business is the people's business. That's the most important thing I learned from my early days at the Wellington.

Most businesses are based on pleasing people. If you want to be successful in business, first you have to be successful with people. If you want to be successful with people, you have to give them what they want. You have to learn and understand what customers need. The best way to do this is not to talk, but to listen. If you really listen, the customers will always tell you.

****

In 1954, I made two important decisions. I married my first wife Josephine Guardino, and left New York for Miami Beach, Florida. The move to Miami Beach was more of a fortunate accident than a well-executed plan. Jo is Italian and the Italians had a custom where they put money in a purse at the wedding as a gift to the newlyweds. We had about $800 from the wedding and decided to use some of it to spend our honeymoon in Miami Beach.

We got there and liked the city and the climate. It was warm and far away from New York City. As it turned out, we never used the return portion of the tickets back to New York.

After more than two years of learning the business from the ground up, I felt ready to try a new hotel environment. Though I felt nervous about leaving what was familiar, Florida seemed like a good place to make a fresh start.

I went looking for a job in Miami Beach and couldn't find one. At hotel after hotel I was turned down because I didn't have Miami Beach experience. I wasn't even sure what that meant, but I continued to leave applications at every hotel I could. After several weeks of job hunting, I finally found a job, not in a hotel as I had hoped for, but at Burdines Department Store. I was hired to work in the basement, removing suits from boxes and placing the suits on hangers. The pay was about $45 a week.

After a month of hanging suits, I received a call from the manager of The President Madison Hotel in Miami Beach. He had reviewed my application and was ready to interview me. I saw an advertisement in the newspaper that the job the manager was calling me about paid $75 a week. When I was offered the job, the pay was $65 a week. I pointed out that the ad said $75 a week, but the manager said he was offering $65 and I could take it or leave it. It was more than I was making at

Burdines and it was in the industry where I wanted to try and make a career, so I took the job.

The night manager was an alcoholic who was much more interested in drinking than he was in working. He basically let me take over all the responsibilities of his job, while giving me none of the credit or any additional pay. The conditions at that hotel were terrible. I was doing everybody's job. Any time somebody didn't want to work, they would call me. I was the broom of that outfit. Everybody gave me the business, but I didn't care. I did what they asked. I knew that they were taking advantage of me, but I needed to learn the business, to get an education, so I went along with it.

On New Year's Eve and Christmas, when nobody wanted to work, I always worked. When they needed a cashier in the bar, I did that. When the housekeeper went on vacation, I went to work as a housekeeper. One time she was out for four weeks, so for four weeks straight, I pushed the maid's cart and cleaned rooms and bathrooms. Whatever they needed, I did without complaint. After a while, the owner began to trust me a little bit.

I moved steadily from one job to the next. Each job learned was another hour of study earned in my on-the-job degree in hotel management.

There were all kinds of crazy things happening at The President Madison Hotel. I kept my eyes and ears open and learned a lot of things, both what to do and what not to do, in running a hotel. I was getting a good education on how things should not be done, and sometimes this lesson is more important than learning how to do it right.

I worked out an arrangement with taxi drivers. When one would recommend The President Madison to a fare, we would give the driver a little money called turkey money because it kept food on everybody's table.

One night, a regular turkey money cab driver dropped a man and woman at the hotel. The man looked familiar. I asked the cabby who the fare was, but the driver didn't know. The man came up to register. I asked him to sign in and pay in advance. The customer shook his head. He had no intention of paying in advance. I told him at The President Madison that was how everybody paid. He turned around and left. The couple got in the taxi and drove away.

The next day the Miami Herald ran a front page story about Rock Hudson, who had just married his secretary. The man in the picture was the same guy who never paid in advance. Hudson and his fiancee had gone to The Fountainbleu Hotel where advance payment was not required.

One of the things I learned at The President Madison was that things are not always what they appear to be. A group of young women from New York arrived at the hotel for Easter vacation. We were overbooked and had no rooms available. I apologized and explained we would put them up in a different hotel across the street, but they didn't want any part of that. In fact, they got upset and began to cause a commotion.

When the hotel manager heard them, he came out of his office and called me every name in the book. I was stupid, he said. I was finished at The President Madison. History. Fired. He sent me to his office and told me to wait for him.

As I watched the women cross the street, I wondered where I could go and find another job. When my boss returned, I began to plead my case. He held up his hand and explained it was all part of the game. I wasn't fired, he said, just go back to work.

Good cop, bad cop. I never forgot that.

* * * *

The President Madison employed a lot of corrupt and lazy people, so when another employee named Florence suggested we both leave and start our own restaurant, it didn't take long to convince me.

Florence had a secret recipe for southern fried chicken long before Colonel Sanders created Kentucky Fried Chicken. She believed we could create a successful restaurant and it seemed like a good idea to me. I thought it could be a big success and make a lot of money. And besides all of that, owning the business, any business, was very much a part of what I thought it took to find the American Dream.

I borrowed a thousand dollars from my friend, Lester Jacobs, and Florence and I started a small restaurant and bar on Seventh Avenue in downtown Miami. Though we worked very hard, the restaurant did not succeed. The chicken tasted great, but nobody came to eat it. Secret recipe or not, we weren't selling any chickens.

After a few weeks without customers, Florence went back to her old job. I continued operating the restaurant, waiting tables, taking orders, cooking the food, serving the food and washing the dishes.

I got to the point where I couldn't buy supplies for the restaurant. We had a convenience store in the back, and any time somebody ordered something off the menu, I'd run there, buy the stuff, cook it and serve it. Once a customer came in and ordered a steak, but the only steak in the convenience store was frozen. I dropped it in the deep fryer till it was done, threw it on a plate and carried it out. The customer didn't complain, but he didn't come back, either.

One afternoon when business was non-existent. I got a call from my wife asking me to bring home some juice, milk and bread. Jo needed supplies for the family. I looked in the cash register and realized I didn't have enough money to buy even those few staples, let alone the restaurant supplies.

I couldn't buy any milk or juice or bread. I sat down and thought about what I was going to do. Jo needed these supplies for all of us. There was no way that I could continue doing what I was doing. Nobody would sell me a piece of bread unless I could pay. I had no customers, no business and no money. I realized I couldn't continue with the restaurant.

The decision wasn't hard. I didn't even say good-bye to the guy who had leased the restaurant to us. I turned everything off, took the key, closed the restaurant, tossed the key into the street and took a bus to The Fountainbleu Hotel.

I told a friend who worked there I needed to get a job that day. I'd take anything. My friend told me I was crazy, nobody hired that fast. I asked him about hopping bells. He said that a man named Harry the Horse controlled that part of the hotel and he had to like you before you could hop bells. Harry the Horse had a kickback arrangement with all the bellhops in the hotel. He liked me and held out a uniform. If it fit, he said, I could start that day.

I made sure that uniform fit me and lined up at the three o'clock bellmen inspection. We didn't use racks, wagons or pull carts. We carried all luggage by hand. If a guest had six suitcases, we had to stack them like books and manage to carry them somehow.

That day I made $18 and to me, it was the biggest day in my little life. I stopped and bought what Jo wanted. When I came home, I was so happy and proud. I hadn't had any money in my pocket in a long time. I figured I could make up to $120 a week at the hotel. This meant I could pay off my debts and provide for my growing family.

I came home to find Jo sitting on the bed, asking where I had been all day. She had tried to call me at the restaurant and was worried when I wasn't there. She even smelled my shirt to see if I smelled like chicken grease. If I had been at work, that was how I would smell. I laughed and told Jo that I had made $18 hopping bells at the Fountainbleu. My days in the chicken business were over.

****

After working a month at the Fountainbleu, my old boss from The President Madison Hotel called. He wanted me back as the night clerk. The problem was I made $120 a week hopping bells at the Fountainbleu, twice what Mr. Raffle had paid. He couldn't afford me.

But three days later, he called back. He and his partners agreed to pay me $120 a week and give me the title of assistant manager. When I reported back to work at The President Madison, I was now in charge of the same people who had taken advantage of me before.

After working the front desk for a few months, I began to get a feel for the way things should be done. Then the manager was fired when he got caught stealing whiskey in coke bottles. Just like that, I became temporary manager of The President Madison Hotel.

Though my salary didn't increase, my responsibilities did. The next day, I fired a couple of drunks. They were bad for the hotel but had been there for more than a decade. Mr. Raffle was furious till I explained they were drunk, lazy and criminal. These men would rent rooms but not list them as rented. That way, they could pocket the money.

Mr. Raffle decided that I had the hotel's best interests at heart and supported my decision. He gave me free rein to run the hotel as I saw fit. During this time, I began to like my work and realized I might have finally found my place in the world.

My answer to hotel problems was to try out solutions that were best for the customer. I never forgot that the men and women renting the rooms had many other places to choose from. The hotel prospered under my management. So much so that Sid Raffle called me into his office and complimented my performance.

One thing led to another and I really began to understand how the hotel business worked. I had learned the business from the ground up. Now as a manager, I was trying out my ideas and they were working.

It struck me that I might have a genuine talent for the hotel business. Like a musician who had learned to play his notes on the piano, I had the basics down and felt ready to make a little music of my own. Riding the crest of my first business success, I had an accidental meeting with the man who would change my life forever.

The first time I met B.G. McNabb I had no idea who he was. To me, he was just a guest at the President Madison Hotel, not the General Manager of the Intercontinental Ballistic Missiles Division for General Dynamics. He turned out to be a very important man in the building of America's space program. He had been put in charge of making the space program come to life at Cape Canaveral. I didn't know any of this then.

When B.G. McNabb went to the Cape in 1955, he realized his most significant problems both related to a lack of housing in Cocoa Beach. He needed to create homes for the permanent employees coming in from all over the country, and he also needed to create lodging where the transient workers could stay. He had to build it all, including a motel to house the people who would construct the site.

Cocoa Beach offered no hotel or motel of any kind. McNabb went to Holiday Inn, Ramada, Congress Inn, all the big hotel corporations at the time, and tried to get one of them to build a hotel there. They laughed. Cocoa Beach was such a tiny speck, they weren't willing to build him a garage there, much less a hotel.

McNabb wasn't sure who would build the motel, he only knew what he was going to name it: *The Starlight Motel*. The men who were going to reach for the stars were going to live there. From the guys who ran the electronics to the astronauts who flew the rockets, they would all come together like magic. They would accomplish great things, and they would live at The Starlight Motel.

CHAPTER 2

Before honor is humility.
 – The Holy Bible: Book of Proverbs 22:4

Someone referred McNabb to Sid Raffle at the President Madison on Miami Beach. He portrayed Raffle as a seat-of-the-pants kind of guy who could get things done. The two men met and McNabb explained if Raffle would build the motel, the Air Force would guarantee it would lease a minimum of 30 rooms per year for 365 days a year. Boeing, North American Rockwell, Lockheed and the other contractors all had the same problem and were willing to make similar guarantees. When Mr. Raffle finally opened his motel, he had 90 out of 99 rooms leased by all the various contractors. Back then, motels that were less than 100 rooms paid less taxes, which is why builders constructed so many 99 room motels.

As funny as it sounds, a two dollar necktie led me to one of the most exciting parts of my life. While he negotiated the contract to build the Starlight, B.G. stayed at the President Madison. The dining room required men to wear a necktie. He didn't have one.

He came up to the front desk and asked where he could purchase a tie. I gave him mine, the only tie I owned. "Here," I said, "you can borrow this one."

After dinner, McNabb returned the tie to me and we chatted for a few minutes. He noticed my accent, asked me where I was from, handed back my necktie and that was that. I put my tie back on and didn't give this any more thought. McNabb was just a customer. It was my job to help him. I did things like that all the time.

Shortly after that, B.G. McNabb and Mr. Raffle began construction on the motel that would change my life.

The Starlight Motel was almost finished and Mr. Raffle introduced McNabb to a man he had chosen to manage the motel. McNabb didn't like him at all. The man talked too fast and too much and didn't seem as though he would work well with all the VIPs who would be staying there.

McNabb asked the man to leave the room so he and Mr. Raffle could talk in private. If Raffle insisted on this guy as manager, McNabb said, he would cancel the government's contract for the 30 rooms. Raffle didn't want to lose the guarantee to rent a third of his rooms and asked what kind of person McNabb wanted.

What happened next was a continuation of the magic that I have almost come to expect from my life. I did not know it then, but my fourth life was ending and I was embarking on my fifth life, the one which would help prepare me for the most important time still to come.

McNabb remembered this guy at The President Madison Hotel who had loaned him a necktie. He couldn't remember my name, or even what I looked like, but he remembered I had funny accent. Mr. Raffle knew B.G. was talking about me. That's how I got the job as manager of The Starlight Motel.

Mr. Raffle got the impression that B.G. didn't like my accent. I could be the manager of The Starlight Motel, he said, but the accent would have to go. Mr. Raffle told me to go to one of those speech schools where they teach you to speak English properly. I didn't have much money then. Paying seven dollars per lesson seemed like a fortune to me, but becoming manager of The Starlight Motel was a great chance and I didn't want to mess it up.

I tried my best to fix my accent, but it didn't work.

After several English lessons, the tutor said, "Henri, you're a nice guy and I know you're trying very hard. But I can tell you right now, if I continue teaching you, I will talk like you. There's no way that I can teach you to speak any better English than you speak right now. You might get a better vocabulary, but your accent, forget it."

I panicked. I saw my whole future going up in smoke. I told Mr. Raffle, "I'm sorry. I let you down. My tutor just quit. I'd better turn in my sheriff's badge over there in Cocoa Beach and you can get somebody else to run The Starlight Motel."

Sid Raffle, was very kind and had no intention of letting me resign from the project because a $7 an hour tutor threw in the towel. He sent me to The Starlight to take care of accounting and set up hotel procedures. He told me to work behind the scenes, try not to talk to the guests or be visible out front.

That was the beginning of something wonderful. When I look back, I wonder if it hadn't been for the first bellman's job, where would I be today? If a lazy manager hadn't stolen whiskey, what would have happened?

* * * *

Raffle sent me and Julia Doyle to run The Starlight. Julia and I began a long and wonderful working relationship in 1954. Julia helped me a great deal in running The Starlight. When I was running around, she was staying behind putting all the little pieces together to make a whole. She was my secretary, my confidante and a tremendously loyal friend. We had a great professional relationship which began at The President Madison Hotel in Miami Beach where she worked with me as a cashier.

My personality, accent and all, seemed to be an immediate hit with the local clientele. When I got there, The Starlight Motel was maybe 80 percent finished. I was asked to go up there with a fellow by the name of Bob Killarin, who was a very talented food and beverage manager. His responsibility was to set up all the food and beverage operations. Mine was to set up the systems at the front desk, housekeeping and accounting. We had a divided responsibility. My main job was to keep an eye on the money and try to stay in the background.

In 1957, The Starlight Motel was nearing completion in an area that was almost completely deserted. There were lots of palmetto bugs and more than a lot of mosquitoes, but the town still only had one restaurant and two gas stations.

McNabb is who I remember best during those first months. He was a little short guy, real brown from the sun, who was always yelling and screaming and threatening. I was young and I wanted to do well, but B.G. was very strict with me. He demanded a lot. But there were two sides to him. On the one hand, he could be tough and had a great deal of power. On the other hand, he always watched out for me and helped me when I got in trouble.

He summed up his early days at the Cape by saying, "There was a feeling in the air that what we were doing was important, damned important to the future of America. The people who came to work at the Cape all shared in this sense of mission. It was an incredibly focused time. Men worked their asses off in the day and partied their asses off at night. That's just the way it was. There wasn't so much of a class thing as there is today. The NASA boys and the building contractors and the fly boys, everybody was together. We worked together and we played together. And together, we built the Cape."

The Government had in fact studied four primary sites to serve as the home of America's space program: Alaska, Texas, Mexico and early long shot,

Cape Canaveral. McNabb was chosen to sit on an eight-man committee to choose the best of the four locations for launching rockets into outer space.

He had launched the first guided missiles from China Lake, California at the Naval Weapons Test Center in 1945. He had also served as special director of research on the hydrogen bomb project, handling the transportation of liquid hydrogen. It has an extremely low temperature and McNabb had to figure out how to move it and then build a system from the ground up. B.G. went to General Dynamics in San Diego to try to convince them to build a hydrogen-propelled missile. He was convinced that this was the best way to move the space technology forward. Impressed with McNabb's experience, the vice president offered him the job of building America's rocket launching center.

Before they could launch anything, they had to figure out the most basic principles. McNabb headed up the Atlas program to develop the data. How should the rocket be shaped? What propellant should be used? A thousand questions led to other questions. The task was enormous in its scope.

In 1956, Charles Lindbergh came to the Cape and McNabb took him on a tour of the missile building facility, showing off one big missile in a hangar. Lindbergh climbed into the missile and crawled all the way through it. Then he turned to McNabb and said, "When do you put the wings on?"

"It doesn't have any wings."

"If it doesn't have wings," insisted Lindbergh, "it can't fly."

After Lindbergh left, B.G. looked at the rocket and decided it looked like a bunch of big tin cans welded together. He wondered if Lindbergh was right.

* * * *

When Cocoa Beach was chosen as the home of America's space program, there were a total of 823 registered voters. The area had little to offer in the way of amenities. In fact, it was little more than a mosquito-infested swamp. The job to convert such a location into a launching facility, was enormous.

While Sid Raffle was overseeing the building of The Starlight Motel, McNabb built 139 homes in a twelve month period for the people who would have permanent positions at the Cape, mostly the conceptual analysts, the physicists and the aeronautical engineers.

It was such a busy time. There was always a commotion. Resources all over America were mobilizing to support America's space effort. Key components of the missiles were being developed on the West Coast. Engineers and designers flew back and forth to Cape Canaveral on a daily basis.

A design problem would be discovered at the Cape, and McNabb would get on the phone and bring three or four experts out from the West Coast to help him figure it out. With the development of Project Mercury, a boom began in Cocoa Beach the likes of which residents of that area could never, in their wildest imagination, have envisioned. They all wanted to come, because by that time, The Starlight Motel had opened.

* * * *

From the day The Starlight Motel opened, it was a huge success. Room occupancy was almost capacity 365 days a year. The Starlight Motel had 99 rooms, a bakery and coffee shop and a dining room, but The Starlight Motel became most famous for its bar, *The Starlight Lounge.* The lounge at The Starlight Motel became the social center of the people who were living there and the people who were building the Cape.

Everything happened at The Starlight Lounge. Anybody who came to Cocoa Beach had to go to that bar. Every single important thing that was going on was happening in The Starlight Lounge.

I had high quality black lights put into the Starlight Lounge. I had some local artists paint space pictures all over the place that showed up in the black lights. It was really unusual and helped create a unique atmosphere.

"I loved The Starlight Lounge," astronaut Gordo Cooper said. "It was decorated with special paint, that when you put fluorescent light on it, black light, you had lunar scenes all painted with landing vehicles sitting near big craters. When you turned those black lights on, the place would kind of glow. It was really quite a spacey looking place. I thought it was neat, and it fit the clientele, which was basically pilots and dreamers who were working our butts off to get into space."

The Starlight Motel began hosting the top talent that I could book including Rip Taylor, Mack Gwenn and singer Barbara Velasca. An awful lot of important people had some great times in that lounge. If you had been there in those years, you would shake your head at the famous people that you saw in such an out of the way place and say,

"I don't believe it." The Starlight was just a different world when you walked through the door.

The Starlight became the unofficial space headquarters and everyone's home away from home. We had a world class cocktail lounge and a jumping night life which I encouraged by hiring the most beautiful, personable women I could find to work in the lounge and dining room. Our dining room manager was a beautiful lady. B.G. called her the hostess with the mostest and a lot of the guys working on the Cape came to The Starlight just to see her. I have found that a great serving staff helps bring the customers back over and over again, especially when the servers are beautiful and have great personalities.

The clientele was pretty good looking, too, remembered Jake Luther, a private contractor who helped construct Cocoa Beach housing for B.G. McNabb. "I was 23 years old then and single. The place where the girls were, and I mean the best looking girls you've ever seen, was at The Starlight Motel. In the daytime, the girls were by the pool and at night they were at the bar. Every one of them was hoping to meet an astronaut. If you were smart, and I was, you could pretend a little bit and go out with the best looking girls in the world. I used to tell girls I was John Shepard! I didn't even have their names right. But that didn't stop most of them from going for a ride on the beach."

The magical thing about The Starlight was the diversity of people that came together there. From the chairmen and presidents of America's biggest companies, to the guys laying the cable and digging the ditches. The Starlight brought them all together. It was one heck of a great hotel.

The swimming pool was very large and it had cabanas all around it. I remember the cabanas because Tom Wolfe was always hanging around out there. Nobody knew him then and nobody paid any attention to this guy. He was just another writer, one of hundreds, there to cover the story of the space program. No one knew then that he would write *The Right Stuff*, chronicling the whole adventure of America's early space program.

In those days, everything was on a deadline. The Russians were ahead of us and it was a real significant thing to catch up to them and to pass them and take charge of the heavens. It's hard to describe now the sense of urgency we all felt to get our astronauts up into space.

98

Each of the companies rented 10 or 20 rooms, so we were full the day we opened. The Starlight was the center of the universe for everything that was happening at Cocoa Beach. Without exaggeration, the money was just coming through the windows. We couldn't do anything wrong. Everything we did was just great.

The Starlight Motel became the home for those men and women who built America's space program. The pressures of the space race with the Russians were enormous, and The Starlight Motel became the place that those feeling the pressure the most would go to let off steam.

* * * *

In the course of "letting off steam" The Starlight Motel became the stage for countless practical jokes. Everyone who stayed at The Starlight Motel during the glory years remembers the jokes and the atmosphere that made it possible.

We loved to play practical jokes on people. Once the jokes got started, it became a matter of outdoing the guy who had played the joke on you.

One joke I remember was with me and B.G.'s boss, Wally Withy. Withy was a pretty serious guy and he was having breakfast with me one morning at The Starlight Motel. Wally teased me that the only thing different in eating at The Starlight and at his home, was that his wife was at home with egg splattered on the front of her bathrobe and her hair up in curlers. Well, the next day, when Wally came in for breakfast, I had a surprise for him. I had one of the older waitresses dress up in an old bathrobe with egg splattered all over it. She had her hair up in curlers. She went over to take Wally's order. She made him feel right at home.

America's first astronauts were real heroes to me. Being with them in those early days was one of the best, most memorable periods of my life.

* * * *

The reporters set up their headquarters at The Starlight Motel. Every time there was an important event, the AP wire service and UPI wire service and the three networks, would bring in their equipment and set up shop.

Writers are fun guys when there is a bar around. They have great stories to tell and are fun company. Many of them loved to talk and trade stories.

Some of America's great journalists and writers spent a lot of time at The Starlight Motel, and later at the Holiday Inn and the Cape Colony Inn. I first met Walter Cronkite, Frank McGee, Eric Sevareid, Chuck von Freund and other great journalists at The Starlight Motel.

Chuck was the first CBS reporter to come to Cocoa Beach. He was a great journalist and friend, and when he got sick and died of cancer, we had a memorial at the Cape to honor Chuck and his wife and children.

Three hundred of Chuck's friends came to the service. Eric Sevareid went up to the podium and gave a beautiful speech and introduced Walter Cronkite who also gave a beautiful memory of Chuck.

Then out of the blue, Walter looks at me and says he would be remiss if he didn't ask Chuck's other dear friend to say a few words. I was wondering who he was going to introduce when he said my name. I was called up to follow Eric Sevareid and Walter Cronkite. My feet were completely glued to the cement. I couldn't get up. I finally made it up to the podium. I had absolutely no idea what I was going to say. Even for Chuck, those two guys were a tough act to follow.

* * * *

One year into my tenure as manager of The Starlight Motel, Jerry Granger, one of Sid Raffle's partners, paid an unannounced visit to the motel. He didn't like certain things and started changing the dining room, the coffee shop and basically interfering with operations. I asked him to talk to me and I would make the changes, not to undermine my management.

That was something else Mr. Granger didn't like. He told me it was his hotel. If he wanted to take every chair out of the place and throw it onto the street, he could do it. I worked for him, and if and when he wanted my opinion, he'd ask for it.

We argued and I took a stand that I believed would cost me my job. I told Granger if he really wanted to run The Starlight, to go ahead, but he didn't need me. Then I called Sid Raffle and told him that Granger's wholesale changes were detrimental to The Starlight. I couldn't, in good conscience, support them.

Raffle told me not to be upset. He agreed to fly to Cocoa Beach the next day so the three partners could sit down and talk. When Raffle arrived, he brought the third partner, who also owned a piece of The Starlight Motel. The three men closed themselves into a room.

100

I thought right there that I was going to be fired. I was history for disagreeing with one of the guys who owned the motel. After about an hour the three men came out of the room where they had been deciding my fate. Instead of being fired, Mr. Raffle came up to me and said Mr. Granger would not be interfering any more with hotel operations. I was in complete charge of The Starlight Motel.

Raffle went on to tell me that the partnership was flourishing under my management and they appreciated my efforts. He gave me a raise and told me to keep up the good work.

The encouragement and the compliments were much more important to me than the money. I worked at The Starlight 18 hours a day. Part of my success there was gained at the expense of my home life. I almost never had dinners with my children. It was difficult. But at the time, the sacrifice was worth it to me. I was building something for the future.

One memorable dinner that I was at home for took place in our tiny house in Cocoa Beach. Jo's mother, Nana Guardino, was a wonderful Italian cook. She made the best Italian food you could imagine. One day I invited Arthur Godfrey, Bob Considine, Frank McGee, Walter Cronkite and the Mercury boys to our little house to eat Nana's wonderful cooking. Everybody showed up and we had a great time and the best meal ever. After dinner, every one of the guys was hugging Nana telling her what a great cook she was.

That dinner was a perfect example of how it was. We all came together, the rich and the famous and the not so rich and not so famous. We were all involved in the same wonderful journey of America's space program. The only ticket you needed to belong was to share the dream and the wonder of it all.

CHAPTER 3

It was divine nature which gave us the country,
and man's skill that built the cities.
                    –Marcus Terentius Varro (27 B.C.)

"Cape Canaveral," Tom Wolfe wrote, "was not Miami Beach or Palm Beach or even Key West. Cape Canaveral was Cocoa Beach. That was the resort town at the Cape. Cocoa Beach was the resort town for all the Low Rent folk who couldn't afford the beach towns farther south."

"That's true," astronaut Gordon Cooper said. "Cocoa Beach was a down to earth place. At first there wasn't much there but a rock hard beach and a couple of joints on A1A, but that changed as the space program moved forward. Cocoa Beach suited us just fine."

The "us" Cooper was speaking of was the Mercury 7. America's first astronauts. The group consisted of Cooper, Alan Shepard, John Glenn, Wally Schirra, Scott Carpenter, Gus Grissom and Deke Slayton.

America was hungry for heroes and the Mercury 7 lived up to the name more than anyone since Charles Lindbergh. Everywhere the astronauts went they were in the spotlight. The exception was Cocoa Beach. At Cocoa Beach they *were* the spotlight.

"The Cape," Cooper said, "was like Edwards Air Force Base was supposed to be in the early days. It wasn't fancy, it was a place where the pilots went and tested their machines. Of course, we weren't flying at Cocoa Beach. So we had to find other things to do."

What America's first astronauts found to do at Cocoa Beach was driving fast, and drinking, and playing world class practical jokes on each other. In many ways, those first days at the Cape were like a giant fraternity party.

The head of NASA, Robert Guilruth, stayed at The Starlight Motel for all the early launches. Mr. Guilruth liked double martinis. After every launch, I left a pitcher of Beefeater martinis in his room as a personal celebration of NASA's accomplishments.

"The early days at the Cape," Alan Shepard remembers, "were like something happening in a movie. We were based at Langley, but the Cape had been chosen as the launching site for the Mercury flights. We had to do quite a bit of our training at Cocoa Beach. Most of us enjoyed going there quite a bit. We stayed in Henri's hotel right on the beach. In those days, we trained hard and we played hard."

The play included going fast. If the Government was not going to let the astronauts log flight time, they would have to satisfy their thirst for speed elsewhere. In the case of Shepard, Schirra, Grissom, Carpenter and Cooper the jets were replaced, albeit a poor substitute, by the fastest cars on the planet.

Jim Rathmann, who won the 1960 Indianapolis 500, owned one of the largest Chevrolet auto dealerships in the area. At that time, Edward Cole was the president of Chevrolet, and like the rest of America, he was infatuated with America's astronauts. Rathmann had become friends with the Project Mercury team, and Cole wanted to be a part of that friendship.

In those days, the astronauts were paid their military salaries and a small stipend for flight pay. When they were grounded, as they were most of the time at the Cape, they did not receive this extra money. Since each of them depended on the extra money earned by logging as much flight time as possible, being an astronaut imposed a financial burden on them and their families.

It was not unusual for business owners like Rathmann to provide products and services to the astronauts at little or no cost. He offered the astronauts a great lease deal on sports cars and everyone but John Glenn and Deke Slayton jumped at it. Though the deals were perfectly legitimate, John and Deke were always very self-conscious about appearances.

Scott Carpenter opted for a Shelby Cobra, at the time one of the fastest racing cars on the planet, but he still wasn't the fastest driver. The wildest driver was Gus Grissom. His blind runs through the sand dunes around Cocoa Beach became legendary. Pilots like to go fast. The faster the better. The funny thing about guys who fly is that they don't drive too well. They all think they drive great, but they don't. A good rule of thumb in those days was to bring your own car to the party, or else you might end up begging a ride with one of the boys.

"I leased a Corvette from Rathmann," Cooper remembers. "And that little car could really haul. I remember Al and Gus had Corvettes, too. Wally had a Maserati he loved."

Wally prized the car so much that Gordo decided to do something about it. He had gone out fishing when the blues were running and brought in a couple of good sized ones. He hid one in Wally's Maserati. It took Wally a couple of days to find the source of the bad smell in his sports car, and to this day, he does not look amused when discussing this story.

* * * *

The astronauts were represented in all public and private business dealings by a Washington tax attorney named Leo DeOrsey. He was asked to take the job by Walter Bonney, who was then the head of public affairs for NASA. The intent was to keep the astronauts from unfavorable publicity that could reflect badly on the space program. DeOrsey ended up becoming a great friend to the astronauts as well as to me.

Leo DeOrsey was a great guy and a great practical joker. He looked out for the astronauts like they were his own sons. Leo was one of the funniest guys alive. Every opportunity he had to play a joke, he took advantage of it. He was joking all the time.

One of the jokes DeOrsey played on me occurred in 1961 at The Kenilworth Hotel. Leo had set up a meeting to discuss the Project Mercury astronauts and me going in as partners on a hotel venture. I flew to Miami to meet with DeOrsey and Alan Shepard. When we got to the hotel, Leo told me the hotel was restricted, that Jews were not allowed. He asked me to cover up my head with his raincoat and walk through the lobby to the service elevator. I fell for it and walked to the service elevator with Leo's raincoat draped over my head.

When we got to the elevator, Shepard and DeOrsey were laughing so hard they had tears in their eyes. I started planning immediately to get DeOrsey back.

Leo knew I was going to get him back, he just didn't know when.

I got my revenge on Leo in spades. My number one rule, where practical jokes are concerned, is simple: if someone plays a joke on me, I pay him back in triplicate. The first part of the payback with Leo's name on it happened when I met Leo's plane in Orlando. I arranged for a stewardess to run up the stairs and kiss him, making sure she got lipstick all over him. I had a hidden photographer taking pictures. The stewardess told Leo she had seen him on television and she just couldn't control herself he was so handsome. Leo didn't catch on that he was being set up. Part two came on State Road 50, the highway leading from the airport to my hotel. I had arranged with the captain of the State Highway Patrol to stop the car and for the officers to harass Leo. This time, Leo caught on and applauded me for getting him back, thinking that was the end of it.

The coup de grâce came later that night when Leo returned to his room from an afternoon golf game. I had put a beautiful young woman in Leo's room dressed in a hotel towel. Leo opened the door and the woman started to hug and kiss him. My photographer got it all on film. I had the pictures developed by the UPI photographers who were staying in the hotel. I made sure no copies were made, because Leo was married and also a very public person. We loved to joke around with each other, but at the same time we were careful not to let the jokes get out of hand in a way that could actually hurt someone.

* * * *

One of the first things DeOrsey did on behalf of the astronauts was to negotiate an exclusive deal with Life Magazine for rights to the astronauts personal stories. As a result of the deal with Life, each of the astronauts would make about $70,000 spread out over the five year period Project Mercury was scheduled to run. For guys who made under $10,000 a year as military officers, this amounted to a fortune.

"DeOrsey was a real friend to all of us," Alan Shepard said. "He never asked for anything. He just genuinely wanted to help us out."

One story that elaborates on the type of man DeOrsey was took place prior to John Glenn's flight.

Leo wanted to make sure Annie would be taken care of if John didn't come back. Without telling anybody, he bought an insurance policy on John's life for a million dollars from Lloyd's of London to cover the four and a half hours of John's flight. Annie was the only beneficiary. He paid $15,000 for the policy. I was with him when he wrote the check. He did it out of his own pocket and without any fanfare. That was the kind of guy he was. He always put protecting the astronauts and their families above everything else.

* * * *

Before the astronauts could be launched anywhere, much less into outer space, a great deal of preliminary missile testing had to be

106

accomplished. The Atlas Program was designed to develop data needed to launch a manned rocket into outer space.

In the early days of Atlas they still had not had the first successful flight. I worried just as much about how the program was doing and whether it was going to be successful as the astronauts did. Being around them, it was very hard not to be personally involved.

After the first successful Atlas launch, there was a ton of data for McNabb and his team to analyze. They worked for about eight hours after the flight and came back to The Starlight Motel where we had a big celebration. The drinks were on the house. I had a band waiting for them out in front of the hotel. We made a real event of their success. This became one of our traditions. We shared in their success by celebrating it with them. These guys were working night and day in this remote location away from their families. By helping them celebrate, we helped pass on the pride all Americans were experiencing through their achievements. The space program was such an American undertaking that it just pulled you in. I was awed by the work these men were accomplishing and I felt it was an honor to celebrate them when things went well, and to help boost their morale when things weren't going so good.

* * * *

I remember a very big accomplishment that took place in December of 1959. The United States engineered a launch of an ICBM into orbit around the earth. It was the first successful launch by America of a rocket into outer space.

"That damn thing was just kinda bootlegged into orbit," B.G. McNabb said. "I didn't know if it would make it off the pad, much less into orbit."

The ICBM was an unmanned rocket that had a capsule with a tape recording of President Eisenhower's holiday greeting of peace and goodwill for the world. The rocket was going around and around the earth making contact with the whole world and wishing every country Merry Christmas and peace in the world. It was a wonderful accomplishment. I was thrilled. It seemed like such an American thing to do.

I wanted to celebrate B.G.'s accomplishment. I took a driver and a limousine, put B.G.'s wife, Iris, into the limousine and sent the car to the Cape to pick him up. The driver brought them back to The Starlight.

B.G. had an assistant who was an ex-FBI guy named Jack Kirby. Jack was assigned to protect him. We met the car outside and the band played. I told B.G., "I don't know how to thank you on behalf of all of America. But I know you've always been a frustrated hotel manager. Well, this is your turn to manage. You are the manager of this hotel. You can do anything you want. Whatever you want. Go for it."

McNabb smiled ear to ear when I turned over the reins of The Starlight to him. He told Jack to get on the phone and call every single guy at the Cape. Every one of them and get them over to The Starlight. He opened the bar. Free drinks and free food for everybody. Hundreds of guys showed up. The party just kept getting bigger and bigger. I went over to B.G. and said, "I hope you're having fun, because it looks like I'm going to go broke now!"

The reporters from Time and Life magazines covered the event. Both magazines wrote about the party that followed the launch. The reporters said the champagne was flowing at The Starlight Lounge.

* * * *

In 1959, news media did not have direct access to the Cape. Everything was secret and the military had orders to keep the press in certain locations. The press didn't like this restriction because there was not much they could find out looking at the Cape from a distance.

The way the press figured out what was going on was by watching who was coming to The Starlight Motel. Who was checking in and who was checking out. If the Navy admirals started showing up, they guessed that a Polaris missile was going to be tested. If the Army generals checked into The Starlight, the press knew that a Jupiter missile was going to be launched. When the Air Force came, it was probably going to be an ICBM.

I was the only outside guy who knew in advance exactly who was going to come to The Starlight Motel. I was asked not to talk about it to the press and keeping it secret was kind of an unwritten trust between me and the military. I never disclosed the presence of anybody. Not once. I always knew though what was going on. If Lockheed Aircraft sent their top engineer, I said to myself: "Polaris is going up." It was an insider's game, and I was on the inside, wide-eyed at the mystery of it all.

Many of the best reporters in the country were covering the Cape and they were no dummies. It was their business to find out what was going on and report it. They had "arrangements" with bartenders and cocktail waitresses to keep them informed on what was going on.

The Eisenhower Christmas-message launch was covered by more than 200 reporters from around the world. It was the first night launch and it was expected to provide a spectacular spectacle for the on-lookers. The weather had turned unseasonably cold and the reporters who were assigned to the launch were freezing on the beach waiting for the rocket to go up.

"I covered the launch for The Miami Herald," said Dave Johnson. "It was cold and miserable. The weather kept delaying the liftoff and we had no way of knowing what the officials were going to do next. This was way before CNN. Everybody was afraid to leave the beach, even for a minute, because the damn thing might go up and we'd miss the event we'd been sent to witness for the world."

I had many friends in the press and knew that they had to be uncomfortable outside. I went to the motel bakery and gathered up all the baked goods they had. I took coffee and other food from the restaurant. Next, I went to the bar and got all the good brandies that we had and took all the bottles off the shelves and packed them in with the food. I called the police and asked if they could escort a truck down to the jetty where the reporters were.

The police agreed. I went with about a half a dozen waitresses down to where the reporters were shivering in the cold.

I can't tell you the reception we got. I was the biggest hero for those freezing guys that night. The Miami Herald wrote an article that called me "hero of the day".

That started a tradition. Whenever a launch was scheduled, I sent food, coffee and brandy to the reporters. The writers were a hardworking bunch of guys and I became good friends with many of them.

For all the accolades I was receiving, the things that mattered most to me were still the small, traditional, non-material things. I am a man of simple traditions. I try to live by the Golden Rule: Treat others as I would want them to treat me. If there is one secret to my success, that is probably it. Pay attention to the small, personal details. The little things matter to people.

The space shots were very special to me. If a launch was scheduled, the coffee shop was opened all night. During the early days, that coffee shop was like Times Square. The party to celebrate the Christmas launch and President Eisenhower's message of Peace was one of the first real big parties at The Starlight Motel.

* * * *

One by one, I became well liked by the corporations and the people working at the Cape. I was coming out of my shell and I stopped being afraid of meeting people. At The Starlight I was truly becoming a full-fledged manager. I was still trying to stay in the background, like Mr. Raffle wanted, but the customers wouldn't let me.

The Starlight was the beginning of something very big and very special. A lot of people were making a lot of money. They were buying land all over by the Cape. They were planning and building hotels. There was activity everywhere and many people were becoming really wealthy. The land was dirt cheap. Every single transaction that you can possibly imagine, and every single important person who came into town, ended up at The Starlight Motel.

One of the clauses that Raffle had negotiated with the government allowed The Starlight Motel to sublease rooms. The room rate in 1957 was $6 a night. Even at that seemingly meager amount, the motel was making a fortune.

We had an arrangement with the contractors who rented multiple rooms that allowed us to make extra money. If the companies didn't use the rooms, we could rent the room to someone else. If we couldn't rent the room, the company still had to pay for the room. This was a wonderful arrangement. If nobody was in the house, it didn't make any difference. We were still full.

It was during the first year at The Starlight Motel that I met the presidents of many of America's biggest defense contractors.

It became very complicated. We had the presidents of McDonnell, Boeing, Grummond...all the big defense contractors. Cocoa Beach had become a boom town and had attracted all kinds of people. Everyone who came to Cocoa Beach was brought by the smell of money. That's what happens in a boom town. You get all types of people, the good and the bad.

The people The Starlight was designed to serve were primarily government contracting types, and NASA officials, and the military. The press came in droves to cover the space program, and a thousand and one hustlers came to see if they could make a buck.

It was nothing for a four-star general to come into The Starlight Motel and need a room, when there wasn't a room to be had. I became a nervous wreck trying to manage the room space at The Starlight. Everybody wanted rooms and the number of rooms was only 99. I started doubling up people all the time. My nickname became Double-up Henri. The guys would think up all kind of schemes not to double up and have their own rooms. They always said, "My wife is on the way. She's going to be here tomorrow. She was delayed, but she's on the way." You know, all kinds of schemes to have that precious privacy.

****

I became the unofficial host of Cocoa Beach. If someone needed something done, no matter how impossible it seemed, I would get a phone call. I tried never to say no. If someone said they wanted a polar bear, I'd try and find a way to get one. It goes back to my basic belief that to have happy customers, you must give them what they think they want, not what I think they want. I developed a network that stretched out all over the place and rarely was a request unfulfilled.

CHAPTER 4

My heart has followed all my days
Something I cannot name.
      –D.R. Perry Marquis [1922]

Almost two years to the day after it had opened, two Chicago lawyers walked into the motel and presented me with a letter from Mr. Raffle. The Starlight Motel had been sold as of this day, the letter said. The new owners wanted me to continue working there. I was shocked and hurt. I felt like Mr. Raffle had thrown me in as part of the deal.

Had he really sold the motel without so much as a phone call to me? I called him and he said the Chicago investors had made him a great deal. He didn't tell me because he was afraid I might have found a way to block the sale. He was sorry, but business was business.

It really was a shame, but I couldn't blame Mr. Raffle. A motel is sold based on the occupancy rate of the year before. The Starlight had a nearly 100% rate of occupancy. Selling it was good business and Raffle made a lot of money.

In a state of near disbelief, I took the new owners on a tour of the Starlight. We walked into the dining room, and who was sitting there but B.G. McNabb. I introduced him to the new owners. B.G. stood up and shook hands and thanked me for introducing him to these guys. He then proceeded to tell them that he was the best customer The Starlight Motel could even imagine. He told those guys that he wanted them to tune into one fact, and that one fact was that I was The Starlight Motel. If they messed around with me, he was pulling out and he was going to use his influence to empty their motel.

I may have been speechless, but B.G. was never at a loss for words.

The Chicago investors didn't understand the guys who worked at the Cape. They came in and changed everything. They had me remove the copy of the famous Brussels statue, the Manique Apis, part of a fountain that had water flowing from a child's private parts. I'd installed the Manique Apis in the front of the hotel and felt a sentimental connection to it, since Belgium is my birthplace. The statue has a history and a legend and people who came to the Starlight loved that statue. They thought it was funny.

From the day I installed it, no one loved the statue more than B.G., who had just finished building a large home in Cocoa Beach. He came home from work at the Cape and found the statue sitting on his front lawn, a housewarming gift from me. He set the statue in a place of honor in his garden.

Losing the statue was the first of a series of things defining the new ownership. Another thing the new owners did was fire everyone who had made the motel a successful operation. They didn't fire me. I resigned.

* * * *

In 1959, The Starlight Motel was still the only game in town. Other developers were looking to build properties there, but the Cape still depended on The Starlight.

I didn't know what to do. Unlike others during the boom at the Cape, I had not profited financially. I had little money and there were no other motels I could go and work for. I wanted to stay in the area. I really loved Central Florida. The space program had gotten into my heart and I wanted to stay and watch their success.

Jo and I decided to make a go of it on our own. A bank president friend lent us $10,000 and we leased an old fourteen-room motel right on the river about halfway between Titusville and Cocoa Beach. We called it the Space Motel, but we could have called it anything and it wouldn't have changed the fact that Titusville was a completely dead town. It had nothing. Zero. My friend Tony Rocko managed a company called Aerojet and he told me that things were growing so much at Cocoa Beach, that pretty soon things would have to expand out to the Titusville area.

In the meantime, things were really difficult. We had no money and making a success of that place proved to be hard work. We had two sons, Gary and Greg and we all moved into an apartment in the back of the motel. I started right away to remodel the bar and dining room.

I painted day and night and named the restaurant The Space Room. The boys from the Cape gave us space pictures to put up in our bar and all kinds of space things. A t-bone steak at $1.75 was the priciest thing on the menu. I worked the bar and restaurant and Jo ran the motel, acting as front desk clerk and housekeeper.

The boom the Cape enjoyed hadn't caught on in Titusville yet. Our main clientele was ironworkers that were working on the west end of the Cape. They were union guys, kind of a rough, blue collar crowd. They almost owned me and The Space Room. They were really our only customers. The bar was doing okay, but the rest of the operation wasn't having much success.

* * * *

Before leaving Cocoa Beach, I had become friends with a young newsman named Walter Cronkite, one of the most widely recognized personalities in America. Walter was the voice for our space program and appeared on television and radio every Sunday night.

When he returned to the Cape to do a story on the astronauts, he was surprised to find I had moved from The Starlight to Titusville. He called and said he and his wife, Betsy, would like to come up to our restaurant and spend the evening with us.

Walter and Betsy came to our hotel and had dinner with us. During dinner, I said, "Walter, if we get a couple of customers, why don't you just go ahead and take them to a table? Maybe that will help business." Walter was a real sport. He said, "I'll do that Henri. I will do anything to help you." Some people came in and Walter took them to a table.

Then I said, "Walter, nobody really recognizes you here. You're not helping that much. Why don't you go in the bar and mix around with the boys, with those ironworkers. Maybe somebody will recognize you." He said, "You really want me to do that?" His wife, Betsy, is very fun loving and humorous. She is a great, wonderful girl. She said, "Walter, I think you should do that for Henri. That's the least you can do. Just go over to the bar and help him out."

Walter Cronkite went into the bar and mingled with the ironworkers. Not a single person recognized him. Not one. Walter came back to the table and shook his head. "I guess you're going to have to make it on your own, Henri."

I love that story because it so typifies the great guy that Walter is. The most popular guy in the country and nobody recognizes him! That has been a joke for a lot of years now between me and Walter and Betsy.

* * * *

Walter Cronkite mingling with the ironworkers or not, things continued to go down hill at our motel. We were struggling, desperately

115

trying to hold on to the business and make it into a success. I decided our only hope was to focus on the entertainment side of the business and try to make the bar into a money maker.

I called a couple of friends who used to work for me in The Starlight Lounge, Jackie Ray and Martin Shear. She sang and he played the piano. They lived together in Daytona Beach. They were really a popular and talented couple.

I told them the problem I had and asked if they could help me for a month or so to entertain these people and try to build up the business. I told them I didn't have any money to pay them, but they came anyway. I put them up in the motel and they started to perform. Almost overnight, the business started to go up and up and up. I was able to hire a bartender and even able to pay Jackie and Martin. The Space Room became the center of things in Titusville. It was starting to be a lot of fun, reminiscent of the original Starlight Lounge. We were constantly doing little things to try and make it better. One night I stapled egg cartons to the ceiling of the bar to produce a better sound.

At the height of the bar's popularity, we had standing room only on Saturday nights. On one busy Saturday night, two men came into the bar after eleven o'clock and ordered dinner. I told them that the restaurant closed at eleven. The two men, alcohol and beverage agents, shut us down on the spot. They informed me of a state law I didn't even know I'd violated. The Space Room had a restricted alcohol license, requiring that as long as liquor was being served, food had to be available.

The next Monday morning, Jo and I drove to see the ABC supervisor of Orlando to try and save our business. The supervisor went over the list of violations and told us we would have to pay a $500 fine to re-open. We didn't have the money.

After several minutes of discussion, the ABC agent told me the real story. The Space Room had been reported to the State for having illegal prostitution and gambling.

Nothing could be further from the truth and Jo reacted immediately. "There is no way you are going to say that to me or my husband," she said. "I am living with my children there. You are not going to accuse us of anything like that."

The agent, trying to calm Jo down, told us the rest of the story. We had been reported by a jealous competitor across the street from The

116

Space Motel. The person who reported us operated a motel called The Mount Vernon Inn. The ABC agent went on to tell us that they had staked out our business for three days and we were clean as far as the gambling and prostitution charges went. But he also told us we were in violation on the other charges. Finally, he said we could reopen without a fine if we would agree to keep the dining room open as long as we served liquor and if we kept enough dishes to serve 200 people. That was the best deal I was likely to get and I quickly agreed.

On the way back to Titusville from Orlando, Jo fumed. She told me she'd had enough. This was the last straw and she wouldn't stay in Titusville any longer. She was done trying to make The Space Motel and The Space Room succeed.

Trying to make the motel work was a hard life, but we were on our own. That was very important for me. I thought maybe The Space Motel was our big break. Most of us coming to America from Europe wanted something little, but something of our own. The thought of giving that up hurt me deeply.

* * * *

A week before the ABC agents closed us down, I had been contacted by Holiday Inn to oversee the building of the Cocoa Beach Holiday Inn and to manage it when it opened. I turned the offer down because of The Space Motel. Jo's unhappiness in Titusville forced me to reconsider.

The events that led to the building of the Holiday Inn started in late 1959. Holiday Inn Corporation decided that they could make money building a hotel in Cocoa Beach. Robinson Callen came down from the corporate headquarters to look around. He found out that B.G McNabb had negotiated with Sid Raffle to build The Starlight Motel, and that McNabb also controlled where a significant percentage of the government contractors spent their motel allowances. Callen met with McNabb to discuss the possibility of developing a property at Cocoa Beach. McNabb invited Callen to his home and they spent several hours talking about the ideal design of the motel.

The two of them actually sat on B.G.'s living room floor designing the hotel on a scratch pad. Callen asked B.G. what the chances were that he could get the business he was giving The Starlight Motel. B.G., ever my advocate, told him that he had one requirement before he'd even consider it, and that was that Callen hire me as the manager.

The next day, Callen drove up to my motel and offered me the job as the manager of the new Holiday Inn. A week later I called Callen and asked him if the job was still open. He said yes, so I took it.

* * * *

I went back to Cocoa Beach and started the job with Holiday Inn. For the first time, I had the chance to oversee a major construction from the ground up. I learned an awful lot helping them build that hotel. There is no way to teach all the things that go into building major construction. You have to experience the problems, the successes and failures, from one day to the next.

I called all my friends from The Starlight and told them I was back in town. The minute the Holiday Inn opened, it was a huge success.

The day the Holiday Inn opened, the very same day, The Starlight Lounge burned to the ground. Suddenly we had all the business in the area. I hated to see it destroyed, though. It had been an historic place and a great part of my life.

Unbelievably, the police asked me if I knew anything about the fire. Of course, I didn't, but it was still strange that our opening coincided with The Starlight's fire. The police determined the official cause of the fire to be faulty electrical wiring. It began in the wall and burned the building and a lot of wonderful memories to the ground.

We called the bar in the new Holiday Inn the Riviera Lounge. I named it from the Italian Riviera which was receiving big play that year in Life Magazine. It became the place to be on Cocoa Beach, but we needed the astronauts to move from the Starlight to the Holiday Inn.

One day, I saw Deke Slayton in the Riviera Lounge, smoking a big cigar. I went up and asked, "Deke, what is the chance of you boys moving here to the Holiday Inn?"

"Well, I don't know, Henri," he said. "We're pretty well set over there and we have a little privacy."

If the astronauts made the move, I promised, Holiday Inn would extend every courtesy to their families and I would personally do whatever was legally allowed for them in the way of special rates and amenities.

Slayton called me back the next day and said he had talked it over with the other astronauts and they all agreed to move with one condition: they had to be guaranteed a room. No exceptions. When they were in town, they had a room. Deal.

Without telling me, McNabb went to Jim Dempsey, who was responsible for the Air Force contracts, and told him that I would be managing the new Holiday Inn and he would like to take the business that the government sent to The Starlight Motel and send it instead to me at the Holiday Inn. Dempsey saw that the Holiday Inn got the contract to house all the Air Force personnel. This was another step in the coup which brought the Project Mercury Astronauts and all the primary players at the Cape to the Holiday Inn. The Mercury astronauts were a key part of the Holiday Inn's success.

Wherever the boys were was where everybody else wanted to be.

****

Preparations mounted for Alan Shepard's first American manned space flight and the Holiday Inn was at 100% capacity. The media was spending a lot of time and attention focusing on the chimpanzees that were being launched into orbit. The pilots were irritated by some of these stories and wanted to prove that it mattered whether or not a man was on board the space rocket.

The Associated Press needed a room to set up almost three truckloads of equipment. I called Scott Carpenter and asked him if he could move to a different room so AP could have enough room for their equipment. Scott told me no. I thought he was kidding, but the next day he came up to me and said he'd talked to his lawyer and he told him that I couldn't move him without his permission. Scott was acting very serious and said, "Don't touch my clothes, Henri, or I'll sue you. I won't like it, but I'll do it."

I asked Scott to stop kidding around. The AP guys were getting nervous. Scott held his ground. The next day I called him at the Cape and asked him one last time to let me move him. He said no. While he was at work, I had all the furniture, every piece of it, including the bed, removed from the room. When Scott Carpenter returned from the Cape he found a totally empty room. Except for his clothes, which were untouched in the closet. I told him I rented him the room, but nobody ever said anything about furniture!

Scott finally gave in and let the AP wire boys have his room. He was going to play his joke to the end, but even an astronaut didn't want to sleep on a bare floor.

Shepard's flight was scheduled for May 5, 1961. A few weeks prior to the flight, my friend, Harry Reasoner came in from New York to do a story on Shepard. I was working the night desk and I had no reservation for Harry Reasoner. The hotel was completely booked. There was not a single room available.

Harry looked at the guest ledger and saw the name of his friend Dick Whitken. Perhaps they weren't such good friends because when I called and asked if he would share his room with Harry, Whitken said no. Harry ended up sleeping on the lobby couch.

Years later, Harry served as guest speaker at the Holiday Inn International Convention, with over 5,000 delegates from around the world. "I'm very familiar with the Holiday Inn System," he began. "It just so happens that I've slept in quite a few of them. One Holiday Inn I remember quite distinctly is run by a friend of mine..."

Harry Reasoner was a great friend and one of the best reporters ever. He had a terrific sense of humor, and he could always make me laugh.

John Glenn could make me laugh, too. We had a running joke about towels.

"I was down at the Cape," John Glenn remembers. "I had a reservation and I went and got a key and went up to the room and there weren't any towels in there. So I went back down to the front desk acting very serious, although I was really joking. I went in and banged on the desk and there were some people who were checking in. I just kept banging on the desk. I said, why can't I get some towels? Can't this place keep towels in the room?"

I heard John making a lot of noise and came out to see what was the matter. He started yelling that he couldn't get any towels and he should have towels in his room. After giving me the business for a few minutes, John laughed and told me he was only kidding. I sent a housekeeper up with some towels and he thought that was the end of it.

I knew John was coming back in a couple of weeks. I made sure to be ready for him.

"The next time I checked into the Holiday Inn," John said, "I checked in and got my key and went up to the room and opened the door and you wouldn't believe it. Henri had a truckload of towels, thousands of them, put into the room. The tub was filled with towels. The vanity was filled up so you couldn't see yourself in the mirror. The bed, literally you could not lay down on the bed, it was covered with towels to the ceiling. You could hardly close the door there were so many towels in that room."

I made sure John had plenty of towels.

After the towels, anything done in the way of a practical joke against me was fair game.

"During the early days at the Cape, we began a non-stop competition of practical jokes," remembered Alan Shepard. "I don't know how the practical jokes got started. Probably because, as a group, the astronauts were very intense and very competitive for the task at hand; and when you are working in that environment, there's always the need for comic relief. As for Henri, he just liked to pull pranks. He was always thinking of the next gag.

"It was my turn to get Henri back. One morning after John's flight, a couple of the Mercury astronauts who shall remain nameless were invited to go alligator hunting. A friend of ours had a big orange grove plantation of several hundred acres. Alligators were all over the place. This guy would go out after dark with a miner's cap with a light in it and walk around and shine the light until it reflected off the red eyeballs of the gator. Then he'd aim between the eyeballs and bang. The alligator would roll over. He'd pull them out and sell their hides for boots.

"Well, we got one little one, about four feet long, and went back to the ranch, when we realized it was still alive. We put some water in the bathtub and threw him in. The next morning, we took the alligator back and put him in Henri's pool at the Holiday Inn."

＊＊＊＊

With stakes so high, letting off steam was essential. I think we all knew that laughter was the best medicine. Nobody sat around talking about how to be funny, it was just part of the atmosphere at the time.

One day, my long time friend, comedian Bill Dana decided to one-up Gordo Cooper. I was sitting with Bill Dana at The Cape Colony when Gordo Cooper's flight was going up. The hotel was packed, so we went to Gordo's room to watch the flight. Gordo had an extra space suit in the room with his name on it. The rocket had just gone up. Bill Dana told me that he was going to put on the suit and go running through the lobby and yell, "I missed my flight! I missed my flight!"

The suit turned out to be too big for Bill so he talked me into doing it. I put on the flight suit and helmet and ran all over the hotel. One of the maid's heard me shouting. "I missed my flight!" and the poor thing almost fainted.

We pulled these stunts just to release tension, but sometimes we went too far. Like with the boat in the swimming pool. That one nearly gave me a heart attack.

B.G. McNabb had just bought a 19 foot cabin cruiser. He and Leo DeOrsey decided they should launch it and christen it by breaking a bottle of champagne over the bow. Leo, who loved a good joke, especially if it was on me, suggested they take it over and launch it in the Holiday Inn swimming pool.

It was around four o'clock in the afternoon, the cocktail hour, when DeOrsey and McNabb hooked the boat up and hauled the trailer over to the Holiday Inn. DeOrsey decided it would be funnier if they got the press involved. He called his buddies in the press pool. A joke on me was always better if the whole town was in on it.

Those guys were crazy. They had an afternoon cocktail party on B.G.'s boat in the hotel pool and nothing would stop them. The only thing I could do was have a drink and hope the boat didn't sink.

Two weeks after the boating incident, I arrived at work around eight o'clock in the morning and found Gordo sitting at the edge of the pool with a fishing pole. I walked over to Gordo and asked him what in the world he was doing.

Gordo looked up at me and said, "Henri, I came here to fish and I'm fishing,"

"But this is a swimming pool," I insisted. "You're fishing in my swimming pool."

Gordo dumped a cooler of live fish into the swimming pool.

"I'll catch these," he said.

I thought fishing in that pool was the funniest thing I'd ever seen, and it certainly made the best-practical-joke-ever list.

****

I went up to Walter Cronkite's room one time when he stayed at the Holiday Inn and found him talking with Don Hewitt, who now produces 60 Minutes, and Sandy Sacalow. Don and Walter thanked me for my hospitality and asked me if there was anything they could do for me. I couldn't think of a thing, but Don turned to Walter and asked him if he would broadcast his fifteen minute Sunday Evening News segment in front of the Holiday Inn sign. Walter thought it was a great idea.

That Sunday, Walter Cronkite stood in front of the Holiday Inn sign for fifteen straight minutes. At the time, Walter's weekly broadcast was the highest rated television show in the country. I don't know how many millions that kind of advertising would have cost Holiday Inn, but he gave us tremendous exposure. Holiday Inn was just beginning to grow with only 200 hotels in operation then. After Walter's broadcast, the number began multiplying rapidly.

Jack Ladd, vice president of Holiday Inn franchise London, was sitting in his office watching the news and he saw Walter standing in front of the Holiday Inn sign. He started calling all over the country to find out who was responsible. He tracked me down and I became a big hero with the company. Those fifteen minutes had a big part in my later success with Holiday Inn.

Later that year, Holiday Inn presented their one and only special lifetime achievement award to me for being responsible for Walter Cronkite broadcasting in front of the corporate logo. Overnight, Holiday Inn had become a household name because of something Don and Walter did as a favor to me.

My attempts to publicize Holiday Inn didn't end with Walter's fifteen minute advertisement. In 1962, more than 2,000 reporters from around the world gathered at the Cape to witness John Glenn's orbital flight. The flight got delayed repeatedly and the reporters looked for fresh stories.

I had an idea to put all 99 United Nations flags, including Russia, in a half-moon around the front of the Holiday Inn. This would give the reporters something to frame their stories against. The flags of the world would be a natural backdrop for the cameras and they couldn't get the shot without getting the Holiday Inn logo, too.

I called Memphis to get approval from Holiday Inn's corporate headquarters to spend $600 on the flags. I had already arranged to get the poles locally at no cost. I was convinced that if I put the flags up, the reporters would start snapping pictures. I called my boss, a little fellow named Robert Hall, and told him about my idea and asked him if I could spend the $600. Mr. Hall said no. It wasn't in the budget and he didn't think it was such a great idea anyway.

I argued with Hall that this idea would pay for itself a hundred times over in the publicity it would generate. Hall told me no and that his answer was final.

I asked Mr. Hall who his boss was, because I intended to go over his head. I knew my job was on the line, but I was convinced that this idea would be another big winner for Holiday Inn. Hall angrily told me his boss was the chairman of the board of Holiday Inn, Kemmons Wilson. I hung up and dialed Wilson's number.

Wilson, who I knew and liked, gave me permission to purchase the flags on the condition that when Glenn's flight was done, I would return the flags for use at the corporate headquarters. The idea was a big success. Hundreds of news stories were broadcast and shot in front of those flags. After John's flight, I sent the flags to Memphis. Wilson erected flag poles lining both sides of the corporate headquarters and they are now a permanent part of the Holiday Inn image.

CHAPTER 5

Wherever you are it is your friends who make your world.
—William James [1899]

I became attached to all the Project Mercury astronauts and their families, but our closest family friends became John and Annie Glenn. The friendship that began in 1960 in Cocoa Beach's Holiday Inn grew so that John and I would often have dinner together and he would come to our house and see my family.

To me, John is the living example of what is right with American values. He's very sincere and totally honest, he loves this great country and is committed to his family.

I love to talk about John Glenn. He is such a unique person. A story that shows what he's really like, took place on New Year's Eve in 1961. John was scheduled to go on his flight in the middle of February. We were all on our way to celebrate New Year's Eve with a late dinner and then a party. As we were walking into the lobby, a couple of high school kids recognized John and they asked him if he would mind talking to them. The kids wanted to ask him some questions about being an astronaut and going into space. When the party began at midnight, John was still there, sitting on a corner talking to a spellbound bunch of kids. He has always been so open to children and believes exactly what President Kennedy said—children are our future.

John and Annie are the godparents of our daughter, Lisa—a Jewish father, an Italian-Catholic mother and Presbyterian godparents! Lisa has all the bases covered.

Another example of John's generosity happened at his home in Texas. He and Annie had invited Jo and I to spend Thanksgiving with them in Houston. I didn't have much money then and the only way we could afford the trip was to piggyback it onto a business trip. I arranged to look at a hotel in Rosenberg, Texas and to evaluate it as a possible Holiday Inn site. Holiday Inn covered the airfare and that way, Jo and I could visit our friends.

The day we arrived, John picked us up in the brand new Chevrolet station wagon he had just picked up from the dealership. When I told him I had to get to Rosenberg to report on the hotel, John told me to take the car.

I drove off but on the way back from Rosenberg, sure enough, I got in an accident and tore up John's brand new car. I called and right away, he asked if I'd been hurt. I assured him I was okay. Then he asked if the accident had been my fault. It was.

Don't worry, John said, it's just a car. He could always get another one. He's truly a wonderful friend. But to this day, he isn't crazy about driving with me.

****

1200 eggs
300 pounds of sugar
190 pounds of butter
250 pounds of flour
100 quarts of milk
160 pounds of powdered sugar
60 pounds of margarine
60 pounds of mixed fruit
65 egg whites
1 quart of mocha mix
2 quarts of vanilla

The recipe Chef Mitchell came up with for John's cake had space-like proportions.

I wanted to do something really special to celebrate John's first orbital flight, something really spectacular. I arranged with my chef, Henry Mitchell and my food and beverage manager to create a cake for him. I wanted it built to the exact measurements of the space capsule, which is six feet by nine feet. It had to be ready when he returned from the mission so we could roll it out to him at the celebration. And it had to be kept a secret. The two men couldn't even know the name of the space capsule.

My staff was challenged, but undaunted by the request. They told me such a cake, while unprecedented, was possible. They would make a combination fruit and pound cake to the exact dimensions of Glenn's capsule. The two men left the office to plan the cake.

The very next day, the chef and food and beverage manager are back in my office. They said, "Mr. Landwirth, we can't bake the cake." The two men explained that they had a problem, a big problem. The men fumbled back and forth, neither man wanting to give me the bad news.

Nobody wanted to tell me what the problem was. Finally, the chef said the door from the back kitchen was only three feet wide. The cake I ordered was supposed to be six feet. Once the cake was built, there would be no way to get the cake out of the kitchen. I told them to let me think about it. I wasn't ready to give up on the cake yet.

128

I contacted a trucking company and rented a two and a half ton truck. It was a tremendous truck. I put the truck outside the kitchen and told the chef to bake the cake in parts and assemble it in the truck. Everything was going great until the delays with John's flight began. We were trying to keep a secret with that darned cake! Well, the reporters had a field day, because I wouldn't let them close to that truck. And you can't keep a secret from reporters for long. It was the biggest joke with everybody. Once they found about the cake, I asked them not to write about it and they didn't. They were just kidding me daily. That was the price for them keeping the secret.

John Glenn's flight was on its third delay. The chef came to me and said the cake was starting to spoil. I decided to purchase an air conditioner and a generator and stick it in the truck to preserve the cake.

After the air conditioner was hooked up. The chef innocently asked me how they were going to get the cake off the truck after Glenn's flight. I asked him what he was talking about. The chef said, "Well the cake weighs at least 900 pounds. We're going to need a pulley or something to move it."

When in doubt, call on the experts. I called McDonnell Aircraft and I said, "Fellows, I'm in trouble. I have a 900 pound cake I can't get off a truck. Can you rig up something for me?" They said, "No problem; we are going to build you a lift." They built me a special lift for the 900 pound cake. The lift was on special rollers and I could put it anywhere I wanted to.

The biggest secret – the one the press still didn't know – was the name of John's capsule. I needed the name so the cake could be completed and put into place for John's triumphant return to earth. No one outside of NASA's inner circle knew what the name was.

I called some of my friends at the Cape and I asked for a picture of the capsule. I told them I wouldn't tell anyone and I wouldn't put the name on the cake until the flight. They said, "Henri, this is classified stuff. You are asking for something that can get us all in serious trouble." I wouldn't give up on the cake and they told me to look for an envelope that might show up in the next few hours.

When the envelope came, I felt like a full fledged spy. I was shaking in my boots just having the name of the capsule. It was called Friendship 7. The perfect name. I locked the picture of the capsule in the hotel safe.

129

I got a visitor the next day, Walt Williams, the project manager of the mission. He walked into my office and pointed his finger at me. "I understand you have a picture in your possession. You should be arrested right at this moment. What you have is top secret. Henri, we've been friends, but this goes beyond that. If word of the capsule's name leaks, I'll come right after you. I promise you." He let me keep the picture locked in the office safe.

Friendship 7 finally broke the earthly plane and soared into orbit with astronaut John Glenn at the controls. He orbited the earth three times. After the first orbit, I called Charlie Buckley, the head of Cape security and began my story.

I said, "Charlie, I want to get this 900 pound cake to the Cape and have a ceremony for the top boys over there from NASA and the government and the Air Force. Everybody who had anything to do with John's success."

Charlie Buckley was getting a little tired of my cake. "If you say one more word about that cake, I'm going to have you arrested. I'm tired of you. I'm tired of your cake. I'm tired of everything you're doing with that damn cake."

I had come too far to be disappointed this close to victory.

"Charlie," I said, "we've been around for a long time. Why don't you just be a good guy? Don't be excited, let me go out with the cake and have a little ceremony?"

"How many people can your stale cake feed?"

"About 2,000."

"You want me to let you poison 2,000 people! There's no way you can serve that cake to VIPs. I wouldn't have my dog eating that cake."

"I'll make a deal with you, Charlie. You send some of the dietitians over here and let them taste test the cake. If the cake is good, you let me bring it out to the Cape. If it's not, it stays in the van."

Charlie reluctantly agreed. The dietitians came and okayed the cake for human consumption. I took the cake to the hangar where John Glenn had taken off from and where he would be brought back to after he landed.

For John, the funniest part of the cake story was the inconvenience his flight delays caused me. "My flight was all set and I was supposed to go the next morning and then the flight got canceled. Delayed for a week or something. Henri didn't know what to do with the cake. They found a big

Navy refrigerator or something and put it into the truck where the cake was. This would cool it down and try to preserve the cake.

"It became a whole great big project down there to keep this darned caked locked up and to keep it a secret. They didn't want anybody to know they had it.

"I made the mission and was on Grand Turk for three days and came back. I was going to fly down to Key West with the family. I was going to be down there over the weekend and come back up and meet JFK at West Palm and then fly up there on Air Force One with him for a parade. So when I got on the plane, I heard they had this big chunk of cake that was about the size of a suitcase waiting for me. It was good. Henri's 900 pound cake, his giant cake, was still edible."

It made history, too. As John was coming down, he said over his radio from Friendship 7, "Henri, I'm coming home. Get the cake ready!"

* * * *

I had other special plans for John Glenn's triumphant return from outer space. John's original itinerary called for him to fly to the Cape to meet President Kennedy and Vice President Johnson, who would be arriving on Air Force One.

I was sitting in a bar with Mayor Kenney of Cocoa Beach and Sweet Smith, who owned the local radio station. We were trying to figure out how we could divert John Glenn's plane to land at Patrick Air Force Base so we could have a parade for John in Cocoa Beach. Patrick AFB was on the south side of town, and if John arrived there, we could drive him through town on the way to the Cape to meet the President.

We called the guy in charge of coordinating John's trip with President Kennedy's arrival and he agreed to see us in his suite.

What followed began to snowball almost as soon as the three of us walked into the coordinator's hotel suite.

We start to lie, and I'm talking about lying. I mean after a few drinks, the more lies we were telling, the better it sounded. The mayor said he was proclaiming the day a holiday and closing the schools. I chimed in and said we were going to have twenty high school bands. We just kept going on and on, and finally, this guy says okay. He'll call his boss.

131

He gets on the phone with us right there in the room and gets Pierre Salinger on the line. He said, "Pierre, I have the mayor of Cocoa Beach here and a couple of the local big shots, and they have an idea..."

He recounted all the stories the Mayor, Sweet Smith and I had just finished telling him. Pierre Salinger listens and said, "I'll talk to the Chief and get back to you."

I leaned over to Mayor Kenney and said, "So we've lied our way all the way to the President. You don't go any further than that."

Within the hour, Pierre Salinger called back. JFK okayed the idea of John Glenn's plane being diverted to Patrick contingent on John and his entourage being at the Cape to meet the President's plane. Logistically, that was okay. So the plan moved into motion. They would divert John and Annie to Patrick. A motorcade would then drive them through town and the parade on the way to the Cape to meet Air Force One.

We had some work to do. We started by trying to remember all the things we had lied about. Twenty bands...kids out of school... local holiday...

The first call went to the superintendent of schools. He said there was no way he was going to close schools in Brevard County. Without the kids, the plan would backfire. Sweet Smith used his radio station, the most powerful one in the area, to get the community involved with the project. He started broadcasting non-stop about the upcoming parade. The station urged parents to let their kids participate. It's educational, the DJs said, it's all American, it's a once-in-a-lifetime experience. Whatever they thought would work, they announced over the airwaves.

I called the superintendent of schools in nearby Orange County and explained our predicament. I asked if all the high school bands in the county could participate. The superintendent liked the idea and promised me all the bands we would need. One thing led to the next, and we managed to deliver everything we promised. It turns out we didn't lie, after all.

John Glenn's motorcade after his successful space flight

We got every leader in the county to drive a car and take all the dignitaries in their cars. I had Pierre Salinger in my car. Pierre was my hero for helping us set the whole thing up with the President.

There were thousands and thousands of children, families and bands. There were bands on almost every street. Cocoa Beach's most exciting day all started because three guys had been drinking a little too much in the bar!

CHAPTER 6

The future enters into us,
in order to transform itself in us,
long before it happens.
  −Rainer Maria Rilke [1900]

In 1962 my future with Holiday Inn was far from secure. After I challenged my boss Robert Hall, and went to Kemmons for approval to put the international flags around the hotel, I did not think that my short-term future with Holiday Inn looked that terrific. Shortly after John Glenn's flight, a man named Walter Rose contacted me and said he was going to build a hotel right across the street from the Holiday Inn. He was going to call it The Cape Colony Inn and he offered me a ten percent stake in the hotel if I would leave the Holiday Inn and go run his hotel for him.

I called my friend Leo DeOrsey to discuss the opportunity with him. I thought The Cape Colony might be the perfect opportunity for the Mercury astronauts to get involved in the hotel business. We could be partners with Walter Rose. Leo was their business advisor and he had to approve the idea before it could go forward.

DeOrsey liked the deal and the Mercury astronauts and I went into business together at The Cape Colony Inn. To take the job at the Cape Colony Inn meant resigning from the Holiday Inn. I decided to fly up to Boston to tell Holiday Inn executive David Stone about it in person. I had to change planes in La Guardia Airport, and when I got there, police had staked it out and everybody was running around.

I asked what all the commotion was about and true to the magic fairy tale ride my life has been on since the war, I learned John Glenn would be arriving for a big ticker tape parade being held in his honor. I decided to take a later flight to Boston and headed over to the parade site.

Though it was cold out, millions of people lined the streets. I was freezing. I hadn't planned on being outside and I wasn't dressed properly, but I didn't care. Wedged about three rows deep in the crowd I managed to catch the eye of a passing police captain.

135

I explained to him that I was a friend of John Glenn and I had heard Glenn was in a building across the street from where I was standing in the crowd. I asked if I could go across the street and say hello to my friend.

"You know John Glenn like I know John Glenn," the police captain said.

I continued to plead with the officer and finally he escorted me across the street. The first person I saw was my friend Charlie Buckley, head of security. Charlie took me by the arm and told the officer I was indeed a friend of John Glenn.

"Henri!" Charlie said. "I'm so glad to see you. Stay here for one minute and let me check something."

A few minutes later, he came back and said, "Henri, you are in the fourth car. You will be riding in the limousine with John's children."

Riding in John's motorcade with David and Lynn Glenn was an unbelievable thrill, one of the best moments of my life. I cannot describe the size of the event. Millions of people were everywhere. The ticker tape filled the entire sky and the wind blew the paper everywhere. It looked like the whole world had come to cheer for John. I felt so much pride and happiness. To me it was a uniquely American moment.

I would later be a guest at the White House during the Bush administration, but I never forgot my early encounters with America's political elite. I participated in America's democratic system in a way I could never have dreamed of when I was a child trapped in Hitler's Germany. To be a witness to these men who made history, to share in those moments with them is something I will never forget.

John remembered it fondly, too. "That day at the parade in New York City was wild!" he said. "You know someone told me a long time ago that they judge these parades by the amount of refuse they pick up and cart off. I think ours was rated as 3,700 tons of paper. That was a record for all ticker tape parades.

"Recently someone told me that record will never be broken. I said, come on, that's not true. Every record is made to be broken and this one will be broken some time, and they said no. The buildings in New York are now constructed so you can't open the windows. And everything is computerized. You don't have as much ticker tape. Now what they do, maintenance people gather as much paper as they can. They take barrels of this stuff up on top of the roof and then they chuck a little bit over the side to make it look like a ticker tape parade. It ain't nothing like they used to have! That one was a real biggie. It was like a blizzard. It was quite a day."

Following the parade, Time Magazine gave a dinner at the Time Building honoring John. The guests were a combination of celebrities and top government officials and military brass. After dinner, the party broke up to move to a smaller, more intimate gathering at the Waldorf Astoria Hotel.

We were all at the Waldorf waiting for John and Annie to come outside. I was standing with the press. John came out and everybody started snapping pictures. He waved me over to him and said, "Henri, come here with me. I want to show you what kind of towels they use in this place."

The towels again! We had come a long way from the early days at The Starlight Motel. Prime ministers, presidents, ambassadors, you name it and they were there, all dressed in formal clothes. Except for me, there in my little Florida summer suit.

The next day, the city hosted a lunch in John's honor. Again I had no invitation, but ended up sitting with the governors and senators of Pennsylvania and New Jersey. Senators from both states were also at the table. They would introduce themselves and I would say, "Hi, I'm Henri Landwirth."

No one asked me what state I represented.

After the luncheon, I got to attend a command performance by Lena Horne in John's honor. I sat with Mayor Daley of Chicago, a funny, entertaining man. It was a great show and I remember looking around at John and the famous people who were all around and thinking, "Little Henri Landwirth, here with America's hero! What a great country."

I topped off this most wonderful evening by having a drink with Walter Cronkite and listening to Walter's perspective on America's space program.

The next day, I flew to Boston and gave my notice to my friend, David Stone. On the flight, I noticed the tattooed number from the camps on my left forearm and thought of a John Glenn story from the first days that I knew him.

In the early days of the space program, the Mercury astronauts liked to spend time around the hotel pool when they had time off from the Cape.

They would sit around the pool talking and they would be wearing Ban-lon short sleeved shirts. I would always wear a long sleeve shirt and one day John asked me about it. I rolled up my sleeve and showed him my tattoo and I will never forget what he said, "You should be proud of that! If I had that tattoo I'd wear it like a dad-gum Congressional Medal of Honor!"

I no longer hide the tattoo. Occasionally children ask me about it. Some even ask me if they can touch the faded blue numbers. When their tiny fingers trace those numbers I tell the children it is not a good thing to be thought of as a number. It is much better to have a name.

* * * *

As I began overseeing construction for the Cape Colony Inn, I came up with the idea of building a press center on top of the convention center as part of the hotel. No other hotel in the country had one and I wanted to build offices and specifically outfit them for the needs of the media. I first took this idea to the Associated Press, who rented space on the spot. Next, I flew to New York and met with executives from CBS, NBC and ABC. All three networks rented space. My next idea took me to National Geographic Magazine. I told them we would have a specially equipped photo lab with multiple darkrooms available and they signed on. Next, Life and Time magazines bought space in the Cape Colony's press center, too.

Overnight, the idea to make the press an intricate part of the Cape Colony had turned into an instant, huge profit center for the hotel. We were making money before we ever rented a room.

My next idea for the Cape Colony was to capture the social side of the equation. I wanted to create a private place where business and socializing could take place. I called it The University Club. It was a private part of the hotel that only members could use. It had a nice little bar, pool room, lounges and private seating. Many historical meetings among some of the most important people in the world took place in The University Club.

The Cape Colony created a venue for access between the press, the government, the astronauts and the most powerful movers and shakers of private industry.

The University Club allowed me to have a place where I could help patch up the inevitable differences arising on a routine basis between those who were involved at the Cape. That type of thing took place all the time. Life, Time, Look...all the reporters writing whatever stories they could find. They would write some things that would upset people. I'd try to get them together over a glass of wine and most of the time we worked it out. I saw my job as keeping all these different guys and personalities friendly and together.

I do not like confrontation, especially among friends. Whenever tempers flared at The Cape Colony Inn, I would try and get the boys together in The University Club to work things out. I thought it was important to the country and the space program to keep all the personalities together. I saw my job as making sure everybody got along.

****

I also wanted The Cape Colony Inn to have a great restaurant, one of the finest ever in Cocoa Beach. I didn't have a chef, so I came up with a truly off the wall idea. As far as I know, it had never been tried before. I leased an out-of-business restaurant in Cocoa Beach and ran ads looking for a chef. Any time a chef applied for the job, I sent him over to the restaurant to cook his specialty. I invited anyone who was at the hotel, the astronauts, the carpenters, the presidents of different companies, anybody who wanted to have lunch, to join me. This went on for several months. I was testing the food of the chefs who applied. You don't know how good a chef is until you actually taste his food.

A young chef named William applied for the job in the Cape Colony Restaurant. I sent him over to the restaurant and told him to prepare lunch for about a dozen people. The chef went to the kitchen and returned a couple of hours later with the meal.

It was one of the finest meals I have ever had in my life. I couldn't believe how good food could be. I asked William to come to my house that night and prepare a full-blown dinner for six or eight people.

Chef William showed up at my house with a toolbox filled with culinary tools. He took over the kitchen, and hours later, served another fabulous meal. My guests that night, including Gordo Cooper, Wally Schirra and Gus Grissom all agreed the food was the best they had ever tasted.

I hired William on the spot. He accepted the job and left the kitchen without washing a single dish or pot. Jo got stuck with a tremendous clean-up job in the kitchen. She probably never forgot that.

Word about Chef William spread around the Cape. Everybody in town wanted to try the food that the astronauts said was "out of this world." The grand opening of The Cape Colony Inn was a big success. The dining room was filled to capacity. There wasn't a single chair available. I had hired a beautiful, talented pianist named Helen to play. Everything was perfect: the ambiance, the clientele, the full house.

But no food came out of the kitchen. I ran to the back to find out what the problem was. Chef William just shrugged and said good food took time to prepare. If the guests wanted good food–and that was the only kind of food he prepared–they would just have to wait. Those who could wait were rewarded with one of the greatest meals in the world. But of course, most people can't wait a couple hours for their food to be prepared.

Chef William, as extraordinary a culinary talent as he was, had to be replaced. I let him go and hired the best chef working in the area from a competing restaurant. The man's name was Chef Neff, and he and I would have a long and sometimes difficult business relationship well into the future. But at the time, Chef Neff solved the problem of a first class chef able to operate a restaurant.

I managed the hotel and the bar, which was, according to Alan Shepard, "The greatest bar in the world. Great entertainment...a lot of interesting people. They were always doing something for the press or the astronauts. They always had something special going on."

Suzy Walton, who was one of the few female reporters for the AP, and later a writer for National Geographic Magazine remembered the Cape Colony as being the quintessential place for writers to write. "We could drink all night long and not even have to leave the hotel to go to work the next day. The Cape was more of a boy's club, but I'll always remember the Cape Colony and how it catered to the press. I've never been anywhere since that cared so much about the comfort of reporters."

****

The Cape Colony Inn, already something of an institution among the space community, was chosen by the State Department to house any dignitaries visiting the Cape.

We entertained them and made sure they had the proper atmosphere for their visit. Most of the time, when the head of a country comes in, security occupies the rooms they'll be using the night before. A couple of security guys stayed in the suite where the Grand Duchess of Luxembourg would be staying. Just before her arrival, I checked the room and found they had left their clothes hanging in the closet. I was glad I found them, not the Grand Duchess

Her favorite flower, I learned, was a long-stemmed red rose called the Charlotte Rose. I looked all over Florida for them and finally found them in South Miami. I flew someone down to pick them up and presented them to her when she arrived.

Prime Minister Nehru of India was visiting the Cape with a large entourage.

Indians are primarily vegetarian, but no one in the hotel could cook Indian food. I found a well-known chef of Indian cuisine in Miami and flew him and two assistants to Cocoa Beach. Money was no object. Most of the time the State Department reimbursed us.

The chef came in and cooked some beautiful food for them. We had security in the kitchen as the food was being cooked. The dinner started and it was beautifully prepared and elegantly served. After everybody got served, the Prime Minister called me over. He said, "My people in India are hungry and this is too much for us to have to eat when they are hungry. I want half of what is on this plate." So I took his plate back to the kitchen. With that, every single person in that room asked to have his food go back to the kitchen.

We had scenes like this happening all the time. We had the king from Afghanistan who required a throne be built for him. And if it wasn't a throne it was something else.

As the official facility for hosting dignitaries for the State Department, we were getting all different segments of the world community coming to The Cape Colony Inn. Most of these people were very important to our country. I was truly getting very nervous about it on a daily basis. The only way I could manage my nerves was to treat everybody the same. Kings or Queens, or the kid bringing in the produce, it didn't make any difference; I decided to treat everybody the same. That has been my style of meeting people ever since.

* * * *

"The space program became a reality under President Kennedy," Senator John Glenn said. "It was a sad and tragic day for America when he was assassinated. One of history's true bright lights extinguished before he completed his work."

Few events in my life hit me with the impact of President Kennedy's death. Like everyone else in America, I remember precisely what I was doing and where I was when I heard that President Kennedy had been shot on that terrible November day in 1963.

I was at the AP wire bureau right there at The Cape Colony Inn, standing with Howard Benedict, the executive director of the AP wire service, when it came over the wire. First, that President Kennedy had been shot. Later that his wounds were fatal.

I started to shake. I was upset. I got very weak and I was shaking all over. I cannot express the way I feel about this country, about how much I love this county. The loss of a president, especially President Kennedy, was something very personal and horribly bad.

For me and the Mercury astronauts, the countless good things that happened after the assassination, were always slightly touched by a tinge of sadness over the loss of the President.

****

As the first generation of astronauts made way for the Gemini team, I felt more committed to the space program than ever. The hotel focused on the people involved in the space program. We became like a family, pulling together and cheering for each other.

NASA timed the addition of the Gemini astronauts to the program to coincide with Gordo Cooper's space flight, so when it was time for his flight, we wanted to do something special for him. Up until then, the Project Mercury astronauts stayed with each other and the Project Gemini astronauts were a little too intimidated to infringe on the group.

Pete Conrad, one of the Gemini astronauts who would eventually go to the moon, became a good friend. Together, we decided it would be a great idea to get the Mercury and Gemini astronauts together on a social basis. They represented the best of America and I wanted them to all be friends.

To loosen things up a little, I called Chef Neff and told him I had arranged a party for fifteen of the sixteen astronauts. I explained the joke I wanted to play on the boys.

We started off with a fabulous cocktail party. Leo DeOrsey came and it was a wonderful party, just beautifully done. We had a big square table with the Gemini and Mercury astronauts set up so they could all talk to each other.

Alan Shepard recalled, "We were celebrating Gordo's flight and a visit by Queen Wilhemenia of the Netherlands. Henri told us that the State Department was letting him pull out all the stops. We had fancy menus that said the main course was veal cutlets and baked potatoes. The room was filled with fancy white tablecloths and fine china. There were plenty of waitresses and waiters and so on. Wine was being served in these lovely little crystal wine glasses. It was really elegant. Nobody had the slightest idea what Henri was up to."

After the astronauts had relaxed and gotten to know each other, I signaled Chef Neff that it was time to serve the main course. Gordo sat next to me. I was the only person at the table who was in on the joke.

Chef Neff and his staff served the meal and the astronauts started to cut their veal cutlets.

"Nobody could even get a knife into it," Cooper remembered. "Henri had the cook take thick pieces of cardboard, bread them and deep fry it so it looked like veal. On top of that, the damn potatoes were raw, but the cheese on top was melted so you couldn't tell. I finally cut through the veal, and I was thinking this is some tough piece of meat."

Alan Shepard cut into the cardboard and decided he could do without the veal. "I couldn't get my knife to go through it. I tried the vegetable, broccoli I think, and it was raw. I didn't even bother with the potato."

I watched Gordo, so he wouldn't put this cardboard thing in his mouth, have to have his stomach pumped and mess up his flight the next morning. After a few minutes the boys caught on and tossed those veals at me! That was how we broke the ice between the old and the new astronauts. The band came in and we had a fabulous party.

Because this was Gordo's first mission, I wanted to do something special for him that was serious and not a joke. We had built the cake for John, so I decided we would build a capsule made out of flowers for Gordo. I got many women from garden clubs and different places involved in growing and cutting tens of thousands of flowers. We made a capsule out of spring flowers that was the most beautiful thing.

* * * *

143

Frank Borman and his wife Susan were staying at The Cape Colony Inn when they got involved in our practical jokes.

Susan was a very funny girl, kind of a comedian. Frank and Susan always had a little nap in the afternoon. Susan, one day, just to be funny, put a basket of cleaning supplies, like soap and detergent, in a basket outside my door with a note. The note said it would be a good idea if the maids would use the supplies and clean the rooms a little better. If this didn't work, maybe it was time to change the maids.

That same afternoon when they went to their room to sleep, I put a sign on their door that said EMPLOYMENT AGENCY. I started sending maids up for interviews. One after another knocked on the door and said they were applying for a job as a maid.

Finally, Susan called down and asked me to cut it out, that they were trying to get some sleep and the interruptions were keeping them from getting any rest.

I told Susan if she wanted to get some rest, she'd better hire some new maids.

CHAPTER 7

There are two ways of spreading light: to be
The candle or the mirror that reflects it.
                                    −Edith Wharton [1916]

To avoid the appearance of a conflict of interest, the astronauts decided to sell their part ownership in the Cape Colony Inn to Walter Rose. This action eventually forced me to leave Cocoa Beach for Lakeland. I wanted to leave the Cape Colony shortly after the boys left, but I had signed a five-year non-compete agreement with Walter Rose, which prohibited me from working in another hotel in Cocoa Beach for five years. I asked Walter Rose to release me from the agreement, but under no circumstances would he let me out of the contract. I had no other choice but to leave town and start a new life in another city. I chose Lakeland because it was reasonably close and offered the best opportunity.

The fortunes of the Cape Colony Inn went quickly downhill after we left. Walter Rose ended up in bankruptcy, selling the entire property for only $50,000. When I was still there, Rose turned down an offer to sell the hotel for two million dollars.

In the early days at Lakeland, Florida, I became friends with the management and players of the Detroit Tigers baseball team. The team had their spring training headquarters there and negotiated to stay at one of the local hotels. I was overseeing the Lakeland Holiday Inn at the time, and the manager called me one day and said he had been approached by the Tigers about staying at the Holiday Inn. He was against it. He didn't want Black players and other Black personnel staying at the hotel. I didn't want to discuss this over the phone. I arranged to be in Lakeland the next day and we agreed to meet for lunch.

We never made it to the dining room. The manager met me in the lobby and we began talking about the Detroit Tigers. He told me he just didn't like Black people. I told him that wasn't important. He was a manager put there to manage a hotel and to do what was best for the hotel. He refused to budge on the issue. As long as he was manager, there would be no Blacks in the hotel.

I took him to his office and told him to pack up his things. I took his keys. He was gone in five minutes.

147

I contacted the team and negotiated an agreement with them to stay at the Lakeland Holiday Inn. The Tigers had already decided to leave Lakeland, in no small part because of the manager's bigotry, and the town of Lakeland was in an uproar. I was delighted that I was able to step in and solve the problem and save an important revenue base for the area.

I was a hero to the locals. But now the hotel didn't have a manager, so I had to stay at the hotel and take over. It was a 72-room hotel and every time I asked anybody to do something, they just wouldn't do it. The employees had no regard for the guests. In a matter of three weeks, I fired every single person who worked in that hotel except for two people. Out of 40 people, only two were kept on the payroll.

That was an exciting time for us. The Tigers had just won a pennant that year. I was good friends with Al Kaline, Norm Cash and Willie Horton. I used to buddy-buddy around with the players and we used to have some great times together. Jim Campbell, a long-time executive with the Tigers and a driving force in those early Tiger teams, is still a good friend of mine.

* * * *

The same year the Tigers won the pennant, I leased two hotel restaurants from Holiday Inn executive Robinson Callen. A Holiday Inn restaurant in Lakeland and another in Leesburg were both losing money and to Callen, were more trouble than they were worth. I contacted Chef Jim Neff and proposed half ownership in the business. I would watch the front end of the operation, Neff would manage the back end. Neff, who was unemployed at the time, jumped at the offer.

It seemed like a great deal for both of us, but I made a fundamental mistake that almost cost me everything. I assumed the lease included furniture, fixtures, equipment and kitchen appliances. Then I got a registered letter from Borden's Milk Company. I had five days to pay the full amount of the $100,000 lease, or they would repossess all the kitchen equipment.

The Borden attorney didn't want to work anything out. He wanted all or nothing. I had no where near the $100,000 I needed to make things right. I met with my partner to discuss it. We had $2,000. That's all the money we had left. That wouldn't be enough to buy a couple of stoves, much less enough to outfit two full restaurant kitchen rooms and dining rooms.

Neff suggested we go down to Second Avenue in Miami, a restaurant equipment resale district, and try to purchase some used equipment. I didn't have any better idea. We just kept going from one place to the other and didn't make that much headway. Finally, someone suggested we contact a guy named Big Ed, who was the head of the GE Credit Union. Maybe Big Ed would have some repossessed equipment on which he could give us a deal.

I called and got an appointment with Big Ed and we walked to his office about 20 blocks away. I was shocked to see who Big Ed was. It was a friend of mine from Cocoa Beach, who had leased us the furniture and the equipment for the Cape Colony Inn. I had called Ed when I was leaving the hotel to say good-bye.

Big Ed took me into his office. I didn't hold anything back from him and laid all the cards out on the table. I told him we had restaurants in Lakeland and Leesburg that we were going to lose in a couple of days because I had made an amateur's mistake and not properly read the contract when I had leased the restaurants.

Big Ed told me not to worry. He took us to a huge warehouse stocked with whole dining rooms of repossessed furniture, whole kitchens, stainless steel, the most beautiful modern equipment, almost brand new stuff. He told us to have a field day, pick anything we wanted.

I got everything I needed for Leesburg and for Lakeland, about ten van loads of equipment. Back in Big Ed's office I got the deal that made all the difference in my life.

He asked me to sign a note for ten cents on the dollar for $150,000 worth of equipment and didn't make me pay a deposit. Not a dime. Without Big Ed's help, we would have gone bankrupt.

Stories, miracles like Big Ed's, follow the path of my life. I seem to have lived my life under the watchful eye of a benevolent God with a good sense of humor.

* * * *

In no time at all, we made the Lakeland Holiday Inn Restaurant the most popular restaurant in the area. When we started to make money, I told Jim Neff to keep doing what he was doing and I would look around and start investments for both of us. Lakeland could only grow south or north, so I concentrated on buying properties on the south and north sides of the city. The property values just skyrocketed.

I became interested in a piece of property being sold by the City of Lakeland. I called the City Hall and I talked to the city manager. I asked him about the land. It had been for sale for eight years, and to buy the land I would have to pay the amount assessed by a city-approved appraiser. After that, I would have to send a check for the land to the city commissioners. I followed these instructions to the letter.

The appraiser assessed the property at $220,000, the city commissioners approved the sale, and the next day, the Lakeland newspaper headline proclaimed I'd almost stolen the property from the people of Lakeland.

I didn't want to steal anything. I called City Hall and told them if they wanted the property back, they could have it back, because I didn't want to start my life in Lakeland that way. The City of Lakeland returned my check.

Six months later, I called them and asked them about the property. They told me it was still for sale. I bought it for the same price, $220,000.

Sid Raffle, Leo DeOrsey and the astronauts bought in with me. Each of the astronauts had 5 percent, Leo and I each had 10 percent. I bought eight percent from a couple of the guys who wanted to sell, and ended up with 18 percent. We parceled it and sold it one piece at a time and made over two million dollars by the time we were through.

* * * *

Around this time I decided I wanted to build a barbecue restaurant. I called it Jimbo's Barbecue and it was an immediate success. It is still in operation today. Harold Lehman, a nice young guy I hired to manage Jimbo's, became the owner and got his brothers involved. Today there are Jimbo's all over the place.

Chef Neff and I continued to have great success with our restaurants. I had successfully lobbied to change the local liquor laws in Lakeland from being dry to wet. I built several cocktail lounges which were all very successful.

The hotel and restaurant business gives you a million ways to go broke. You can lose your shirt overnight and be finished. I've been inches away from being there. But I always survived. It seems to me now as if my journey was a perfect plan leading me toward my destiny.

Everything in my business life was going great. New opportunities were popping up almost daily. The only thing that was going bad was my marriage. My marriage to Jo was not looking good at all. After 13 years of marriage, and three children, we were getting a divorce.

* * * *

One of my first experiences in reaching out to others occurred in Lakeland, Florida in the late sixties. Before Lakeland, I collected a very small salary for what I was doing. It was just barely enough to live on. When things started to go well for me, I started to look around for some other work to get involved with. I became involved with the mentally and physically handicapped children in Lakeland. These special children moved me so much that I became an officer and a director of the Foundation.

The thing that really struck me was the amount of talent in those children. These children had difficult problems, but they also had such a willingness to do good. I started a nursery project where the children could grow and sell plants. They enjoyed caring for the plants and it became a regular source of income for them.

We built some houses for the children, and it was then that I got the idea that I could employ some of the older children in our Holiday Inns. Maybe even get something started in all the Holiday Inns across the world.

For my work with the disabled children, the State of Florida presented me with its Man of the 'Year award. At first, the recognition embarrassed me, but I have learned awards enable you to spread the word to others, to get them involved.

I have had some success in getting other industries to hire these special people. It is very uplifting. We have some real success stories. Putting children in a regular environment helps them in many ways. They have to work and they have responsibilities that they sometimes don't normally have. Many of them grow and develop in a wonderfully positive way. Some of our employees in this program get married, or learn how to drive, or just become more independent and self-sustaining. We even have one young man who went into the Army and became a successful soldier.

I spend a great deal of my time trying to increase the state's involvement for people with special needs. This led to my involvement at the Cerebral Palsy Clinic. I became a director of the CP chapter in Lakeland, and in this position was able to help implement many positive actions, but my power was limited. I decided these children needed a special home, a place with a special clinic designed to serve the needs of the children afflicted with cerebral palsy. To accomplish this, I became president of the CP chapter.

After I won, we built a clinic and a pool with special access for the children. I became a primary fund-raiser for cerebral palsy. My friends would cross the street when they saw me coming, because they knew I was going to ask them for things that were almost too much to donate. I remember calling a friend of mine named Ron Manser, a builder, and asking him to build a pool for the kids.

Ron, by now used to my requests, said, "Henri, you obviously have no idea how much a pool costs or you wouldn't just pick up the phone and ask me to build you a pool."

The end result, of course, was the kids got their pool, and Ron Manser helped bring joy to a great many children.

During the building of the CP children's home, I called my friends at Florida Tile and asked them to donate all the center's tile and the carpeting. They did. And it is amazing how history repeats itself, because Florida Tile would come through for me over and over again in the years to come.

My special empathy for children is probably a result of the difficult circumstances I survived as a child. I have a need to help children who cannot help themselves. I am drawn to children who are in trouble. In the concentration camps, handicapped children were killed in the first minute the Germans saw them. Terrible things happened to children of all ages and in all states of health. But the disabled had not the smallest chance to survive. In today's world, physically and mentally challenged people are making contributions every day. The value they bring to our lives and communities makes the world a better place for all of us.

152

CHAPTER 8

I have more memories than if I were a thousand years old.
–Charles Baudelaire [1861]

In 1969, I left Lakeland for Orlando. Disney announced that they were thinking about bringing Disney World to Orlando. This was big news. Later, I was riding in a car with a friend who owned several Holiday Inns. I mentioned a new market in Orlando that would be opening up because of Disney. I told him that I thought I could get Holiday Inn franchises, and maybe even get John Glenn to join us.

Years earlier, I had been promised by Holiday Inn president Kemmons Wilson, when I was financially ready to become a Holiday Inn franchisee, all I had to do was pick my spot and I could have it.

My friend liked the idea of having John Glenn's name involved with the partnership and agreed that we would be equal partners and apply for a franchise location in Orlando.

There was nothing in writing. We applied for a one-third, one-third, one-third partnership. We applied for two locations. We got a promise from Holiday Inn for one franchise.

I remember trying to figure out where to put the hotel. If you look at central Florida on the map, the place that was most likely for anything to happen, the place where all the highways were coming together was I-4 and Highway 27. That was the place where we decided to build a 125-room Holiday Inn.

I suggested to John Glenn that we go to see the Holiday Inn boys in Memphis and apply for a franchise on our own. This one would be ours, his and mine. We went to Memphis and came way not with one franchise but several. On the return flight to Orlando, the guardian angel that follows me brought me even more good news. I met John Quinn. He had just applied for and received a Holiday Inn franchise in North Orlando's Altamonte Springs. At the time, I owned five Travel Park franchises that I was trying to get rid of when we got the Holiday Inn franchises. I didn't want to be in competition with myself.

That plane ride started something very special. I invited John to see our operation in Lakeland. He came to see us and we hit it off right away.

In time, John Quinn, John Glenn and I formed a three-way partnership. John Quinn gave us a two-thirds stake in the Altamonte Springs Holiday Inn, and we gave him one-third of the rights at the Disney East Holiday Inn.

John Quinn, with his background in commercial real estate and financial planning, took over many of the financial responsibilities. He put together the mortgages and assured the money. John Glenn's background is in politics and mine is in hotel management. My responsibilities were focused on overseeing the actual building of the Holiday Inns, and the eventual management of the properties.

Our original plans called for 200 rooms at the Altamonte Springs location and 156 rooms at Disney East. As soon as we broke ground for the construction, I contacted my partners and urged them to expand the Disney construction by 72 rooms. It would be more cost effective to do it now. It turned out to be a good business decision. The hotel is located three miles from Disney's front gate. From the day we opened, the property has operated near capacity.

The Altamonte Springs location catered to business travelers. It was a commercial property and we had problems attracting customers. With one booming property and one in need of extra attention, I turned my focus to the area surrounding the hotel, which had lots of kids, students and people working for Disney, living in apartments. They didn't have any place nearby to go. The young people needed a place where they could meet and have a beer and spend time together. We started a bar in the hotel called The Why Not Lounge. From the day the doors opened, business boomed.

I set a special area of the lounge aside for the kids to socialize. We charged a dime for omelets. Any time of the day or night, you could get an omelet for ten cents. The kids didn't have much money. They'd come in with half a buck and could eat five omelets if they wanted. Next, we added Cuban sandwiches for a dime an inch.

We started a club for girls where drinks were a nickel. This attracted the ladies, which in turn brought the guys in. Each night we tried to encourage some kind of participation between the sexes. Best dressed, best dancers, you name it.

I hired a couple of bands. When one would stop playing, the other would start. As the bar's reputation grew, we expanded into the dining room. For eight straight months, I spent almost every night at The Why Not Lounge. I decided that the location of the band wasn't in the right place and ended up moving it four times. Each time I moved it, we added a new dance floor. We became the only place in town with multiple dance floors. We were attracting kids from all over the area.

Our hotel customers were still primarily commercial travelers who could be very demanding. As a gimmick, I bought a parakeet and kept it in my office. I taught that bird some catch phrases by placing a tape recorder in the parakeet's covered cage each night. The idea was to amuse our customers. The bird learned phrases like: "Stop pestering me!" and "Why don't you go back home!" Even a talking bird couldn't keep the hotel's occupancy rate up.

Playboy Magazine wrote about the bar. The place was making money like it was going out of style. Even though the hotel didn't do well, we had money to pay down the mortgage. We sold the hotel at the height of The Why Not Lounge's popularity.

John Glenn and John Quinn have been my business partners in a number of hotel ventures. John Glenn and I have been partners for 35 years. John Quinn joined our partnership 26 years ago. We've had a lot of business and financial success together and I attribute that to the fact that we trust each other completely. Each of us knows that the other will be 100 percent honest in everything we do as a partner. If we tell each other something, mark it down and take it to the bank because it is going to happen. You don't need a contract, our word is good enough.

* * * *

Annie Glenn had a big birthday party for John one year, bringing in people from all over. It was quite a party. We were over at 1789, the restaurant. I had some important papers for John to sign. Right in the middle of dinner, I remembered the papers, pulled them out and asked John to sign them. I put the papers down and John pulled out a pen and signed the top one. I took that one away and he signed the next one, and the one after that until he had worked his way through the pile. I put the papers away and we finished our meal.

Afterward, people were saying nice things about John, taking turns telling stories about their relationship with him. Then John's turn came to make a few remarks. He began talking about the way we did business with each other. It struck him how he had signed a stack of papers I had given him without a second thought. It demonstrated perfectly what our relationship meant. How many partnerships have you ever known when one of the partners would come in with some papers, plunk the papers down and without even looking at them or reading them, just say, it's okay and sign them?

* * * *

I love meeting people. Everyone has a story to tell, and to me, learning those individual stories is a wonderful part of life. I am blessed with a good memory and this has helped me considerably over the years.

One first meeting, which turned into something special, took place in 1975 with a very pregnant young woman named Terry Whaples.

Today, Terry is a minority partner at Holiday Inn Sunspree in Lake Buena Vista, near Disney World. But in 1975, when she was nine months pregnant and recently fired from an employer who didn't think a new mother could carry the workload, I hired her as a C.P.A. Not only could she do the work, over the years, I came to trust her more and more.

In the seventies, there still weren't too many female managers in the hotel business. Orlando was home of the good old boy network. When I appointed Terry controller, most of my colleagues thought I was crazy.

From the day I hired Terry, she has looked out for us. It was always very important to her for everything to be done 100 percent properly. I remember she gave me a bill for some stamps that I used on a couple of letters. They were personal business and even though I was one of the owners, she gave me a bill for three bucks for the stamps. I knew I had made a good choice in hiring her when she gave me that bill.

One year, we gave a party for key employees at John Quinn's house in Maitland, Florida. The staff brought over all the supplies for the party, including two large plastic garbage pails to hold ice and drinks. After the party, when they cleaned up, they left one of the cans behind. Terry assumed John kept it and sent him a bill for $5.00.

She is a perfect example of what can happen when you give a hard working person a chance to be successful. She grabbed every opportunity. We made her a partner, and she was very grateful, but I told her that it was her honesty, her hard work, and her pursuit of excellence that had earned this chance for her.

* * * *

At our hotels, we've always committed ourselves to the family and family values, to get past the black and navy blue suits. The business traveler is a father, a mother or a grandparent, an aunt, an uncle, a single parent. If you fulfill the needs of the person in the hotel, you will be able to fill more rooms.

This commitment to family has enabled our hotels to boast an incredibly high occupancy rate of 95 percent. Last year, we had one of the highest occupancy rates in the Holiday Inn system.

What we do at our hotels is to try to appeal to the children. If we can make a place for the children, then the parents will follow.

Holiday Inn Sunspree is designed with children in mind. The children's room concept that has been in use for 13 years at our hotels, was expanded and modernized to include several special amenities for children. The architecture in the kid's areas of the hotel is built on a kid's scale. Terry and our general manager, Jim Olson, recently built an innovative "kid's suite" which was the first of its kind. Our rooms are oversized and Terry and Jim decided we could take some of that space and carve out a special place for the children. Within the rooms, we've built a private kid's suite which has bunk beds and a separate phone and television. The kids love it. They feel private and very safe at the same time. Other amenities for the kids in the hotel include a special dining room and day care center, video games, puppet theater, and most uniquely, there is Max.

Max, the Holiday Inn mascot, is named after my father. He is the face that all the children remember. He walks the hallways during the day and tucks the children in at night. To Max, the children are the VIPs.

We always get the names of the children and their ages and address a little note to them from Max welcoming them to the hotel. If the child is old enough, we make sure he has a handful of tokens to play video games. We want to get the children involved in the experiences, the fun they can have by coming down to the clubhouse with the other children. Once the kids see Max, they're hooked.

* * * *

My success in life has been a partnership. I owe a tremendous amount of my success to people that helped me get to where I am today.

159

Many people helped me, and maybe I helped some of them to where they are today, too.

We shared a common goal, to do the best we could with whatever we had. The goal was not my success, or his success, it was our success. I have always cared for the people who work for me. I've been where they are. I've worked the jobs that they are holding today. I always put myself in their position when I talk to them. Every time a maid works for me, I am the maid. Every time an employee comes in to talk to me, regardless of their job, I am them because I have done their job. I base my management style on this. I always ask myself, if I were sitting where they are, how would I feel and what would I need to make things right?

We spend over half of our lives working. Work can affect our personal life tremendously, the same way our private life can affect work. When I was still involved in the day to day operations, I tried to help our 650 employees reach a place where they can be happy in both their work life and their private life. Work should be fulfilling and sustaining to a person's feelings about themselves. If it is not, if people do not like their work or enjoy their work, they would be much better off if they left and found something they like better.

People are more afraid of change than they should be. It is much worse to stay where you are unhappy. The worst feeling in the world is to go to work hating to be there only because you have to make a living. The same person who is miserable in one job could be very happy right across the street doing something else.

By far, the best part of being an employer is the feeling I have for the people who work for us. There is a lot of love between us, we are like a family.

CHAPTER 9

I stood tiptoe upon a little hill.
−John Keats [Poems - 1817]

I came to America with little and never dreamed of attaining the success I have achieved. Kemmons Wilson gave me the opportunity to have the Holiday Inn franchises. Because of Kemmons, I became wealthy.

I have very clear cut ideas on wealth and what it means to a person's life. When I was younger, I had a drive and an excitement to make my first million. The hard part comes after you make the money; how do you hold onto it? Many people have had millions and millions of dollars only to have nothing today. A lot of people have a talent for making money, but have no idea how to hold on to it. My desire to make money is gone.

Most people don't use money because of fear and insecurity. They stash away as much money as they can. The more they stash, the more they want so they can stash away even more. Greed takes over and there is a constant fear that all the wealth can disappear as quickly as it came.

It can, but I don't believe life can be enjoyable or meaningful unless a person gives something to others in some way. If a person cannot give something to others, that life is hardly worth living.

If you don't share of yourself or give to others, and you take all this money you've made and you don't do anything positive for others with it, what does that say about you?

How much can one man possibly consume? How many steaks can you eat? How many bottles of wine can you drink? How many comfortable chairs can you sit in? How many trips can you take? After a while, after you have done all these things, you get very depressed, frustrated deep in your heart because there is nothing else to do, nothing else to have.

I believe giving to others helps make a person whole. It doesn't matter what type of help you are capable of giving, what matters is being able and willing to give.

I don't believe there should be any hunger in this world. Turn on the television and we see the dying thousands in Somalia and Bangladesh and

163

a hundred other forgotten places. Right in front of your eyes, a child dies. How can we allow that to happen? We have so many resources. We understand so much more about the world than we did thirty or forty years ago. Why do children starve in this world of plenty? I can't understand this.

Having spent five years fighting starvation, I am particularly empathetic to children who do not have enough food to eat or clean water to drink.

We aren't doing justice to those in need. In this great country of ours, we should be able to figure out how to help people. A person who has been hungry will be psychologically affected for a long time, maybe even for the rest of his or her life. Hunger and thirst are feelings you never forget.

I don't like to tell people what to do. I've learned from my children that telling is not the best way to accomplish anything. But if I were to offer one word of advice, it is this: find someone who needs a lift up, who needs a little help. Offer him your hand. Once you experience the pleasure of helping others, many of your other problems will go away. By reaching out to others, you will help yourself. By sharing a meal with a person who is hungry, you feed your own soul as well.

* * * *

In 1980, the Mercury 7 crew and friends all got together in California to celebrate the twentieth anniversary of Alan Shepard's flight. I asked all the astronauts for a few minutes to talk to them about an idea.

I brought up my idea about forming a foundation. They would hold board meetings at least once a year, and this would insure that the astronauts would stay in contact. The foundation could do good works and keep them together at the same time. They agreed to that.

I obtained foundation status for them and organized what became the original Mercury 7 Foundation, and what today is named the Astronaut Scholarship Foundation. The board of directors included the astronauts, Betty Grissom, Project Mercury flight surgeon Bill Douglas and me.

One of the really wonderful things to come from the Foundation was Space Camp. The boys in Huntsville had decided to build a space camp in Florida for children to visit. I proposed that the Project Mercury astronauts join their program and Alan Shepard, president of the Astronaut Scholarship Foundation, and I began negotiating with them. We eventually became 50-50 partners in the Titusville Space Camp.

164

All the money made as profit at Space Camp goes to scholarships for youngsters. Space Camp is designed to get children interested in space, then help the most deserving ones get an education through scholarships. The students awarded the scholarship can continue for as long as they maintain a B average, all the way to becoming doctors. The Foundation stays with them all the way. Scholarship students can take their studies to the stars and beyond.

"Space Camp is first class," Alan Shepard said. "If it helps motivate young people to get involved in space technology, then obviously our country is going to be much better because of it."

Scholarship recipients are chosen through a selective process that begins by high schools and colleges across the country submitting names of talented youngsters. An independent committee run by Dr. Miller in Ohio makes the final decisions.

Howard Benedict, the AP wire chief during Project Mercury, operates the Astronaut Scholarship Foundation.

"We are successful at launching a lifetime interest in space and technology because our hands-on programs help to ignite the imaginations of youngsters," he said. "Even in kids who will not go on to pursue an interest in the aerospace industry or other high technology careers, Space Camp fosters teamwork, decision-making and leadership. For a young person, these are valuable assets with which to navigate any future course."

At age 19, George Bush was the youngest American fighter pilot in World War II, just a few years older than the kids who attend Space Camp. During a visit to Space Camp in 1991, President George Bush told trainees, "This is probably the same thrill and experience for me as it is for you. I'm absolutely convinced that what we're seeing here today, including the education of young Americans looking to the future, in terms of science and technology and the emphasis here on space, is absolutely vital to our country. I'm inspired by the young people who participate in this program, because this really is the future."

A Hall of Fame for the Mercury, Gemini and Apollo astronauts is one wonderful addition to Space Camp. It is the only one of its kind in the world and honors the historic achievements of 31 of America's heroes.

****

Greetings from the moon!
Three American heroes sent me special regards.

"To Henri Landwirth–You never get too far away to enjoy a good joke."

–Neil Armstrong [1969]

"To Henri Landwirth who can really appreciate the effort for this, with my sincere thanks for helping the effort."

–Alan Shepard [1971]

"To Henri, with best wishes. Sorry I haven't been over sooner – but I've been out of town."

–Pete Charles Conrad, Commander Apollo [1969]

166

The connections from the early days continue to this day. The old and the new. I see the little space kids running around with the astronauts. It is a very nice thing. One of the goals I have in life is to connect the younger generation with the older generation in as many ways as possible. The children and the elderly needs us the most. They are the two most disenfranchised groups in our society. We cannot forget the innocent or the old. We are, after all, connected to this life through love and caring. Reaching out to others is what makes a life a life.

I started the Fanny Landwirth Foundation, named in memory of my beloved mother, in 1980 to help as many needy people and organizations as possible. The Foundation has grown to have an endowment worth several million dollars. My children and wife are on the board of directors of the Fanny Landwirth Foundation and help make the decisions on how the money will be spent and what causes it will support.

I want my children to experience the pleasure of helping others. And in order to be fully capable of this responsibility, I wanted to educate them in a meaningful way of the things I experienced first hand.

One of the causes that is dear to me is supporting worthwhile programs and projects in Israel. Over the years, I have worked to help expand schools and day care centers. We even built an Olympic size swimming pool for the children. Because of my roots, I feel a special closeness with the people of Israel, especially the children.

One of the first projects the Foundation sponsored was Witness to the Holocaust, a study of that terrible time, so children would have an accurate history to learn from and to see how it really was in the concentration camps. Many of today's school children do not believe the Holocaust happened. I wish I could sit and talk to each of these children one at a time. I would explain the Holocaust could happen again if they turn away from the lessons of the past. The Jews were destroyed once. Such destruction could happen again. To forget the past can be a very serious mistake.

We donate art works to many temples and charities and schools, and we provide as many scholarships to children as we can. We have helped build computer rooms for schools in Israel for children, and each year we continue to try and expand our efforts from the previous year.

I do not like to be applauded by others. I am a little embarrassed to be writing about these things. Most of my efforts on behalf of those in need remain private. This book was difficult for me to commit to writing for that reason.

I am a very private person. That may appear to be a contradiction since I am in the public eye so much now with Give Kids the World. But I have always been a very private man. I love to be with people. I love to listen to others tell me about their lives, but I'm not really comfortable talking about myself.

One of the secrets to being successful is to follow through with a good idea. A lot of people have good ideas, but instead of acting upon them, they talk about them and don't do anything. You have to have enough faith in yourself to believe in your ideas and to act upon them. If you fail, so what? It is much better to fail than not to try at all. In fact, I'd much rather do something, than talk about doing it.

CHAPTER 10

This only is denied to God, the power to undo the past.
—Agathon [400 B.C]

Relationships, both romantic and personal, are the hardest thing in life to be successful at. My whole life, I've never been afraid of failure, because every time I fail, and I have failed more than once, it tells me a lot about myself and I learn a lot from the failures. We really learn much more from our failures than our successes. This is truer in relationships than anything else. In every relationship, there are moments that stand out from the rest. Moments that define the high points and low points of a couple's time together. One partner might perceive those events in a totally different context than the other. This can happen when the frame of reference is different.

Because of all the things that took place in my youth, I have never attached myself too much to material things. Possessions are like window dressing. I have always been more attracted to people than to things, but even with people there is sometimes a distance that is difficult to overcome. To this day there is a numbness which remains inside of me.

I decided I wanted my children to see proof of the camps for themselves. As painful as it was, I returned to Matthausen with them to allow them to witness with their own eyes what is real and what is not. We didn't talk much on the way. My memory moved into the past, when this camp had been my only reality. Even in the company of my children, I felt distant and alone.

As we went through the barracks, I pointed things out to them like the wooden lofts a few feet above each other where dozens of men slept almost on top of each other. I could remember how it felt to lie on that wood, so close to others that I wasn't sure if I was touching and smelling them or myself.

I felt very apart from my children and my voice did not sound at all like my voice. We were the only ones in that camp. The man who was at the gate, closed the gate and locked it and went to lunch. He must not have known we were still inside.

When we were ready to leave, we couldn't get out of the camp. I cannot tell you how I felt standing with my children behind that locked gate.

171

I became very frightened, very nervous. Why did I come back to this place? My heart hurt. I was there with my children and we were locked inside. I thought of my own parents, of what it is like to be with those you love more than life itself, that you would die to protect, and to be incapable of saving them.

I know seeing this place in person affected the children. To go into the past in such a physical way is a very sad pilgrimage. I wanted to show the children a terrible piece of history that I had experienced. As my children, by extension, the camps became a part of each of them, too. I am very aware that to forget the past can be a serious mistake. I wanted them to see with their own eyes. I wish everyone could see with their own eyes, so there would be no doubt in anyone's mind that such horrors happened once and could, God forbid, happen again. I want the words "concentration camps" to be more than words in a book. I want children to learn that this was the wrong way. That this camp and hundreds of others just like it were real places. The ovens and the crematoriums were real. The murders really happened.

Later, when we were driving away from the camp, I was filled with thankfulness that my children were living in America.

The highlights of my first marriage centered around the births of our three children.

My children are the source of my greatest happiness.

Jo is a wonderful mother and a fine person. She's very direct and has tremendous honesty. We had Gary in 1955. Greg in 1957, and Lisa in 1961. And raising the children and making our house a home was the most important thing to her. I found a lot of excitement and a lot of fulfillment in the outside world, climbing the ladder of success, learning and doing new things in the hotel business. Jo and I were not together very often.

Most of the years we were together, we were poor. We began to do a little better during the years in Lakeland. But before that, we didn't have many material things. Jo has never remarried and remains a dynamic force in the lives of our children and grandchildren.

After our divorce, I went to Lakeland every single week to see my children. I went every Wednesday. The trip took about an hour each way, but nothing was more important to me than to see Lisa, Greg, and Gary. One day I particularly remember, I came and my little daughter, who was about five-years old, brought a small brown paper bag to dinner. She waited until we were alone and opened the bag and said, "Daddy, I brought you a present...

Lisa gave me her favorite doll. To this day, whenever I move from one location to the next, the very first thing I take is that little doll. I will never forget the day Lisa gave me that doll. It says so much about families who are together and apart at the same time.

My children are the most important thing in my life. I started out to write this book as a private memoir just for them, so they could know me a little better, and hopefully understand why they have sometimes suffered while I put other work above being with my family. The idea to use this story to help Give Kids the World came later.

With my pride and joy, my children, Gary, Lisa and Greg

With Admiral Alan Shepard and Senator John Glenn, each of whom donated a $100 bill to Give Kids the World for the privilege of holding granddaughter Rebecca

I am so proud of Gary, Greg and Lisa. Each of them, in their own way, is the source of my greatest pride. I love them and respect the lives they have made for themselves. Gary is a veterinarian by training, but is working with a charitable foundation in Orlando. Greg has a factory which manufactures fishing lures, and Lisa is working hard to develop the skills to take on more and more of the responsibilities of the Fanny Landwirth Foundation. It is an honor to be their father.

One of the real extra pleasures of having children is when they have children of their own. Having four grandchildren is a joy without limit.

Greg and his wife Lisa have two children. Rebecca is six-years old and Max is four years old. They live in Tampa and come to Orlando often so I can spend time with them.

My daughter Lisa, and her husband Bill Ussery, also have two children. Sarah is five-years old and her younger sister, Emily, is almost three. Lisa's family lives in Jacksonville, but like Greg and his family, they often come to Orlando so we can spend time together as a family.

My oldest son, Gary, lives in Orlando. Like the other children, he is keenly aware of the importance of being together. My children and I spend all of the most important days with each other. It is wonderful. At this point in their lives, my children are each becoming more involved in the importance of giving. Each of them is active in the Fanny Landwirth Foundation and the work it does.

I hope in my heart, that each of my children finds peace and satisfaction in how they spend the precious moments of their lives. We are each our parents children. I am the son of Max and Fanny Landwirth. Much of what I am is because of those few simple words: the son of Max and Fanny Landwirth, and like it or not, much of what Gary, Greg and Lisa are is because they are the children of Jo Guardino and Henri Landwirth. That is one unalterable piece of their destiny which will never change.

It is important to me that my children understand that my eyes have witnessed a changing world from a perspective that very few people share. I have had the misfortune of being at death's door in a Nazi prison camp, starved and ravaged, and the good fortune to meet and dine with heads of state in splendor and magnificence. I have been so poor I did not know where my next meal was coming from, or how I would pay the rent, and now my family is financially secure. What a remarkable journey life has taken me on, and how empty it would be without my children to share it.

My son Greg points out that his mother is a survivor, too. I survived a difficult past and she has survived a sometimes difficult life. We both have similar values that emphasize honesty and family. I see my children with their children and I am proud of the wonderful parents they have become. This is a gift passed on to them by their mother for which I will always be thankful.

I want my children to look at the world around them with eyes wide open. I lost my parents to the brutal cruelty of the worst of human nature, yet I now have the great gift of serving as a surrogate parent to the thousands of children who benefit from Give Kids the World.

The world around us is seldom seen in black and white. Things are just not that simple. I am constantly assessing and reassessing America's changing role in world politics and I want my children to do the same thing.

* * * *

After my first marriage, I decided that I would probably never remarry. I kept that promise for 14 years, then I met my second wife, Carol Rosenberg. She had three little girls, the youngest was six and the twins were eight years old. But that marriage did not last too long, about five years. I am still close to my stepdaughters, Lisa, Dina and Jenny.

***

I am lucky that my children are healthy. It is a sad fact of life that there are all too many parents who cannot say those few simple, but so important words. To watch a child fight an illness is a very difficult thing for a parent. We want to protect our children, to keep them safe and out of harm's way. When serious illness strikes a child, and it can occur anywhere at anytime, the families rally around the child in every way possible. They provide love, caring, emotional support and so much more. But what resources are available to help them as a family?

I started looking for the answer to that question because of a tragic story about two such families. That search led me to the best idea I have ever had and that is what the rest of this book is about: *Give Kids the World.*

Donated to Give Kids the World by my children, the statue of mother and child, sculpted by Heisman Trophy artist Frank Eliscu, is an enduring symbol of our work.

PART III

The Miracle of Give Kids The World

God will bless all children, but we have to help.
                                    –Mother Theresa [1989]

Part V: A Moment in Time

He touches a child's hand,
Her flesh warm as summer sand.
A smile brushes across her lips,
He traces it with his fingertips.
Innocence, afflicted without reason;
Death, stealing life in spring season.

Words fail him, they cannot explain
Any reason to justify a child's pain.
She smiles again, does not complain,
Her mother, nearby, nearly insane
From searching for the smallest grain
Of hope amidst such a fruitless plain.

Her child's body has turned against her,
Like cruel winter wind against the shore.
Her spirit learning from her body's pain,
Such a price for knowledge gained!
Tears whisper across sallow cheeks,
Her life measured in days, perhaps weeks.

He has brought them here, a last request,
To provide a memory of the thing loved best—
Mickey Mouse in his Magic Kingdom
Free from disease, worry or harm.
Disney's magic wraps sickness in its arms,
And, for a child's moment, works its charm.

Part VI: Full Circle

Her tiny hand traces his graying cheek,
Her struggle is long and she is weak.
There are questions and angry shouts,
But not from this child's mouth.
She leaves the anger for other lips...
Today, Snow White is at her fingertips.

If love could only save her!
But it can at best deter
The unseen stalking thing
That seeks to steal a child's spring.
Yet for a week, illness has no say,
Memories are made for another day.

He sees himself in this child's eyes,
And again a little piece of him dies.
She comforts him,
Strength moving from her limbs.
A child, mother to the man,
Ready to embrace God's plan

As He has written it.
Facing crisis with wisdom and wit.
While others have seasons many
A springtime child hasn't any
Dream past tomorrow's peace.
When springtime sleeps, even angels weep.

CHAPTER 1

Unearned suffering is redemptive.

–Martin Luther King [1963]

Amy was six years old in 1986. She had incurable cancer. Like so many other children in wish foundations, Amy told her mother if she could have one wish, it would be to meet Mickey Mouse. Such a simple wish would bring her joy. It did not happen because the arrangements took too long. Amy simply ran out of time.

Jim Olsen, my hotel manager at Holiday Inn East, told me Amy's family canceled their trip, because their daughter had tragically died while the arrangements were being made. Though I never knew her, Amy's death became the catalyst for building Give Kids the World and has affected everything in my life since.

I hurt for the family's loss, but I also felt angry. How this could happen? How could we allow a child to die before she could see Mickey Mouse? How in America could we not fulfill any child's last wish?

For days I couldn't stop thinking about Amy and her family. What if it happened again? What if another family simply ran out of time? That thought bothered me and I began looking a little deeper into how the wish foundations worked. I discovered the wish of nearly three out of four terminally ill children is to see Mickey Mouse. Most of the children and their families have never traveled outside of their communities and their resources are limited. I found out that almost every foundation in America took six to eight weeks to process the many components, including hotels, transportation and tickets, necessary to arrange a trip for the families. Sometimes six to eight weeks can mean the difference between life and death. It was with this thought that my sixth life, the most remarkable part of my life's journey, began.

With Amy's death, the seed that would grow into Give Kids the World had been planted in my heart and soul, but I didn't know what to do next. Over the years, I had developed a good relationship with the management at Disney. Seeking their help seemed a logical place to start, so I arranged an appointment with Dianna Morgan, at that time the head of Disney's public relations department.

181

When I walked into her office, I had two things on my side that others with similar proposals may not have had. First, I had a reputation with Disney. And second, I was willing to back my proposal with money from my mother's foundation as well as from my own pocket.

At this point in my life, my children were healthy and successful. My hotel businesses and other investments were profiting. I had attained a level of comfort light years away from where I had begun. Yet something was still missing. And as I began to tell Dianna what I wanted to accomplish, I had a sense of discovering that which had been missing from my life.

A man is not defined by what he has. What matters is the values he lives by and what he does for others. Without being consciously aware of it, I was getting ready to make a commitment with my life that I'd never imagined making.

But that awareness came later. When I was talking with Dianna Morgan, I was thinking of Amy and how time had run out on her while she waited six weeks to see Mickey Mouse. It was clear to me that time was the greatest enemy of these special children and I vowed to cut through all the planning, paperwork and red tape. I wanted Dianna to understand the situation from my eyes, because my eyes were seeing it through the eyes of a sick child wanting nothing more than to see Mickey Mouse.

I explained my idea to bring together foundations, corporations and individuals working as one for the benefit of the children and their families.

I knew from experience that Disney never gives an answer right away. You can go to Disney with an idea and they receive you like royalty. They always listen closely to what you have to say, but you can never get an answer from them until they are ready.

When I had finished my presentation, Dianna agreed to give me everything I asked for and more. I couldn't believe it. Disney gave us an answer on the spot and it was yes! I was so excited that I kept asking Dianna if it was really true that Disney was going to support Give Kids the World. She said we could count on it. With Disney behind us, I knew then, really knew, that it was going to happen. Once Disney gives you the stamp of approval, you know you're on your way.

Excited, I got in the car and drove to Sea World to meet with their president, Bob Gault. He received me, and I told him about Disney. I asked him if he would join us at Give Kids the World. Without a moment's hesitation, he said, "Henri, you've got whatever you need from me."

And Gault meant it. He volunteered his marketing department, with Sue Schoening in charge, to create a brochure and logo for Give Kids the World. The artist for Sea World came to me with two ideas for the logo. The one we chose was the mother and child. We put this picture of mother and child with the words Give Kids the World, and that's how we named it. Sea World put these ideas together in our first brochure. Bob is now the head of Universal Studios Hollywood and his enthusiasm for Give Kids the World has only increased.

Once Disney and Sea World committed to the project, things started happening very quickly. I found myself faced with a difficult task. I've always been very conscious of not abusing friendship or asking people to do something as a favor to me, but I wanted Give Kids the World to succeed. I asked each of the Mercury astronauts to help us. Not one of them turned me down. They committed the support of the Astronaut Scholarship Foundation as well as their personal support. I contacted Walter Cronkite and Art Buchwald and asked them for their help. Both Walter and Art agreed to do whatever they could.

Art even became one of the first Advisory Board members and contacted Equitable Insurance Company to help arrange financial support for Give Kids the World. Equitable Insurance gave the foundation its first corporate money. I went to New York to receive their check for $75,000.

I walked out of their Seventh Avenue office with that enormous check and looked across the street to the Wellington Hotel, the first hotel I ever worked for. I remembered manning the Wellington front desk for $42 a week just years before, then patted my pocket with the $75,000 check from Equitable. I had to laugh. It could only happen in America.

We were just getting started but we were already picking up momentum. I converted a storage room at the Holiday Inn into an office and staffed it with one secretary and a telephone. We began to build our dream with a hundred square feet of office space and a commitment that there would be no more Amys.

* * * *

The months that followed were a whirlwind. I spent every single day going from one business to another urging people to participate in the foundation.

183

Our original program brought families in to Orlando for three nights and four days. One of my first responsibilities was to arrange the housing for the families. Eighty-seven Orlando hotels agreed to join our efforts. Any hotel that had a hundred rooms agreed to give us five rooms a year. This meant that for a hotel with 500 rooms, the commitment was 25 rooms. We used these rooms as needed. As Give Kids the World grew, we were able to get the rooms any time they weren't sold out. We worked it out informally, without lawyers drawing up reams of contracts. We just had a verbal agreement to help the children.

The first year, we brought 380 families to Orlando and expanded their vacations to four nights and five days. In those days, many of the hotels were booked to capacity and we often had problems securing rooms. Almost from the start, the need was greater than the supply.

The demand was so great that we were having trouble serving all those families with special children who wanted to meet Mickey Mouse. This is when the idea for the Give Kids the World Village changed from a nice thing to dream about into something we had to build. But like most good ideas, moving from imagination to implementation did not come easily.

I had experience in major construction, but I had never tackled a problem this size before. One person could not do it alone, so I decided I would do what I have done so many times since. I asked our dear supporters and friends for their help. But before I could do that, I had to go shopping.

* * * *

I knew that the first question potential supporters would ask me was where the Village was going to be built. I thought it was extremely important to have a real place to show them, so they could see the land and realize what we wanted to build with their help. I decided the best thing we could do to help ourselves was to purchase the land.

I took my checkbook and began searching for the perfect location to build the Kids' Village. I found it almost immediately in Kissimmee on a 35-acre lot. The land had 20 acres of wetlands, the rest dry. I planned to clear the 15 acres of grove and use it for the site to build the Village.

I bought the land, both for its central location near Disney, Sea World and other major attractions and because I could look at that overgrown orange grove and see how the Village would appear when we built it. In front of me were rows of burned out orange trees, but I didn't see that.

I looked at the land and my imagination saw the Village as it would one day look. I could see the villas, and a place for the children to fish, and the castle. I could see it all, as if my dream had already come to life.

During this early time, Bob Allen, then Disney vice president, learned about Give Kids the World. Bob, an extremely innovative and inspiring guy, was also a close friend. He told me if we needed anything for Give Kids the World and it was within his power, he would make sure we got it. One of the things he suggested to me was to create a video about Give Kids the World to show to people. This became a very important tool for us.

Bob's son, also named Bob, worked in Disney's video production. We met and Bob explained, "Henri, we're going to give you a video. My dad asked me to do that, but you have to get somebody to narrate."

The first person I thought of was Walter Cronkite. I got on a plane to New York and went to Walter's house to ask him in person. He opened the door and as I walked into his house, he started to tell me how busy he was, how many projects he had going on. On top of all this, Walter would be flying to Vienna later that day.

With friends Walter and Betsy Cronkite

We spent the next several hours talking, and I didn't feel I could impose on my friend. Before I left to return to Florida, I gave Walter some promotional material about Give Kids the World. I also handed him a tape of The Today Show, which had done a five minute feature on Give Kids the World and me. I asked Walter to look at the material if he had a chance.

I didn't hear from him for quite some time, a couple of months, maybe. Then one day I got the warmest, most beautiful letter from him. He apologized for not reading the material and promised to do whatever he could to help. I called Walter and told him why I'd really come to visit him. He agreed to narrate the video.

The video quickly became our biggest fund raising tool. With it, we can show potential contributors and volunteers what the foundation is accomplishing.

Shortly after Walter made the videotape, I traveled to San Diego for the Super Bowl as a guest of one of the Holiday Inn franchise holders. The Holiday Inn people already knew a little about my work with

Give Kids the World. When I got there, I made sure they knew everything. I gathered everyone together and showed them our videotape and asked for the money to help build the Village.

That year, the second year of Give Kids the World, we served more than 700 families, almost doubled from the first year. The year after that, over 1200 families came to us. The need had already outstripped our ability to meet it through area hotels. We needed more housing for the families. Our original plan was to build eight villas with two apartments each. We also wanted to build a pool, a playground and an administration building.

Mike Meeks, a strong supporter of the children from the beginning, took the Village as his project. He said he would take the idea to Mike Ross, then the chairman of the board. Ross agreed Holiday Inn would advance a million dollar loan on behalf of its employees, and would start fund raising around the country.

On March 11, 1988, Meeks, on behalf of Holiday Inn franchisees and their employees, presented me with a check for one million dollars. He said he wanted to help us begin construction immediately because time is the most precious thing the children have. I thought of Amy, the little girl who ran out of time, and hoped

Seed money – the million dollar check with Art Buchwald and John Glenn

such a thing would never happen again. As painful as her loss was, I hoped her parents would someday visit the Village and see what she had inspired for other children, the difference her young life had made.

* * * *

I have always tried to do things instead of talk about them. So much energy can be wasted worrying about the exact way to do something. I think it is better to begin and adapt along the way. Learn from your mistakes, but keep moving forward.

I met with Gary Brown, the president of Welbro Constructors, Inc. and asked him to help us build the Village. I had worked with Welbro building hotel projects and I knew they were a quality company with quality people. Gary agreed to help us raise a million dollars of in-kind services from various builders and contractors.

We wanted the Village built and operational by Christmas of 1989, but still needed more money to meet this target. Jan Silver, my assistant at Holiday Inn, worked with me day and night trying to coordinate the frenzy of activity that was taking place.

Building the Village got difficult, more difficult than it needed to be. One day, I called my secretary into my office and told her I would be leaving. Transfer my calls to the Village, I said. I decided to set up shop there, oversee the construction and get this thing open. I couldn't do it from the hotel. I picked up a pen from my desk and went to the Village for what I thought would be six to eight weeks. I never went back. That's how I finished my life as an active, participating partner in the hotel business.

Building the Village was an enormous challenge. The day-to-day work took it's toll on me physically, to the point where I had a mild physical breakdown. I simply couldn't keep up with the ever growing list of demands. I tried as hard as I could, working twenty hour days, until I just couldn't go on any longer. One day, I just collapsed and had to stay away from the Village for a short time. While I was recuperating, I was thinking about where we would take the Village next. The seed was really starting to sprout and take on a life of its own. I was very anxious not to let my own physical limitations restrict what we could do for the children.

By the time we cleared the land and poured the foundations for the villas, more and more people became involved. It was a real American happening. Different plumbing companies came on Saturdays and Sundays to install plumbing. Secretaries and company presidents came out to the Village every day to volunteer. A group of 100 guys showed up on Saturday to help. One of them opened the back of his station wagon, pulled out a set of golf clubs and teed up on the grass. I asked what he was doing and he said that for as long as he could remember, he'd never missed playing golf on Saturday. He said he was going to hit that ball once and then get to work.

Aerial shot of the Give Kids the World construction

As construction on the Village continued, a real ground swell of community momentum started to build. I saw an enthusiasm driven by momentum that is impossible to buy. Many wonderful people and companies came together in a way that seemed to exemplify the American capacity for caring.

187

The union hall in Orlando volunteered to come to the Village and wire eight villas for us. I explained there might be a problem because this was a non-union job. They said it didn't matter. They wanted to help us, to be a part of the Village.

The electricians came out the next day. One of them said a member of their union hall from Cleveland had a sick child we had cared for the year before. That kind of networking is how Give Kids the World succeeds. We are all connected through the children. Their innocence and the burden of their suffering brings us all together with a common goal.

Seeing what was happening, feeling the spirit of the volunteers, I decided that we shouldn't stop at eight villas but build sixteen, instead. That meant we needed another $700,000. I went back to Memphis and talked to Mike Meeks. He sensed the excitement the project caused but didn't feel Holiday Inn could commit any more funds. I felt we had to take advantage of the momentum generated by the community getting behind Give Kids the World so I went to the bank and signed a note guaranteeing the amount.

Construction stayed right on schedule. Bruce Holmes, vice president of operations for Welbro, worked with me to contact many different associations in the community, from plasterers and painters to electricians and plumbers, and they all donated goods and services and volunteered a variety of expertise. Gary, Bruce and I continued to go to every subcontractor association and trade group we could think of trying to gain additional support. Each time a company or individual signed on, they helped bring in others in their field. The Florida Lumber Association gave us the rafters for the roofs and sent us all the roofs complete. Even today, the FLA continues to support Give Kids the World. They sponsor a support group for the parents that meets twice a week.

Bill Dodson of WM. B. Dodson, Inc. agreed to help with the interior design and furnishing of eight villas. Bill and his assistant Brenda Hall contacted furniture manufacturing companies around the country to help complete the interior of the villas. Over 150 Eastern Airlines employees came in on Saturday and Sunday and built a whole playground. Welbro Constructor sent out at least 100 of their employees and framed all the villas. Area landscaping companies got together and donated about $250,000 in landscaping services. One connection led to the next. A volunteer, who might be a plumber would go home and talk to his friend, who might be a painter. Word of mouth kept the supply of labor and services flowing.

Volunteer commitment was deep. In some cases, it was permanent. In fact, many people who started out with us in the beginning still participate. The Florida Irrigation Society sends people in twice a year to help. The Florida Landscape Society brings its best people in from all over the state four times a year to work on the grounds, keeping the Village looking nice. The last time they came, they brought over 200 men and women to do landscaping.

We finished the first villas in the winter of 1989 and immediately

began work on the next ones. The demand was so great, we could not afford to wait. Our first visitors in the new villas were children from Russia. The Today Show sent a reporter to cover the story.

An architect in California named Henry Conversano saw The Today Show segment about Give Kids the World and

Clown and child creating memories

sent me a note that said, "You're doing a great job. I'm all for you. Here's $5,000 to help you." At that time, this represented our largest personal contribution. I called Henry Conversano to thank him and discovered he had designed the interiors of several of the most impressive casinos in Las Vegas, including the Golden Nugget and the Mirage Hotel.

I told Henry our plan to expand the Village by adding more villas. They were to be residential, but we wanted them to be spectacular. Henry volunteered to create the original drawings for every villa and included everything the families needed: fully equipped two bedroom, two bath houses complete with wheelchair-accessible shower stalls, a whirlpool bathtub, washer and dryer and full kitchen. Henry and Paul Steeleman, an architect on his staff, came up with an elaborate design for the villas.

Welbro loved the designs, but determined they were too elaborate and would be cost prohibitive. Bruce Holmes designed a simpler, more cost efficient plan. Ben Butera, our long-time architect and supporter, then took both sets of plans and came up with the design that would be built. We were able to build the villas for about half of what they would have otherwise cost.

* * * *

189

One day, I got a call from a Dr. Jampolsky in San Francisco who had just read an article about Give Kids the World. I had no idea who he was, but when he said he knew of two families who needed our help, I asked for their names.

"It's that easy?" he asked.

I assured him it was.

That same evening, my daughter Lisa called and said, "Pops, I just put a book in the mail to you and you have to promise to read it." The book, she added, was called *Love Is Letting Go of Fear* by Gerald Jampolsky, the man who had called that morning. Neither one of us could believe it.

Later that night, I got a call from Linda Kaplan, the national executive director of the Make A Wish Foundation. I asked Linda if she had ever heard of Gerald Jampolsky. She said, "Henri, if you had asked me who I would like to meet today, from anybody in the world, it would be Jerry Jampolsky."

Linda would get her chance. Jerry was coming to meet me the following week. The three of us met for breakfast and hit it off right away. He invited us to attend a speech he was making that night. We went as his guests and joined a thousand or so people in the audience.

After Jerry spoke, he asked me to get up and say a few words about Give Kids the World. I didn't want to talk in front of all those people, but once I got started talking about the kids, I felt no shyness, no embarrassment. When I was finished, I got a standing ovation.

Several days later, I got a beautiful letter with a book from a woman I did not know. Her name was Julia Hobbs and she had been in the audience at Jerry's lecture. My talk had inspired her, she wrote, and in turn, her letter inspired me to give her a call.

Julia sounded delightful. She came to Give Kids the World and began work there as a volunteer. Julia is very compassionate and caring. I offered her a full time job as developer of special projects. She accepted more and more responsibility, and for awhile, was our first executive vice president. She is now the CEO of Kaleidoscope Magic and is also on our Board of Directors.

****

I don't like having neon signs all over the Village. We've lost some large contributions because of this, but I believe my decision is right.

We created our foundation without middle men. We don't have to accept donations that come with strings attached. Many people come to Give Kids the World seeking to participate, but with a motive other than the children. Our foundation probably turns down eight out of ten who approach us with different deals and ideas. The only condition we accept is that every penny goes to the children.

Once a wealthy Las Vegas resident offered to send a check for $200,000, with the condition that two small plaques with his name on them be placed on the villas. I told him this wouldn't be possible. The potential contributor couldn't believe we would turn down such a significant donation for what he perceived to be such a minor concession.

Today the Village is logo-free and that is the way we intend to keep it. We salute our contributors on a Wall of Honor in the administration building. To people who share our love for the children and our wish to fulfill their dreams, this is recognition enough.

We finished the Village at a total cost of $3.5 million. We had put up $1.7 million and corporate and community donations paid the balance. Now that the first phase of the Village had been completed, we focused on our next goal: feeding the families who came to visit us.

CHAPTER 2

For I was hungered and ye gave me meat;
I was thirsty and ye gave me drink;
I was a stranger and ye took me in.
The Holy Bible: Matthew 25:35

The way Perkins Family Restaurants became involved with Give Kids the World happened almost by accident. Holiday Inn's Mike Meeks and Donald Smith, Chairman of Perkins Family Restaurants, had come to town for board meetings. They hadn't come for anything related to Give Kids the World but Mike had adopted our foundation as his own, and he invited him and Smith out to see the Village. Construction on the first villas, the administration building, playground and swimming pool had already been completed.

Donald walked around and said, "Perkins supports what you're doing here, Henri. We have Friendly's Ice Cream. We can give you ice cream if you like. "

Do children love anything better? I thanked him and as we continued walking, we discussed where we might serve ice cream.

Donald asked, "Who is serving the meals?"

"No one."

He looked at me and said, "How would you like for the families to come to our restaurants and have breakfast?"

I thought it would be great.

We kept walking and he said, "No, that's not right. How about if we bring breakfast here?"

Even better.

Then he stopped again and said, "How about if we just get some facility here and Perkins will serve breakfast and dinner."

That, I told him, would be wonderful!

After Donald left the Village, he arranged for people from their corporate headquarters in Memphis to visit us. They toured the Village and supported the concept but did not feel it was appropriate for them to build the structure. Perkins did not own the land and a potential for liability and other legal problems existed.

193

If Give Kids the World built and maintained the structure, Perkins agreed to provide the meals for families visiting Give Kids the World. This type of major construction would be expensive. I felt we needed a significant commitment before we could secure the resources to build. Donald guaranteed Perkins would provide breakfast and dinner for at least five years. I accepted the five year commitment on the spot.

Faced with the problem of building the Perkins structure, I went to Bill Plamondon and Herb Luckrow, my friends at Budget Rent-A-Car who had been with us since the day we started. I got right to the point. I told them we had the opportunity to get five years' worth of meals from Perkins, but we didn't have a building for serving food. I asked if they could help.

Herb asked, "How much do you need, Henri?"

"Well, give me $150,000."

"Henri, can you really build something like that for $150,000?"

No, but it would be enough to get me started. That was the beginning of the Gingerbread House. I spoke with Henry Conversano and explained what we wanted to accomplish. I wanted everything to be child scale. The Gingerbread House was for them and all the furniture and everything else would be built to accommodate them. Henry is an idea man and he did the first conceptual drawings.

Two weeks later, I sat at my desk and opened my mail. Inside of an envelope from Budget, I found a check for $150,000. Their check was a sign of the trust that existed between us. Budget did not require a lengthy legal document guaranteeing we would build the structure. Our commitment that we would was guarantee enough.

I took Budget's $150,000 and started a whirlwind tour of the country trying to raise donations to complete the Gingerbread House. Individuals, organizations and companies donated everything from the lollipops and the gum drops on the outside of the building to the interior decorating. It was Bill Dodson's idea to create tables for the children which had real pieces of candy in-laid into the Plexiglas counter tops. He contacted companies all over the country and found a small manufacturer in Washington state to donate the tabletops and a candy company to donate the candies.

By the time the Gingerbread House was completed, it cost over $600,000. The Gingerbread House restaurant has become one of the

Mickey Mouse and Cinderella walk with a wish child towards the Gingerbread House

emotional centerpieces of the Village. Child-sized furniture decorated with peppermint candies, a player piano belting out favorite childhood songs, and a collection of more than 700 dolls from around the world make the Gingerbread House a fun place for the children. The dolls are brought by the families who visit us. They also frequently bring us a flag of their home country. We fly the native flag of each visiting family to make them feel more at home. We also put the family name on the villa where they will be staying.

Donald Smith committed to provide breakfast and dinner for the families, but I didn't know how Perkins would fund the project. The Perkins chain has over 450 restaurants nationwide and Donald got each one involved in the fund raising efforts to pay for the food program at Give Kids the World. Each store owner in turn goes to local suppliers and purveyors and enlists their support for the Gingerbread House.

Every day, across America, employees and patrons of Perkins restaurants help Give Kids the World. They have a "round your check up" program which lets restaurant patrons contribute to Give Kids the World when they pay for their meal. The money is sent by the Perkins stores into a locked box account. All bills are paid out once a month. At the end of the year, any money remaining is donated to Give Kids the World. Perkins runs the program so well that the company has made, and continues to make, a significant financial donation to the Give Kids the World endowment each year.

****

Having overcome the challenges of housing and feeding Give Kids the World families, we turned our attention to our growing transportation needs. Budget Rent-a-Car, a sponsor since our inception, began by providing cars for our first families in 1986. By 1988, our needs for transportation were growing each day. Each visiting family needs transportation.

Budget did not hesitate. Their generosity has grown with our needs. Bill Plamondon feels just as individuals have a responsibility to strengthen their communities, corporations have a duty to support the communities in which they operate. With that from-the-heart sentiment, Budget provides more than 3,500 complimentary automobiles per year.

Not every family drives. Some families require different type of transportation. Paul Mears, president of Mears Transportation, arranged for his company to provide bus service to as many families as needed at no cost to Give Kids the World.

Another problem solved. Next, we turned our attention to the people who would make it all happen.

CHAPTER 3

It is more blessed to give than to receive.
– The Holy Bible – Acts 20:35

In my mind, three integral parts make up Give Kids the World. The first is the children and the families who need us. The second part is the staff and the volunteers who work so selflessly for the children. The third part is the participants, the companies and individuals who help us.

In the 1960s, a new era of volunteerism began in America. As a society we turned our attention outward to focus on the needs of others instead of our own. Volunteerism is a real extension of the American heart as well as being the foundation of Give Kids the World. I watched it begin to beat in earnest. Give Kids the World simply could not function without the dedication of our 58 employees and more than 1,200 volunteers, or as we like to call them, angels. We have a special walkway in the front of the Village called the Avenue of Angels to honor the volunteers. Give Kids the World started with a group of senior greeters called the 39er's. They all help, they all participate.

Requests by wish children to come to Orlando continued to grow. As we completed our first phase of building, we were already contemplating additional facilities. We needed more staff and volunteers to manage the needs of the families.

Look around the Village on any day of the year and you will see volunteers from our corporate sponsors helping us. They may be landscaping, planting trees or cutting the grass. Their support goes beyond the millions of dollars they provide through in-kind services. It is the commitment of their people. Volunteerism is such a beautiful thing. It brings everybody together to make great things happen. It brings the young kids together with the older people. It brings workers and company executives together. It's much more important to many people to give a few hours to their community than it is to write a check. They get much more out of it.

From our ever growing ranks of volunteers, we use more than 500 people per week. Without our greeters, meal servers, groundskeepers, gift givers, transporters, drivers and so many others, we could not serve the growing number of families. We have two full-time employees with the sole responsibility to coordinate the activity of the volunteers.

199

The Gingerbread House uses about 150 volunteers each week. All activities are coordinated by Perkins employee Nancy Knutowski. Her energy and enthusiasm for the children has grown in direct proportion to our expansion. "Our oldest volunteer is Louise Ramellone," Nancy said. "We all call her Lee. She is 92 and inspiration to everyone she meets."

Our permanent staff is among the most talented and creative employees anywhere. They sacrifice greater material rewards they could obtain in other jobs to serve the children. We would not be where we are today without their dedication, their commitment to excellence and their self-lessness. Their work truly reflects what the Village is all about.

Child sharing a magical moment with
Mickey Mouse and Walter Cronkite

The number of volunteers from Disney continues to grow. They help in every aspect of Village operations, from baby-sitting to landscaping. Disney's Volunt-Ears have created a number of special projects for the Village. Their current wonder is building beautiful gates for the Avenue of Angels.

Disney employees have saved the Village hundreds of thousands of dollars in maintenance costs through their adopt-a-structure program. This is how the program works. Each villa and building in the Village is "adopted" by a different hotel. The hotel then becomes responsible for preventive maintenance on that building. Three times a year, painting, repairs and general upkeep are provided.

In addition, Disney's volunteers make the holidays in the Village unforgettable. Each Christmas, the Village becomes a winter wonderland for the Children. Scooter, the man who puts it all together, orchestrates the work of hundreds of volunteers. School children from around central Florida help out, too. Each school adopts a villa to decorate. The children raise money for the decorations and try to make each villa as spectacular as possible. Disney holds a huge Christmas celebration with toys for the children handed out by Goofy and other Disney characters. The music is provided by the Executive Band, a group of swinging Disney executives who love music and love the kids.

We also celebrate Easter with an egg hunt for the kids, and Halloween with a costume party. Whatever excuse we can find to celebrate with the children is a good one.

I dedicate this chapter of the book to each staff member and every volunteer that helps make Give Kids the World a success. You do wonderful, important work, and I can never thank you enough for your help. The love and support you demonstrate day in and day out for the children and their families is an inspiration.

The Caring Center and administrative building are designed to facilitate the work of our employees and volunteers. Built by Meeting Planners International, the Caring Center is one of the emotional touchstones of the Village.

****

More and more families were requesting to come to the Village. Demand continued to grow past our ability to meet it. We needed more housing. We decided to build more villas. This time, they would have a global theme of architecture, with each villa designed in the architectural style of Italy, Japan, Holland, Mexico or France. Ben Butera created designs that satisfied our criteria that the villas be both spectacular and feasible to build.

Once we had the working plans on paper, we had to find a way to build the additions to the Village and pay for it. Each villa would cost about $120,000. That meant for the structures alone we would need at least $1,440,000.

My dream was to keep the Village debt free, to build it through the generosity of the community and corporations supporting the goal of serving the families in need. Gary Brown came up with an idea to help fund the construction. We invited every single builder in the Orlando area to a dinner where we would have this special reverse auction. Gary priced what each design would cost.

Instead of bidding up, the builders tried to bid down. Someone would offer, "I'll build a villa for $100,000." Then another bidder would say, "I can do it for $90,000." The event generated a remarkable excitement and sense of community. Here they were, competitors in the highly competitive construction business, joining hands for the good of the children. It was remarkable and wonderful at the same time.

The ultimate thing a person can do is to give of himself. Many of us can write a check and donate money to worthwhile causes. This is important. But I believe the purest gift is to look inside and give something from the heart. It is this type of sharing that helps the giver as much as the recipient. When you give from the heart, you receive a tremendous gift in return. This is the wonderful secret supporters, employees and volunteers alike soon discover. The more they give, the more they benefit.

One person can make a difference. It doesn't matter that you can't move the mountain of need by yourself. Pick up the shovel and start digging, move some of that mountain one shovelful at a time. Maybe that little bit will help one innocent child who suffers. Maybe if your energy, your compassion, your desire to help the children starts the work, others will grab a shovel and help you move that mountain. Once you roll up your sleeves and pick up that shovel, your life will never be the same.

Gone is the overwhelming size of the problem. Instead, the focus is only on the small patch of rock and dirt right at your feet. It is a place to start. Maybe if you work this one spot as hard as you can, progress will be made. By setting an example, something special happens. Others reach out to help, to share their the power and energy with you. That is what unselfish work inspires in others. The sum of all of our hands working together to move that mountain of need is enough. Through love, determination and hard work, we have learned to move mountains together for the children we serve.

One day, as I drove to the Village, I saw a Jaguar sedan right behind me. I pulled into the Village and the Jaguar turned in and parked. From my office, I saw the driver, a man, walking with his wife and two children. They were pulling our maid's cart.

Later that day, I found Phillipe making the beds in one of the villas while the man and his son made up the other room. The daughter was working somewhere else. I stopped and introduced myself and learned the man was chairman of the board of a large land development company. His daughter had told him about Give Kids the World and he wanted to help.

Winston Churchill said, "We make a living of what we get and we make a life by what we give." These words, the most important words in my life, were given to me in a frame by my daughter Lisa when she was twenty-three. Just as Lisa gave me Winston Churchill's powerful message, so did the chairman's daughter lead her family to volunteer. If we listen, the children and young people will teach us in their own special way.

Sharon Dillon, a volunteer since 1987, knows what a difference giving can make in a person's life. "Give Kids the World has changed my life in so many wonderful ways. It has brought me enduring friendships and an inner joy I did not have. Serving the children has uncovered a place inside of me that I never knew existed. I do things now that I could never in my wildest dreams imagine. It seems that the more I try to give to the Village, the more I receive in return."

* * * *

The wish children and their families quickly become an extension of our family. Our staff tries to help the kids and their parents, to take care of them. More than anything, they just love the kids. They have special feelings for each wish child and want to make their days at the Village unforgettable.

When children from foreign countries visit Give Kids the World, they often require the services of an interpreter. The international cultural office at Disney's Epcot Center is an important liaison in finding interpreters to assist the families. Epcot's exchange program brings young student leaders to the United States for one year. Many of these students work as translators when needed.

Recently, we had two little Chinese girls of five or six, who came in one after the other. One was from Beijing, the other from a nearby province. The children didn't know English and we couldn't speak Chinese, but we communicated wonderfully without language. The children understood us by our facial expressions and our body language. A hug is the same all over the world.

The local Orlando newspaper ran a picture of a banner the children had brought with them from China. The sign said: *Peace And Love* in Chinese characters and was signed by a hundred children from a Chinese elementary school. It was the children's way to call attention to sick children and help raise funds for other Chinese children who were sick and wished to visit Give Kids the World.

One of our volunteers was escorting the Chinese family to dinner with her own two kids. From the moment the children got in the van together, they giggled and laughed and joked. If you weren't looking at them, you'd think they were carrying on this great conversation. They communicated. They never spoke one word to each other in any kind of language other than kid's language, but they communicated better than most adults. The universal language we all share is love.

In no instance was this more clearly demonstrated than the day the Israeli and Palestinian families arrived together at the Village. We had received a request from Hospice and The National Association for Home Care to bring in two families simultaneously. One was from Israel, the other from Palestine. Culturally, their countries had been at war almost incessantly.

The families arrived together and on the first day stayed pretty much to themselves. The next day, they began spending time together. By the time their vacation with us was over, the families had become best friends. Hate was transformed into love. Their children suffered the same. They cried the same way, fought against the common enemy of disease, and were experiencing the same struggle. Children have no hate, only goodness. Through them, a cultural divide dating back centuries, began to narrow.

****

The theme at Give Kids the World is giving as much as we can to support the children and their families. Even when we have visiting dignitaries and famous people at the Village, the attention always goes to the children. We do it naturally. If you work at the Village, whether a volunteer or an employee, your heart steers your eyes to the children. Always.

Each Thursday, we have a Christmas celebration in the Village. The children receive special gifts from our year-round Santa and are delighted that Christmas can come more than once a year.

In the converted railroad caboose, kids can have all the Friendly's ice cream they want. Bill Dodson did the interior design – twice. First laying it out as a game room, and finally as the ice cream parlor. It is one of the most popular places in the Village. When they want to walk off some of that ice cream, the kids can hike along the nature trails that the United States Navy built for them, wearing BluBlocker sunglasses provided by BluBlocker Corporation's chairman Joseph Sugarman. Back in their rooms, they find treats provided by Coca Cola, Oscar Mayer, Procter & Gamble and many others.

****

There wasn't a day that went by at the Village from 1989 to 1999 that didn't involve some type of construction. We grew quickly, eventually encompassing 51 acres, mostly because there were so many families worldwide with sick children who needed us. In 1997, we secured the Village's final 16 acres for $40,000 an acre. That was 400% increase over the first 16, but we needed the land for the children.

Our biggest need was for more two-bedroom, two-bath villas with full kitchens, washers/dryers and entertainment centers. The additional acreage allowed us to build 42 more villas, bringing the total to 96. But we didn't stop there. We needed an extension to the Gingerbread House, so we built an adorable cupcake shaped room filled with sunlight and antique toys where families eat breakfast. We also built the House of Hearts, a reception area where families check-in, designed by New York architect Robert Stern. We turned an older villa into a whimsical Ice Cream Parlor stocked by Friendly's Ice Cream and we built Julie's Safari Theatre where movies are shown nightly along with free popcorn and candy. We also built an addition to the Amberville Train Station, our game arcade, to house a huge model train set.

The Board gave $1.5 million for the construction, but we never used it. Instead, I organized a ten-member Executive Committee of the best and brightest who'd ever been involved in the Village. Each member came to the table with an area of expertise. Paul Katen, on loan from Disney Imagineering for a year, chaired the committee. Thanks to Paul, the Village looks like it was built all at once, not as pieces of a puzzle. Frank Eller, our building superintendent, came on loan from Centex Rooney Construction for a year, but stayed two because we needed him.

Also on the committee: Dick Frantz with Centex Rooney, Dave Kittridge with Boyle Engineering and Ben Buttera with Ben Buttera Architects. Bill Dodson designed the interiors; Todd Hill designed the landscape. Bill Coan with Itech Productions, creator of whimsical things like the banana split icons atop the Ice Cream Palace, designed many of the details that make the Village sparkle in a child's eyes and John Jensen, a retired Disney designer, took over responsibility for the Amberville addition. We all met weekly. It was very organized.

My responsibility was to get the money to pay for all the construction. K-Mart donated $600,000 for the House of Hearts, Perkins Family Restaurants $300,000 for the cupcake addition and John Quinn, a long-time hotel partner gave $60,000 for the Ice Cream Palace. Master Custom Builders (MCB), which builds high-end homes in Disney's planned community, Celebration, built the villas. MCB went to its suppliers who'd profited from all the Celebration construction and asked them to donate supplies. One day 42 whirlpools arrived, another day roofing material, another day drywall, the list went on and on. This brought the cost of each villa way down. In addition, corporations and individuals adopted a villa for $125,000 each. Coca-Cola and Holiday Inn each adopted five villas, money that went into the general coffer.

Although I have no doubt the Village is God's place, I'm not above employing a bit of craftiness to get things done. I went to Jim Berk, then President/CEO of Hard Rock Cafe and asked him for $500,000 for the Amberville addition. I told him he didn't need to pay me all at once, but could pay $100,000 over five years. He agreed to do whatever he could for the children and we shook hands to seal the deal. Then, I went to his fierce competitor, Robert Earl, Chairman/CEO of Planet Hollywood, and asked him to build the movie theatre. I told him Hard Rock was building the Amberville addition right next to the theatre site. Earl, not to be outdone by Berk, also agreed to do whatever he could for the children and we shook hands, sealing the deal.

Both companies went to their longtime suppliers for donations to defray costs but unfortunately things didn't go well for Planet Hollywood. The company filed Chapter 11 shortly after theatre construction began. With only a structural skeleton built, suppliers just walked away and I couldn't get anyone to call me back. So, I went to Earl and said, "Robert, we've got to do something. There's a skeleton in the middle of the Village." He said come back in two days. When I returned, I sat in a chair across from his desk and he put an envelope in front of me. Inside was a personal check from Earl for $200,000. I thanked him, went away and used the money on the theatre but it wasn't enough. I had to return to Earl a month later. "Robert, please help me here. We still don't have enough money." He told me to return the next day, and when I did I sat in the same chair across the desk from him. There was another envelope waiting for me, but before I could touch it Earl made me promise not to return again.

Inside that envelope was a $200,000 check from Sylvester Stallone. We still had to spend nearly $500,000 of our own money to finish the theatre but I kept my promise and didn't return to Earl's office.

CHAPTER 4

Too low they build, who build beneath the stars.
—Edward Young [1745]

Webster defines the word miracle as an extraordinary event manifesting divine intervention in human affairs. The Castle of Miracles lives up to that definition. From its inception, there has been a steady stream of miraculous events. I was sitting in my office in 1994. We had completed the villas, the Caring Center and the Gingerbread House. A woman named Terry Merrill came to see me. She was dressed in blue jeans and sneakers. She told me she would introduce me to people who could help us build a castle for the kids. I agreed and she arranged a meeting with ITEC Corporation.

Hugh Darley, formerly of Disney, was one of the owners of ITEC. He told me that his company took on one charity project a year. He wanted it to be this castle. ITEC imagined a castle rising majestically from the center of the Village which would become the center of activity for the kids. The outside would feature a hand carved, wooden carousel complete with wheelchair-accessible figures. Inside, we would have as many interactive elements as possible, including a fantasy activity center with a talking wishing well, arcade and tale-spinning clock named Father Time. The castle would have a stage where we could hold performances and a game room with more games and activities than a child could imagine.

I loved the idea. The scope of the project was intimidating, but the Castle of Miracles would be a real pleasure for every child who visited the Village, and I knew we would find a way to build it.

Darley said ITEC would design the castle and commit to building the interior, which alone was more than $500,000. I agreed to get the ball rolling, and ITEC got to work creating a rendering of the castle.

As the plans took shape, the project continued to grow until the final cost reached $2.5 million. The Give Kids the World Foundation agreed to start the fundraising by pledging $250,000 and the rest of it would be paid for by our supporters. In typical Give Kids the World fashion, we decided to have another auction.

ITEC created a model of the castle, breaking it into individual components, like separate pieces of a puzzle. Contractors, builders, designers,

209

suppliers, technicians, craftsmen and workers would each take a piece of the puzzle. One company would take the floor, another the walls and so on, until each piece of the castle was adopted. As word of the project spread, more and more companies took part. Eventually, more than 300 companies participated in building the Castle of Miracles.

Hugh, Greg Gibson and Chris Smith headed the design and interior buildout. The entire ITEC team showed incredible talent. Their enthusiasm, vision and creativity seemed to feed off each other, making the sum of the parts stronger than any individual. ITEC's creative team was working around the clock for no pay to make the castle the wonder it became. ITEC's J.J. Jensen was an inspiration to the team's creativity, challenging the staff to stretch their imaginations, to give the kids the best they had to give.

At the auction, Dick Frantz, vice president of Centex Rooney Construction, stood up and said that Centex hadn't had the opportunity to participate in the building of the villas but wanted to build the castle for $52.50 a square foot, and would commit up to $250,000. Bob Moss, Centex Rooney president, and Dick's boss told him he had the responsibility to build the structure. Centex Rooney became the castle's prime builder.

Frank Elder, the building superintendent, was responsible for getting every possible donation from every possible source. He was at the construction site almost every waking minute. Frank worked without an office, carrying a portable phone in his back pocket.

As we broke ground for construction, Frank needed twelve truckloads of dirt for fill. Frank went to the boss of a local company asking for help. He was told the company didn't give things away. One of the business' drivers overheard the conversation and he stopped Frank as he was getting into his car.

"Don't worry," he said. "I know what Give Kids the World is all about. You'll get your dirt. We'll bring it by today after work." Sure enough, that afternoon, a line of twelve dump trucks pulled into our driveway and brought us all the dirt we needed.

Frank coordinated hundreds of small pieces into the whole that became the Castle of Miracles, and was instrumental in facilitating the work between both union and non-union workers.

Boyle Engineering donated more than 1,500 hours working on the castle's structural, mechanical and civil engineering requirements. Dave

Kittridge, the principal engineer, helped solve a critical problem during the construction. Building could not begin until a method could be found to overcome a fundamental challenge to the way structures are normally built. The castle had evolved from a fairly uniform design of a square with a turret on each corner, to an incredibly complex structure with 19 corners, only four of which were square. Dave and the engineers from Boyle developed an innovative system of coordinates to allow builders to layout the foundation on a special grid on the ground.

"Each time a new contributor would come on board, the work specs

changed," Dave remembered. "The dimensions of the project grew as the community's involvement increased. Our engineers had to constantly use all of their creativity to fit the pieces into the whole. It was like trying to put together a moving jigsaw puzzle, with new pieces being added all the time."

With some of our special children in front of the Castle of Miracles

Just as the project began to take shape, an event that could have been a disaster occurred. Hugh Darley sold his company. ITEC was the driving creative force behind the castle and continuing without them would be difficult, if not impossible. I met with new owners Bill Coan and Mark Nichols who assured me they would completely fulfill ITEC's commitments. Greg Gibson left ITEC and came to the Village for five months to ensure the castle would be built the way we wanted.

It was, and the crowning touch came when the carousel arrived from Holland. Vekoma's craftsmen created this unique merry-go-round with full wheel chair accessibility, so children confined to wheelchairs could ride without difficulty.

****

Every life is touched by miracles. Sometimes people just don't recognize them, but that doesn't mean that what they are experiencing is not a miracle. My own life has been touched over and over again by events, by happenings which I cannot define any other way, but to call them miracles.

There were miracles in each of my six lives, but none as profound as what I'm experiencing today. When the Castle of Miracles was under construction, Bob Richards was the general manager of J&N Stone and they were doing some work on the castle. Bob was 46 years old then with five children, and he was battling terminal colon cancer.

"I'm a Christian," Bob explained, "and I believe what happened to me at Give Kids the World is a miracle from God. The more I got involved at the Village, the better I felt. The less I worried about my own health, the more my health improved. I'm cancer free today and I think working at the Village is an important part of the reason why. Wonderful things happen to people who help at the Village."

When we were first opened, we didn't have any blankets or pillows. I gave my assistant, Jan Silver, several hundred dollars and asked her to go to Kmart and buy some pillows and sheets and blankets. As I finished saying that sentence, a big tractor trailer filled with pillows and blankets pulled up right outside my window.

These connections of faith seem to happen all the time. Small wonders. Since Give Kids the World began, I've witnessed dozens of things I would call miracles. As I look back at my life, I can see a steady stream of events, from the survival of my sister and me, to the Mercury Years, to Give Kids the World. Miracles happen. They are real and tangible. There's no question about that. We just have to be willing to see them.

A few years ago, I was with my son, Greg, in Seattle when we got a phone call from Give Kids the World that our computer system broke down. We only had a single terminal off campus and our needs had grown well beyond that. All of our data was temporarily lost. Greg knows computers so I asked him what to do. As we talked about the problem, Mike Meeks came over to join us for breakfast and said all the computers we needed at Give Kids the World were going to be donated.

At Give Kids the World, every child, both the wish child and siblings, receives a toy each day when the family returns from the theme parks. This means that we use more than 60,000 toys each year. Because we use so many toys, I wanted to build up an inventory. I asked Julia Hobbs to write a letter to every toy company in the country asking for donations for the kids. The very next day, a man called from Roxbury Toys in New Jersey. He had a tractor trailer full of toys for us.

The Village provides a library of videos for the children to watch. One day, as I walked through the administrative building, I noticed our

212

video supply was low. I asked one of the staff to call Disney and see if they could send us some more videos. A big box from California waited for me on my desk. That's right, it was filled with videotapes for kids.

The greatest miracle is building Give Kids the World on a handshake and a prayer. The companies have taken the business side out of it. They benefit from the goodwill, but they remove the business from it. This is a uniquely American story.

Our foundation is unique in other ways also. No other foundation gives a vacation for the whole family. None. This is the only one in the world. Our Village is unique because it is the only place that offers the gift of memories for each member of the family individually and the family unit as a whole.

In 1996, our corporate sponsors will provide over $12 million dollars of services and incidentals for the families. The number of people that Give Kids the World serves continues to grow. This year, more than 4,500 families will come to Give Kids the World from 45 countries across the globe and no one will be asked to pay anything. By the end of 1996, we will have served more than 27,000 children and their families.

We have no contracts, no legal agreements. We do this in the spirit of generosity which makes America unique among all the countries of the world. Such kindness, all rooted in our collective love and caring for the children couldn't happen anywhere else.

* * * *

In the modern world, we are less and less likely to extend our hand to another. It is increasingly difficult to see ourselves through the eyes of those who are different or have less than we do. But in Biblical times, a stranger, a passing traveler would be welcomed into your home, just as the old couple in Czechoslovakia welcomed me. Each person felt honor-bound to feed and shelter all who passed his door. Men and women saw themselves in the reflection of the traveler's need.

Give Kids the World has never turned away a child in need. It doesn't matter that the number of requests has doubled and tripled and doubled again since 1986. It is our personal commitment to meet the needs of every child's voice. Families in crisis can reach us through the more than 300 wish-granting foundations, hospitals and other organizations around the world.

213

In our offices is a photograph of Snow White kissing one of the wish children, a girl about five or six-years old confined to a wheel chair. The child's face is lit up with joy. This picture epitomizes Give Kids the World. In that single, magical moment between a fairy tale character and a terminally ill child, a pathos is born of the reality that Snow White cannot help the child transcend the physical straits which hold her captive.

For this girl, and many others like her, the promise of childhood is fleeting. The dreams of growing up, of having a boyfriend, of graduating college, of one day marrying and having a child of her own, are as distant as a shooting star. For the wish children, there is today's struggle. Little thought can be given to tomorrow, because all the energy in that tiny body has to muster the courage and strength to fight today.

One day Snow White was visiting the Village. Her smile could be seen across the crowded dining room in the Gingerbread House and lit up the room like a beacon. Later, after the hugs for the children and posing for numerous pictures, Snow White was alone outside. Tears trickled down her cheeks as she leaned against the door of her car.

"It's so sad," Snow White said. "They're so brave. I wish I really did have the magic to make them well again."

The truth is that all the fairy tale characters in the world cannot heal a single child. But it is also true that the joy the characters from Sea World, Universal, MGM and Disney bring to these children is real. They help create a priceless memory for the children and the families.

One little girl who visited us loved Snow White. When she was at the Village, she dressed like her favorite character, and when Snow White visited, she was beside herself with joy. When this child succumbed to her illness, I was contacted by her family. They wanted to use Snow White on the child's tombstone and needed help in gaining permission. Our friends at Disney gave it, and the child was buried with a Snow White marker on her grave.

****

When a family arrives to visit us, this is what they experience. They are greeted at the airport by one of our many greeters. If they do not speak English, we try to arrange an interpreter or translator to meet them. The greeter assists the family with everything from luggage to transportation. The family arrives at the Village and their experience with us begins.

From the first moments they are with us, we treat them as family. During the first day, there is sometimes a feeling of nervousness, an unfamiliarity. By the second day, that feeling is replaced by a joy that is difficult to describe but wonderful to see. Each employee and volunteer tries to make the wish child and family feel at home. Sprint Corporation takes this one step further by providing the families unlimited long distance phone service. This allows the families to stay in close touch with their support network back home without worrying about the costs involved.

Families come to Give Kids the World ready to celebrate at the area's theme parks, including The Magic Kingdom, Epcot, MGM, Sea World, Universal Studios and Wet & Wild. Each year, through the generosity of these entertainment giants, all the tickets for the children and their families are provided without cost. Meals and amenities are provided to families by such restaurants as the Hard Rock Cafe and Wild Bill's Dinner Theater.

Nickelodeon Studios also provides tickets and gifts and allows the kids to slime the parent of choice when the Nickelodeon Game Lab travels to the Village each month. When the time comes to cool off from all the excitement, Wet N' Wild opens its gates and hearts to all of our families. The water-park experiences are some of the best fun the kids have.

On a busy day, Orlando's theme parks play host to more than a quarter of a million people. The city and its attractions hold a unique place in children's imagination. To them, Orlando is the home of Mickey Mouse, E.T. and Shamu.

The themepark characters visit the children at the Village regularly. Mickey and his friends come to visit every Monday and Thursday. Sea World

sends Shamu for our Monday evening pool party each week, and on Friday, the characters from Universal Studios visit the children. Each Tuesday, the Royal Lipizzaner Stallions are brought to the Village for the children to ride and enjoy. Clayton, Give Kids the World's mayor, is also there to provide joy for the children.

Give Kids the World Mayor Clayton shares a laugh with a wish child

No matter what characters are visiting us, they interact with the children, hugging them and sharing special moments, creating memories. The joy in the children's eyes is wonderful to see.

CHAPTER 5

A man never stands so tall as when he stoops to help a child.
     –Father Flanagan

I cherish memories. So do the families who come to us. They are facing the most difficult times of their lives. Give Kids the World gives them time to make and keep good memories. Sony's video camera program allows each family the use of a video camera during their stay to tape the highlights of their experience.

For many of these families, their time at the Village will be their last time together in a setting other than a hospital. The video gives each family member wonderful memories and reminds them in all their pain and sorrow, there are happy moments, too. We have received hundreds of letters from families who lost their children and now look at the pictures and the videotape and feel great joy that the family had this precious time together.

Give Kids the World celebrates the living, yet it exists because of catastrophic illnesses which befall all too many children. Because the wish children are very sick, special precautions must be taken to provide medical care, should the children require it. Minor needs are handled by House+Med/Medi+Clinic which treats the children at no charge. If a child's problems are more serious in nature, they are sent to Arnold Palmer Children's Hospital for Children and Women.

The reality we have to face is that many of the children who come here will not survive. The hope, of course, is that many of them will go into remission and beat their diseases. We've had wonderful success stories, like eight-year old Veronica who came to the Village with leukemia and is now in complete remission. But the sad fact that many children will not triumph over their illnesses is never too far away. These children are here because they are very sick. That is something as painful as it is, we have to face.

There are several touching stories of wish children who fulfilled their wish of visiting Give Kids the World, and who died at the Village. Some of our children are so very sick when they arrive here that they do not make it back home. The one thing they might want to do is to see Mickey Mouse. They do that, and the next morning, the child passes away. It is

217

almost like they got here and did the one thing they always wanted to do and then were able to die happy. It is very sad, but at the same time, it is a good thing that the child was able to experience their wish.

I recently had a call at the Village. A young mother said that her daughter had only a very short time to live, maybe only 48 hours. We cut through all the red tape and brought the family in the next day. On the airplane, the little girl almost died. When she got to the Village, a miracle happened. She jumped out of the car and went running towards a large topiary sculpted in the shape of a sea serpent. Her mother was shocked. She immediately called her doctor, who couldn't explain it but who advised her to let the child have fun. If she wants to run, let her run. That little girl lived for another six months. Each day a gift to her family.

We name streets in the Village after children who are no longer with us. There is the name of a different angel on each road and street and cul de sac. It is a celebration of their goodness and the joy they brought to their families. It is also a celebration of their spirit and pays a small tribute to their too short lives.

* * * *

Somebody said to me he could never volunteer at Give Kids the World because being around sick and dying children would be heartbreaking. It broke my heart too, at first. When we first built the Village, being close to the children and their families felt too painful for me. That's changed. Now I love to be with them. The children are the source of my deepest joy and gratitude. When I see the wish children here, and you can sometimes tell by their appearance that they have been in chemotherapy, I don't see a calendar behind them. I see a living child with the rest of his or her life in front of them. We try to make them happy. That's our bottom line, sharing joy with our children.

Each day I see children suffering from every disease imaginable – cancer, tumors, AIDS. I thought, over time, that I would get used to it. But that doesn't happen. Instead, after the children return home, their faces and their family's faces join in memory. They become part of every child who is healthy and every child who is sick. There is commonality. Shared suffering and shared hope. Medical healing is not always possible, but spiritual healing is.

We cannot give to others if we do not understand what they are going through, what their needs are. In reaching out to afflicted children, I remember what it is to be an afflicted child. I understand a child's pain and suffering first hand, the feeling that events are beyond personal control. I remember when I had no control in my life, either. I see the suffering of young parents and remember the suffering of my own young parents. Empathy is the ability to feel, to really understand another person. Give Kids the World is built on this foundation.

Working with sick children and their families has special rewards and special pressures. "When I really start to dig into the feelings that I have about Give Kids the World," said Emily, a long-time volunteer, "and the people I meet here, I get very emotional. Saying good-bye to some families is very hard because they just hug longer, you know, a hug that doesn't stop real easy. There are days when the ache for the children is overwhelming, and then you remember there is another child coming in the next day, and you go on.

"Working at Give Kids the World is not an ordinary job. It is very fulfilling. We learn things here that most people will never have the opportunity to learn."

* * * *

When families are faced with the crisis of a terminally ill child, they are challenged in a way that many of us will never experience. Their daily lives revolve around doctors and medical care. Sick children change the focus of normal life from the external world to one which seldom extends beyond hospital walls.

It has been a long time since these families have had normalcy in their lives. A sick child requires all the attention. Parents and siblings forget their own needs in order to take care of the sick one. Relationships between husbands and wives suffer because all their energies and love are focused on the sick child. Siblings innocently wish to be sick to get the attention the sick child receives. All these dynamics constantly rub against each other.

At Give Kids the World, our parent's night out gives Mom and Dad a night out on the town, a date. This may be the first evening in years where the parents can relax without the child's needs taking precedence. We give them a beeper so they are in touch if we need them. Additionally, Bell South provides cellular phones for families who are awaiting transplant notification, or other important news.

219

In 1993, families let us know Give Kids the World needed a chapel. Not a denominational church, but a quiet place where families could pray or meditate, where they could feel closer to God.

The building cost over a quarter of a million dollars, money we didn't have. We went to our friends at Disney for help. Dick Nunis, Chairman of Walt Disney Attractions, was the real force behind building the chapel. He adopted the project as his own. Disney helped build the inside of the chapel. Other volunteers contributed to constructing the outside of the chapel and the beautiful stained glass windows. Money from the Give Kids the World Foundation covered the rest.

This intimate, spiritual place has become one of the most special places in the Village. We keep guest books in there which have taken on a whole life of their own. Instead of visitors writing down their names, they fill the pages with powerful stories. Mothers write of their pain. Fathers scribble their thoughts of helplessness. People reach out and find others who share a similar journey. Some parents who could never talk about their child's story write with touching eloquence .

* * * *

Families in crisis need proper support. We do this at Give Kids the World with support group meetings for the families, a program that lets families talk to each other. They share, give each other strength and realize that they are not alone. Here, we learn the most about what these parents experience.

The mother of a seven-year old boy with bone cancer found comfort in the Healer's Prayer of St. Francis. With misty eyes, she recited:

> *Lord, Make me an instrument of your health:*
> *Where there is sickness, let me bring cure;*
> *Where there is injury, aid;*
> *Where there is suffering, ease;*
> *Where there is sadness, comfort;*
> *Where there is despair, hope;*
> *Where there is death, acceptance and peace.*
> *Grant that I may not:*
> *So much seek to be justified as to console;*
> *To be obeyed, as to understand;*

To be honored, as to love...
For it is in giving ourselves
That we heal,
It is in the listening, that we comfort,
And in the dying
That we are born to eternal life.

She told me how she and her family said this prayer so often it had become second nature to them. "The Prayer of St. Francis reminds each of us, my husband and my two sons and me, that our life exists past the illness of my son. When Jason goes to St. Jude Children's Hospital for his chemotherapy, he reaches out to other children. He tries to live the words in the prayer. He has become my teacher, and as much as it breaks my heart to see him suffer, I think that God is watching over him and is using him to a higher good that I cannot understand in this lifetime."

Values. Parents impart their values to their children. Jason, at age seven, has wisdom that many others will not find in a lifetime that lasts ten times as long. Values are not static, but dynamic. They are constantly being affected by the world in which we live. One of the first things you learn at the Village is how much the children and their families multiply the love they receive. They give us back more than we give them.

One young father recently contacted me at the Village. He had been at the Village with his sick daughter, a wish child, her two siblings and his wife three weeks earlier. I remembered the family because they were in a celebratory mood when they were at the Village. The child needed a liver transplant. The family had finally raised the money and the surgery was imminent.

The father told me that his daughter had died. Too much paperwork, he said. Too much bureaucracy. He told me his family was coming back to the Village and asked to meet. When the family came, they brought a donation of $10,000 to Give Kids the World. The money had been raised by the community to help defray the medical expenses for his daughter's organ transplant. When the child died before the surgery, her father remembered how happy the family was during their time at Give Kids the World. He gave us the money asking that we continue helping families like his.

We all gathered together at the gazebo and said a prayer for three-year old Kaitlin. We named the gazebo after the little girl. She will always be with us, in our memories and in our hearts.

221

* * * *

Emmy Murrell adopted two small children with AIDS after the mother of the children died of the disease. "To me, being at Give Kids the World is almost a religious experience," she said. "Jesus took care of the lepers. He reached out to people that society could not even stand to look at. Today, people with AIDS, like these beautiful, innocent babies, are lepers. Since their mother died, Give Kids the World is the first place we've been that I don't feel any stigma."

Emmy pointed to her children and shook her head. "The oldest child is pretty sick. The other, while HIV positive, is doing okay. I'm fifty years old and these children will probably not live to be five." She looked around the Village. "That's what we all have in common – the time of our children is so very short. That's a curse, I suppose, but in some ways, it's also a blessing. We know that every minute is precious. Every single minute, how precious."

"When you are told that your child is sick, shock is the first reaction," said the father of a four-year old child with an inoperable brain tumor. "Next comes numbness. Right on top of that is anger and fear. One day your biggest worry is the car payment and the next day your child is fighting for her life. It's an awful, helpless feeling. The last year and a half we've been fighting this thing and now we're at Give Kids the World. Yesterday I saw my daughter hugging Mickey Mouse and the tears just came."

After attending her first support group, the young mother who's family so depended on The Healer's Prayer of St. Francis said, "I didn't know what to expect. Every time a mother spoke, it was like looking at myself in the mirror and hearing myself talk. As sorry as I am that these families are suffering like we are, it is a comfort to be together with others who understand, who are feeling the same blow to their hearts as I am to mine.

"I told them The Healer's Prayer. One mother said thank you and we cried together."

At Give Kids the World, no one is ever alone.

* * * *

A number of the families that visit Give Kids the World do not have experience with traveling. For many of these families, it will be the only time they have away from hospitals and the medical environment. That is why it is so important to create happy memories of them together as a family in the short time they are with us at the Village.

I hope you share the story of their American journey, how Give Kids the World happened and how we operate day-to-day. How the kindness and generosity and promise of America are what has made us successful. Among all countries in the world, the American spirit for giving is unique in its capacity to reach out and embrace those most in need.

People like Senator John Glenn, Art Buchwald, Walter Cronkite, Alan Shepard and so many hundreds of others, tell me over and over again, "If it is for the children, and it is within my means to do it, I'll do it." I think the reason people don't say no to us very often is because we are not asking for anything for ourselves. We represent the children. When we need support for the children and the families, we ask for it. If it's for the kids, it's okay to do whatever it takes to make it happen.

When we were just getting started, just the mention of Walter's or John's name brought instant credibility. Their personal integrity was without question. That is what sets them apart. That is why, when Walter was at CBS, he was the most trusted man in America, and why John Glenn, one of America's heroes, would rather talk to kids than to attend events in his honor.

We continue to grow, in part, because everyone who works with us, is always thinking about others instead of themselves.

* * * *

I have a special deep admiration and affection for each of our supporters. The very best of what America is all about is demonstrated every day in what they are helping accomplish at Give Kids the World. They have done so much for us over the years, from landscaping, to building structures, to the millions of dollars of services they donate for the children and their families.

Our partners' help is not limited help. They never say, "I helped you yesterday, get someone else to help you today." They always find ways to support us. Since 1986, I have asked corporate America for a great many things to sustain Give Kids the World and our ever-growing need. No corporate supporter has ever left Give Kids the World. As amazing as that seems, it is true.

Procter and Gamble has been supporting Give Kids the World for the past five years. They started by donating amenities, such as Folgers Coffee, Tide and Jif Peanut Butter and many other items the families could enjoy in their villas. Their involvement has grown tremendously over the years.

In 1991, Procter and Gamble ran its first coupon promotion with us which generated a cash donation to the Foundation in the amount of $250,000. P&G's involvement has continued to grow in size and scope. Their support currently represents almost one-half of the annual operating budget for Give Kids the World.

Kmart sponsors a program each year in its more than 2,100 stores nationwide raising money for Give Kids the World. Each store across America sells paper castles to customers for a dollar donation. The program has grown significantly since it began and continues to grow. Kmart has become an increasingly more important partner in helping raise operational funds for the Village.

Tom Williams, president of Universal Studios Florida, celebrated the grand opening of Universal Studios Florida by providing unlimited complimentary passes to Give Kids the World.

The Flintstones with wish children at the Give Kids the World Village

Universal Studios Florida is a working motion picture and television production studio and theme park. Its production facilities and movie-theme attractions and rides place visitors into the heart of the movies. Universal's generosity allows our special children to become stars for a day. Their characters, from Boo Boo Bear and Yogi Bear to Woody Woodpecker and the Flintstones often visit the Gingerbread House to have breakfast with our rising stars. In addition, Universal helps grant special requests from the children, such as meeting the Ghostbusters or taking the wish child for a ride in the Ghostbuster's Ectomobile.

Sea World, one of our original partners in caring, still participates, providing families unlimited complimentary tickets to its attractions, as well as allowing their characters to visit the Village to bring cheer to the children. Sea World also donated a Pirate Ship used at our Village, and through its generosity, continues to keep the ship in excellent repair. Bill Davis, Sea World vice president, is always looking for ways to support the kids.

Over a hundred of America's greatest corporations have joined hands and hearts with us to use their resources, their goodwill, their multifaceted talents to help those families facing the most difficult struggle of their lives. Give Kids the World would not exist without their generosity.

A Sea World porpoise delights a child

With each addition to the Village, our mission remains the same. We are serving the children and their families. The success of Give Kids the World is not built upon me or any other single individual. Over the years, many kind and loving things have been said and written about me. When I hear and read these things, I am humbled and a bit embarrassed. It is very important to me that your attention remain on Give Kids the World and not on me personally. It is the children that most deserve our admiration, our respect and our hard work. Let the accolades fall to them. We are an organization which exists through your generosity. We serve children and their families through your kindness and support. We will continue this service until, God willing, there is no child in need left.

* * * *

Give Kids the World is one of the most efficient operating foundations in America. Ninety-three and a half cents of every dollar goes directly to the children. The other six and half cents goes to administrative costs and overhead. Few other foundations in the world have a comparable ratio.

But money isn't the reward. For us, it is the relationships. From the Board of Directors on down the line, this is really a people business. Give Kids the World has built its fund raising efforts on the foundation of strong relationships. The people who play an important part decide what they want to give. They give what they can, whether its money or lamps. Most people are inherently good, kind and generous and willing to help worthy causes as often as they can.

In today's world, many worthwhile foundations and charities need and deserve support. One of the most difficult parts of maintaining any non-profit foundation is the on-going burden of fund raising. We made the decision early on that fund raising could be fun. It all happens at the annual black and white gala held at the Peabody Hotel in Orlando.

Many of our corporate sponsors donate valuable goods and services to be raffled off or auctioned. Budget, donates a car. Harley Davidson a motorcycle. Airlines donate trips, hotels offer free accommodations. We auction trips to Paris and London and other of the world's most exciting cities.

We've auctioned worldwide seven-day cruises. All these contributions raise tens of thousands of dollars for Give Kids the World, but no one donates more on this special night than the Peabody Orlando.

The gala all started because we wanted to celebrate the Village becoming a reality. I met with executives from the Peabody about hosting a gala and they told me it would cost so much for this, so much for that. I sat there and multiplied in my head what this would cost. The guest list for any party would have over a thousand people on it and I wanted to know to what amount of money I was committing Give Kids the World.

All of a sudden, it hit me. I could not commit Give Kids the World to such a large financial obligation. I just couldn't do it. It would cost too much. I told the hotel people unless they could give us the party at no cost – everything for nothing – that we wouldn't be having the gala. They looked at me like I was crazy. I told them I was sorry but I just couldn't commit the children's funds for a party.

The next week, the Peabody Hotel invited me over for a meeting. I went feeling very much on the defensive. The Peabody agreed to give us the whole gala for as many people as we wanted. They had only one condition. "Uh-oh," I said to myself. "Here it comes."

The annual Peabody black and white gala

What happened next was another miracle. The Peabody's one and only condition was to sponsor the gala for five years instead of one! And with those remarkable terms, the annual Black and White Gala became a reality.

The Peabody funds the gala in a way similar to how Perkins pays for the thousands of meals it serves at the Village each year. The Peabody invites all their suppliers and purveyors to a lunch. My staff and I give a presentation to the suppliers. We let them know what Give Kids the World stands for, about our mission to serve the families of terminally ill children, and our promise to let the voice of no child needing help go unanswered.

The suppliers donate goods for the gala. The wine merchant donates the wine, the fish supplier makes a gift of the fish, the meat supplier contributes meat, all down the line.

I remember one meeting, a man stood up and said, "I don't know what I'm doing here. I sell toilet paper." We all laughed. He ended up donating cases of toilet paper to us.

The Peabody's five year commitment turned into ten. The Peabody personifies the type of long-term commitment that Give Kids the World is seeking. Tables sell to corporate sponsors for $2,000 each. Every dollar raised at the gala goes directly to Give Kids the World. All costs for the wonderful celebration are absorbed by suppliers and the Peabody Hotel.

"Give Kids the World is the most worthy cause I know," said general manager Alan Villaverde. "We are committed to hosting the first ten galas and maybe more after that. If the children need our help, I'd like to think the Peabody Orlando will always be there for them."

CHAPTER 6

There is always one moment in childhood when the door opens and lets the future in.
–Graham Greene [1940]

The Give Kids the World Village is one hundred percent debt free. All expansion of the Village is very expensive. Ensuring we can pay for what we build is one of our primary goals each year when we set about the task of fund raising. My goal is to grow the foundation endowment to $25 million dollars in my lifetime. This would create enough financial security that the wonderful work done here could continue for another hundred years.

Give Kids the World exists because of selflessness on the part of so many. It represents a purity of purpose, a strength of spirit and true sense of caring that cannot help but positively affect all who come into contact with the organization. These corporations ask for nothing in return. They do business on their word. Their handshake seals deals worth hundreds of thousands, even millions of dollars.

To have wealth in America is a tool that lets you do things you want to do. I work every day with many wealthy people whose values transcend their money. Likewise, I work with an equal amount of people who have very little in the material sense, but they have a lot of compassion and deep feelings of understanding for people and the pain we must go all through in life. Our values are the same. Money does not impress me, kindness and goodness do. Many of the people who built Give Kids the World are much richer in their spirit than in their pocketbooks.

One of the most important elements of our expansion is to provide more hands-on, positive experiences for the wish children, usually kids three to eleven-years old. For many years, I have thought of creating an interactive train station where the kids could play with model trains. This simple thought, with the help of many talented and creative people, has grown into the Amberville Train Station, named in loving memory of Travis and Amber, siblings who succumbed to their diseases after visiting Give Kids the World.

In typical Give Kids the World fashion, a small idea has grown into something much greater. The original concept was targeted at about

$200,000 in construction costs, which was pledged by 23 of the Davidson Hotels. This seed money was the foundation for what is now a $1.2 million center of joy for our children. The construction is scheduled to start soon. The station will have an international flavor with donations from China, Australia, Brazil and Europe.

With the help of Ted Crowell, former president of the International Association of Amusement Parks and Attractions (IAAPA), the organization's more than 10,000 members have adopted the Amberville Train Station as their own. So has the National Model Railroad Association, Inc., Robert Charles, company president, has pledged the full support of his organization. As the creative minds of some or our original supporters came together, the Amberville project began to gain momentum.

One of the unique and wonderful things I have experienced at Give Kids the World is the continuing relationship of our supporters from one project to the next. Our original designer, Henry Conversano is back with us working on obtaining icons for the Amberville Train Station. Designing it is Chris Smith, a former ITEC employee now with Disney. ITEC's presence includes engineers who worked on the amazing effects in the Castle of Miracles. Our old friend David Kittridge from Boyle Engineering recently designed our a warehouse and is also lending his expertise for Amberville.

Dick Frantz, formerly with Centex Rooney, the company that built the Castle of Miracles, is now vice president of DCC Constructors, Inc. DCC is building Amberville, and as he did with the original construction, Dick is insuring the children get the maximum benefit for the bare minimum cost.

Ben Butera, who lent his creative vision since the first villas and the Gingerbread House, is Amberville's architect. When Ben needed renderings of the Amberville Train Station, Give Kids the World paid for the drawings. Ben returned the money, saying he could not take money from the kids. He, and many other talented people, donate their time and talents year after year without ever asking for or accepting payment.

My administrative assistant, Linda Mixter, plays a key role in helping me coordinate the frenetic pace of our continued expansion. "Every day is new and exciting," Linda said. "There is always something more we can do for the children and their families. If it will make their memories with us more special, we try to find a way to make it happen."

* * * *

We are also working on The Park of Dreams which will include an inter-active water park, entertainment center, an amphitheater and a one-of-a-kind wheelchair accessible miniature golf. In keeping with Give Kids the World policy, the Park of Dreams will have 100 percent wheelchair accessibility. Kaleidoscope Magic and IDEAS, Inc. are supplying the design magic to help bring the dream to life and Centex Rooney will build it.

The Park of Dreams is sponsored by American Airlines and its parent company AMR Corporation. American Airlines will fund the construction of the Park of Dreams, and they'll continue to maintain it after it's built.

Robert Crandall, Chairman and CEO of American Airlines and AMR, pledged one million dollars on behalf of his employees for the Park of Dreams, maintenance and the endowment. American recently donated eighty round trip tickets, good for worldwide travel, for us to use any way we see fit. They are also sponsoring trips for 70 families during the construction of the Park of Dreams.

Bob Stoltz has implemented the Ideas In Action Program as the creative vehicle to fund American's participation at Give Kids the World. He encourages American's 120,000 employees to be creative in their jobs and work more efficiently, thereby saving the company money. American then earmarks a portion of those savings to support the Park of Dreams.

American employees are supporting us by volunteering at Give Kids the World in ever increasing numbers. They also buy engraved pavers on our Avenue of Angels. One hundred percent of this money goes directly to the kids.

****

We have expanded our services to include more attention to the spiritual and emotional needs of the families. We have developed a wonderful program called Give Kids the World at Home. According to doctors and psychologists, when wish children anticipate the trip to Give Kids the World, it serves like a magic potion, improving their condition. With this in mind, we decided to extend their experience, making it last after the children return home.

With the help of the International Association of Amusement Parks, Perkins Family Restaurants, Hard Rock Cafe and a growing list of supporters, we give the families a package to take home with them that contains free tickets good for one year. These tickets allow them to access amusement

231

and theme parks near their homes and to restaurants providing complimentary meals and special nights out. They can also go to movies at General Cinema and have portraits made at JC Penneys. The program is already yielding great results. I'm convinced extending the joy of the children helps extend their lives, as well. It gives them one more reason to keep looking forward.

We are also proud of our Compassion Program, in which we coordinate the distribution of tickets from Disney's many area theme parks, Sea World of Florida and Universal Studios Florida. When the parks receive individual theme park admission requests from families with terminally ill children, those requests are forwarded to us to facilitate. Our coordinators then provide the families with the tickets and passes they've requested.

Although children come from all over the world to visit us, more than 500 families right here in Central Florida also have children facing life-threatening illnesses. We've joined hands with Disney and Arnold Palmer Children's Hospital For Children and Women to create the Give Kids the World Kid's Club. We hold monthly events for the local families, sponsor character breakfasts at the Village and give out passes to Disney, Sea World, Gatorland and Mystery Fun House.

We also sponsor nights out for local parents, just as for visiting parents. We care for their children while they spend some well-deserved and much needed time with each other. The parents are connected to us by beeper so they don't have to worry about being out of reach should their child need them.

Another extension of our community outreach is part of the Second Harvest food bank program. This makes groceries available to families at a fraction of their value. This savings helps lessen some of the financial pressures many of them experience.

Every day we try our best to find new ways to make their lives a little bit easier, a little less dominated by sickness.

* * * *

Wherever I go, I am attracted to children. I love their honesty and their goodness. I try to see the world through their eyes and love speaking with them. Recently, I spoke to a group of students at Blue Ridge High School in Cashiers, North Carolina about Give Kids the World. I tried to explain what it means for parents to come to the Village and see their sick children fulfill their dreams.

Making dreams come true is not always easy, but in America, it is always possible. I have a special, deeply rooted love for my adopted country. America has given me unlimited possibility and opportunity. In a way, I feel fortunate so many hardships took place early in my life. It gave me a perspective allowing me to appreciate what America truly represents, how great her promise is for every individual.

I reminded these children of all this country offers. In America, if people are smart enough to trust their instincts, they can take advantage of opportunities there for all of us. I believe that. Those who are willing to try, to sacrifice, to do whatever it takes to make something happen, will find success.

All children can make something of their lives here. I'm not just talking about material success. Our country allows us to live by higher values than anywhere else in the world. Here, there is no penalty for doing the right thing, for making the correct moral choice.

I am Jewish, I told these children, and lost my parents during the Holocaust. Such a thing can happen again if we don't remember the past. Oppression is wrong, wherever and whenever it occurs. When Americans say immigrants have no business here, we forget who we are.

If you are fortunate enough to have your parents today, I told these children, I beg you to be good to them. Try to love them as much as you can. Respect them, and your life will be enriched.

As I said these things, I realized the values linking us are the same. We all want to be loved. We all need food and water and shelter. We want to be comfortable and successful. In America, we believe those things are ours by right. We will work to have them, as we will fight to help those who feel their lack, those who are in need.

* * * *

When taken in its entirety there is a magical, spiritual quality to the journey that has brought me to Give Kids the World. From the child's whistle that united my twin sister and I, parted by the Holocaust, to the magic of The Starlight Motel, to Snow White kissing a wish child. It has really been quite a remarkable and uniquely American experience.

I have spent a lifetime in almost non-stop motion striving to be successful. In the 1980s, whenever the pace around me slowed down long enough to have quiet thoughts, I found myself once again contemplating the suffering of the innocent. These thoughts were not a comfort, quite the opposite. Each time the lack of motion settled upon me, freeing up my mind to explore my deepest thoughts, I found myself a little less willing to return to the normal commotion around me. Instead of finding an excuse to escape my thoughts of the children, I found myself thinking of little else.

I see the connections now. I can draw a link from the past to the present. From the desperation of my own childhood grew the empathy to serve children facing their own desperate circumstances. From survival as a child to fighting to help other children survive, my life has come full circle.

I look at Give Kids the World children and think of children of my time, with so much of our youth taken away from us. I am thankful to God to give these special children a place where their wishes can come true. I believe that is why we are here.

As I approach my seventieth birthday, I enjoy life more now than I ever have. I live in the present. I have for the last fifty years. I never thought I would make it past my teens, so all the time since has been precious. As you go through the years, your life changes. Your taste for food changes. Your outlook and your priorities are different. What has happened to me the last ten years, being involved with Give Kids the World, has created a different set of priorities than I ever imagined I would have.

Because of her business expertise and her talent for managing large groups of people, the Board of Directors choose Pam to take over my job of running the day-to-day operations at Give Kids the World. This allows me more time to manage the work of the Give Kids the World Foundation. Pam has been named president of Give Kids the World and sits on the Board of Directors for Give Kids the World, serving as a primary link between the Board and the Village.

* * * *

Each man's spiritual journey is different. I am not here to say that one answer is right and another is wrong. The only words I have to offer are these – a man is richer by what he gives than he can ever be by what he owns or what he receives. For me, belief in a higher power carries with it the responsibility of action. It's fine to pray for guidance or ask for help in handling a problem or situation, but in my mind, prayers have a better chance of coming true through action rather than passivity. Try and make a difference. Give God a reason to lend a hand. I learned early in my life that it is better to take action than to do nothing. It is easy to sit and wring our hands and bemoan all the bad things that happen in this world. It is much harder to leave the complaining to somebody else and to pick up the shovel and go to work. It is my experience that miracles are real and living things. They are built with sweat and toil and hard work from the foundation up under the eye of a watchful and loving God. Miracles, great and small, take fashion from unselfish action, love, even tears mix into the permanent mortar of miracles.

There is a certain injustice when the innocent suffer, especially children, which touches something deep and profound in all of us. I have learned firsthand that many of life's most painful questions have no rational answers. It is impossible to rationalize why one child is afflicted with a life threatening disease and another is not. Those questions are for a higher power to decide. For me, the questions are much less infinite and much more earthbound. How can we help these innocent children celebrate life, and in doing so, help them and their families find more strength and courage to continue their struggle from one day to the next?

At Give Kids the World, there are no moral dilemmas, no philosophical questions of good and evil to ponder. There is only the children, their special needs and our ability to help them. It is that simple.

****

In 1987, brothers Bill and Val Halamandaris co-founded the Caring Institute and its national Caring Awards program. Each year, the Caring Institute recognizes adults and children who are making a difference in society. I was honored to be recognized by the Caring Institute in 1991. I have been involved with their work ever since and recently had a wonderful experience connected to Give Kids the World.

Several years ago, a wish child named Kelly came to the Village. She was twelve-years old and suffering from leukemia. Kelly was in chemotherapy and wore a baseball hat to cover her bald head. The child asked for a meeting with me and spent the entire time asking me questions about fundraising. Kelly wanted to raise money for leukemia victims after she returned home. I found her to be a truly special, inspiring little girl.

Two years ago I was attending the annual Caring Institute awards banquet in Washington D.C. to honor that year's most caring people.

A woman came up and introduced herself to me. She was Kelly's mother. Kelly was in full remission after a bone marrow transplant from her brother and was among the honorees as one of the world's most caring young people. I was filled with such a sense of joy and gratitude. I invited Kelly to return to Give Kids the World, this time as a volunteer. She came back to the Village and worked for a month, inspiring everyone who met her, and providing hope to other wish children. Kelly is a beautiful, vibrant, caring young woman. From her adversity, she has built a life of giving.

* * * *

I never dreamed of seeing all the things that I have witnessed, of having the wonderful friends I have. It has been a great blessing. Once you reach a certain financial security, and if you're lucky enough to know when to stop, which most of us are not, you have to find something to do with your life that has meaning and will provide fulfillment.

I have found this work to be life-sustaining and spiritually more fulfilling than anything else I've ever done. Early in my life, I lost touch with my spiritual side, abandoning God, as I had felt abandoned. It took me a long time, but I have learned not to go through life embittered by painful experiences. I live on very precious borrowed time, and in order to use this time wisely, I must do my best to change today and not dwell on yesterday.

It is easy to have perfect vision when looking back in time, but I believe now that I survived my past because it is my destiny to bring our energy, talent and resources together to help children and families in need. For more than 27,000 special children and their families, your kindness and generosity has provided sustenance for years to come, a sustenance made from memories created in happiness as a family. By giving kids the world, we have helped rescue the families as well.

The Village exists as a tangible expression of love built to help create a better world for children in need. Supporters of Give Kids the World have created a monument to the values of caring, kindness and compassion.

I believe that there is a spiritual goodness, a power that exists. I do not know what it is or how to define it. I believe that a spark was lit inside my soul when I was a teenage boy, and that spark, call it compassion if you want to, has now grown into a fire that burns for Give Kids the World. From an evil, death-filled place to a good, life-affirming place. That is where God has brought me.

As Give Kids the World became the dominant force in my life, I've learned more about who I am spiritually. At this point in my life, I believe more strongly in God than I ever have before. Jerry Jampolsky and his wife Diane Cirincione helped me so much to find this part of myself. I will always be grateful to both of them.

I sometimes wonder why God has chosen us to do these things and not someone else. But then I look around and I see a whole world needing a helping hand out there. Caring is one emotion there can never be too much of, and as God will tell all who are willing to open their heart and listen, there is enough work for each and every one of us.

We are partners in the miracles and memories that Give Kids the World creates each day. We thrive because of the endless generosity of the corporate sponsors and volunteers which serve the children and their families. That is why corporate America extends its hands to us and why so many other individuals and volunteers participate in making Give Kids the World possible. To my friends and partners who make it possible to help these special children and their families, God bless you and I thank you from the bottom of my heart. We flourish because new people and companies join our work every day. Each of you who donates time, goods and services to the children, stands on every podium with me and shares equally in every accolade and word of recognition that I receive. Thank you for being there with me. I know that it is the sum of all the hands working together against the mountain of endless need that is making the difference.

237

CHAPTER 7

THE MIRACLE OF GIVE KIDS THE WORLD

Now join your hands, and with your hands, your hearts.
— William Shakespeare

here is an adage that Indian fathers use to teach fighting brothers about the futility of standing alone in this world. The father removes a single arrow from the quiver and breaks it easily across his knee. Then he takes two arrows and again shatters them easily. Next he takes a handful of arrows from the quiver and tries with all his strength to break them. He cannot. The lesson he hopes his sons will learn is that there is a power in unity that cannot exist in the singular.

Give Kids the World is stronger with each person and company that joins our cause. The back of any man can be broken. Any single life can be gone in the blinking of an eye. But when a noble idea is joined by the belief and faith of thousands, then that idea is elevated, like a prayer, to a place where it cannot be harmed.

Give Kids the World offers purity of purpose; strength against the oppression of the innocent; and hope for those who's hope has been pushed beyond their ability to endure. Give Kids the World is truly an organization that finds its greatest measure, not in terms of itself or any single individual, but by the sum of its parts. Collectively, those who dedicate their lives to the families in crisis, represent a unity of hope that cannot be shattered.

If a person stands on the shore of a lake and casts a stone as far away as he or she is able, that stone will set off a series of ripples in every direction. Some of these ripples, maybe even all, will not be seen by the hand that threw the stone.

No one can know the goodness that is set in motion by your participation and support of Give Kids the World. Every act of kindness, every service and dollar donated, sets off its own series of unseen ripples.

Imagine for a moment how many lives are actually affected by Give Kids the World. How many people are actually touched by a hand reaching out to help a child? Think of it. There have been more than 27,000 families that have visited Give Kids the World. They are from the four corners of the earth. Their communities helped them get here through more than 300 Wish Foundations and other supporting organizations. Take those 27,000 families and multiply the number by the people who know them, who want to help them in their own home towns. Multiply it by the number of grandparents, and uncles and aunts, and siblings; multiply it by the number of schools and bridge clubs and fire departments and civic groups that want to help the sick children of their community.

Then take that ever-escalating number and multiply it by the number of people who read of Give Kids the World in a magazine, or hear it mentioned on a television interview or on a radio program.

And then take this number and multiply it by the number of volunteers who serve Give Kids the World so unselfishly. And multiply that by the number of employees in all the corporations and companies that support Give Kids the World. And if there is still room in your calculator, multiply this number by the number of healthy children in America, in the world, and multiply that number by two thankful parents for every healthy child.

The progression of lives being affected at Give Kids the World extends around the planet earth. We are all our brother's keeper. Our children are, each of them, our greatest treasure. There is no turning away from this fact. When we feed the mouth of a hungry child, any child, we are feeding our own child. When we offer comfort to the infant afflicted with AIDS, we are comforting our own child.

For every man, woman and child in the world that has helped us, we thank you and wish you happiness, and health. It is our mission to serve the children. It is the right thing to do and we could not do it without your help.

The family of man, in all of our weakness and through all of our foibles, is at our omnipotent, unbreakable best when we stoop to lift up a child. More people lend their hands and hearts to Give Kids the World every day. The vision for the children is growing. Hope is growing. I promise each of you, that as long as there is a terminally ill child who dreams of meeting Mickey Mouse, Give Kids the World will be there. Our promise will remain constant: *No child in need will ever be turned away.*

CHAPTER 8

*All changes are more or less tinged with melancholy,
for what we are leaving behind is part of ourselves.*
—Amelia E. Barr

Timing plays such a big part in life, not just being in the right place at the right time, but knowing when to leave one venture and begin another. Intuition, luck, divine intervention, even sheer fatigue, can all play a role in timing.

In 1999, with construction at the Village complete, it was time to turn in the Sheriff's badge. There was no more land to buy and no place else to expand. The final phase of construction had required so much passion, it had become something of an obsession. When people said, "Gee, Henri, I'd like to donate to the Village, but I already support another charity," I got angry and took it personally. My behavior was becoming unreasonable. I was exhausted and my marriage to Pam Landwirth suffered because of it. I took an inventory of my life, searched my soul and realized at age 72, after 15 years at the Village and the creation of a $37-million endowment to ensure its future, my work there was essentially done. The diamond was cut.

****

The only way I could really leave the Village though was to leave Orlando entirely. I moved to Ponte Vedra Beach, Florida, a suburb of Jacksonville, where I could be closer to my daughter Lisa and two of my grandchildren, Sarah and Emily. Nevertheless, my heart will always be a part of the Village, where I still sit on the Board of the Executive Committee. Pam Landwirth is now the Village's extremely effective President and her tremendous love for the children and the families is displayed daily in her work there.

Still, I cannot wait to be asked back. Every year on my birthday, March 7, Pam organizes a Founder's Day Celebration, which in 2003 proved especially memorable. That year, at 10:00 a.m., an honor guard presented me with an American flag flown over the U.S. Embassy in Belgium. At the same time, on the floor of the U.S. Senate in Washington, D.C., Florida Senator Bill Nelson read a special proclamation into the Senate Record to honor my work with children.

****

Five weeks after I moved to Ponte Vedra Beach the realization set in: I was bored. As a person used to meetings and making deals, whose phone started to ring at 7:30 every morning with calls from business partners and banks and CEO's, I didn't know what to do with myself. Life had no meaning and I felt like I was waiting to die.

I called my daughter and asked her to go to Jacksonville's homeless shelter, the I.M. Sultzbacher Center, with me. I've always felt a bond with homeless people, because for a time near the end of World War II, I was homeless, too.

That's when the Nazi soldier smashed my head with his rifle, leaving a dramatic furrow in my skull you can still feel today. His actions triggered a set of events ending in my freedom, such as it was at the time. Once free, I walked around Germany and into Czechoslovakia for a month. I literally became a wandering Jew foraging for food from garbage cans and stealing apples from markets. I stole clothes to get out of the concentration camp uniform and I stole shoes to give my blistered feet some relief. I had no underwear or socks and carried only a tiny bag with nothing much in it really, but it made me look like a traveler. People probably knew I came from a concentration camp but they didn't bother me. The war was almost over and they didn't care. My legs were infected, the wound on my head was infected and I smelled terribly. I slept anywhere I could; I was half-crazed and never expected to survive. I was indeed homeless.

****

Little did I know what lay ahead when Lisa and I walked into the Sultzbacher Center for the Homeless for a meeting. We sat down with a dozen homeless people and a social worker and I told them I wanted to help. No one said anything so I asked a second time, "What can I do for you, what do you need?" Still no response. Finally, I told them I've been homeless myself so I know what it's like. With that the floodgates opened and almost everyone started talking at the same time. One man said, "We need to get out of here and find a place to live." I told him I really couldn't help with that. "What else do you need?" I asked. Another man

244

pulled down his pants, revealed his naked buttocks, and complained he had no underwear or socks. "Now this is something I can help you with," I said. In that instant, Dignity U Wear, a name Lisa later came up with, was born.

****

After that meeting, I started calling old corporate contacts made during my days at Give Kids the World. One initial call was to K-Mart, where I asked my friends if I could buy all the packages of underwear and socks that had been opened by customers in their stores. K-Mart said sure and before I knew it boxes of underwear and socks began to arrive daily on my doorstep. Friends helped bring some of the boxes to the Sultzbacher Center, which soon overflowed with new underwear and new socks in all sizes. We stored the rest of the boxes in a small, rented storage unit.

Some solicitation calls ended with more than underwear and socks. Sears offered to give us some surplus children's clothing if we promised not to resell it. We agreed and took the clothing, although we didn't have any recipients in mind yet. We figured there'd be a need for it in due time, and there was. Families who'd lost everything in a fire, poor children identified by their teachers at local schools, homeless families at soup kitchens, all became recipients of our clothing.

We soon found ourselves renting bigger and bigger storage units to hold everything. But, the storage units were located all over town and it soon became a time-consuming process to stop at one unit for one thing and another unit for something else. Just one year after our humble beginning at the Sultzbacher Center, Dignity U Wear needed a warehouse.

****

Just how we got our warehouse on Jacksonville's Myrtle Avenue is nothing short of a miracle. Owned by the Spence Family, a prominent name in local real estate, the warehouse sat empty for seven years. When Jeff Spence showed us around I realized why. The warehouse was formerly a giant freezer and it felt incredibly cold and uninviting inside. Jeff offered to sell it to us for $200,000. I looked around, shivered, and thought, "We can make this work." Jeff and I shook hands on the deal.

I had no idea how to pay for the warehouse until a letter arrived at my home several days later. The letter was from the MIKI Corporation in Japan offering to pay me $200,000 to speak to 8,000 of their top female associates in Hokkaido. That was more money than I ever expected to be paid for a speaking engagement and I knew right away the reason God sent me the opportunity was to pay for the warehouse for Dignity U Wear.

****

The MIKI Corporation, a big Japanese company specializing in health products like MIKI Prune Extract, wanted me to speak about philanthropy. It knew of my work with Give Kids the World through a Japanese television show called "Super Teachers," produced by NHK, Japan's public television network.

NHK selected me as a super teacher of philanthropy and produced a segment at the Village. Cameras followed 14 Orlando school children and me around for a week. I gave the children assignments, including one to go home and not eat for 24 hours so they could get an idea of what it's like to be hungry. Some of the children couldn't wait that long to eat, others went to bed early and slept through their hunger pangs, but a few learned a good lesson about food and taking it for granted.

The "Super Teacher" show on philanthropy was very well-received in Japan, where public giving is only now becoming part of the culture. When I spoke to the 8,000 MIKI associates, I explained why and how we started Give Kids the World. The women were amazed that Americans would build a village for sick children they didn't even know.

By the way, NHK is still eager to expand on the "Super Teacher" show on philanthropy and on a growing mood of public giving in Japan. It has translated this book, Gift of Life, into Japanese and a portion of each sale in Japan will return to Florida to help Dignity U Wear and Give Kids the World.

****

The speaking engagement in Japan was an exhilarating but exhausting experience. I went there with Linda Mixter my longtime administrative assistant and my very best friend, who was soon to become

Linda Landwirth, my sweet, adorable wife and partner in life. On our way home we stopped in Kauai, Hawaii for two days to see Herb Scheidel, a friend and philanthropist. I ended up staying six weeks and seeing Herb's holistic doctor who treated me for exhaustion. The doctor wanted me to stay in Kauai under his care for eight months, but I just couldn't. I had to return to the mainland for an important meeting with Wal-Mart for Give Kids the World.

****

After two months away, I returned from Japan and Hawaii to find Dignity U Wear in a shambles. The operation was not the way I wanted to see it and the financial status was not good at all. Night after night, I fought with myself as I seriously considered closing Dignity down. When I approached Linda about this possibility, she looked me in the eye and said, "Henri, you can't do that." She strongly urged me to take charge and try to do whatever was necessary to turn things around. If you don't, she said, thousands of people will not get the help they need to improve their lives.

I realized she was right and began a series of sweeping changes at Dignity U Wear. I changed systems, policies and personnel and hired Executive Director John Arrowsmith, a retired division president from Tree of Life, a health-food company based in St. Augustine. I utilized the services of an extremely committed public relations professional, Maria Coppola, Vice President at the McCormick Agency, who spreads the word about us at no cost. And I also knocked on the door of one of Dignity's oldest friends, Jacksonville-based retail giant Stein Mart.

****

From day one, Stein Mart has been a great friend to Dignity U Wear. Of course it helps that we're both in the clothing business and therefore a natural fit for each other, but I often wonder where Dignity would be today were it not for Stein Mart.

In the early days of Dignity U Wear, we spent a lot of time talking to vendors, explaining what we were all about and trying to get them to donate clothes. It was a time-consuming process that took us away from our main mission, which is giving new, properly sized clothes to people

247

who need them. So I asked for a meeting with Jay Stein, the Chairman of the Board of Stein Mart, a retail company with stores in 30 states. Not only did Jay agree to help Dignity get clothes, he also gave $100,000 to Give Kids the World.

Jay asked his buyers to call manufacturers and ask them to send us overruns, the sample clothing they cannot use, so we could give it to our clients. He simply picked up his telephone, called his Chief Merchandising Officer and asked him to put the word out to all the other Stein Mart buyers. Jay even offered to pay the bills if manufacturers wanted to charge us for those overruns.

The response from Stein Mart's vendors was incredible. We finally had what we needed most: a pipeline to manufacturers. Clothes started arriving daily at our warehouse. These days, we have more than 80 vendors with new ones like Levi-Strauss and Limited Brands signing on at this writing. But, it was that early support from Stein Mart that landed us some of our biggest corporate manufacturers like Cotton Couture, Silk Club, Izod, and Rafael. These companies, along with others we landed on our own like Sears, K.I.D.S., Universal, Disney, Fishman Tobin, Erin London and Venus Swimwear, all gave us new clothes. We in turn gave them to children and adults, often with life changing results.

****

One of the goals at Dignity was always to take our small, grassroots organization nationwide. Since we're based in Jacksonville, we work closely with many organizations there, including the local Jacksonville school system. But we really wanted to get Dignity into as many states as possible in order to expand our work and help more people in need.

So, I arranged a meeting with the person in charge of Stein Mart's community outreach programs, Julia Taylor, Director of Boutique and Agenda. She liked the idea of expanding our partnership and got me together with Jack Williams, Jr., Vice Chairman of the Board, Mike Fisher, President & CEO, Gwen Manto, Vice Chairman and Chief Merchandising Officer, Mike Ray, Senior Vice President, Store Operations and Hunt Hawkins, Senior Vice President, Human Resources. Together we all focused on ways to create a national partnership between Dignity U Wear and Stein Mart, an association we labeled "Partners for a Brand New Life."

Key to this partnership is the 20,000 associates and the 160 agenda consultants at Stein Mart's nearly 300 stores nationwide. The agenda consultants, along with the help of store associates, pick a charity in their town that meets certain criteria and could benefit from Dignity's services. For instance, one Stein Mart in Cincinnati chose a non-profit organization called Tender Mercies as its recipient. Tender Mercies owns and manages seven apartment buildings for homeless people with histories of chronic mental illness and provides supportive services to those residents.

By choosing local beneficiaries, the associates and agenda consultants feel a part of the decision making process, and become both cheerleaders and fundraisers for Dignity. The associates can see the results of their in-store fundraising at work right in their own community. They can see firsthand how lives are changed for the better with something as simple as new clothes.

Meanwhile, we at Dignity are able to expand our services and help people we've never helped before. In addition, Stein Mart associates become our eyes and ears all over the country. We can now be doubly sure the new clothes we're giving to people are going where they're needed and are not being resold. It's truly a win-win partnership.

****

Just how a large, publicly traded company like Stein Mart adopted a small non-profit like Dignity U Wear and made us their corporate charity, is a management lesson that should be used as a case study at Harvard Business School. In short, Stein Mart was careful not to force us onto their associates. Instead, the company came up with ways to create genuine interest and enthusiasm in the mission of Dignity U Wear. The results have been a winning partnership, not just for us, but for Stein Mart, too.

It all started in 2003, one day before the company's national Manager's Meeting in Orlando. That's when Stein Mart organized a focus group of ten managers representing all size stores. With Julia Taylor at the helm, the company introduced this focus group to myself, to Dignity, and to Give Kids the World. Julia said she wanted the managers to know about the Village from Day One because she wanted them to understand just how big Dignity could become with their commitment.

Julia also asked the managers to brainstorm workable strategies for rolling out Dignity to their associates back home, and eventually to their customers. The focus group came up with great ideas like Dignity Dollar Days where associates pay $10.00 for a Dignity/Stein Mart polo shirt. The money goes to Dignity and the associate earns the right to wear the shirt to work, along with either jeans or khakis, on that day. The next time Dignity Dollar Day comes around, the associate pays just $2.00 to wear the polo shirt again, along with his or her jeans or khakis. It's a simple but effective way to fundraise, because lets face it, everyone likes to wear jeans or khakis to work.

Another rollout idea from the focus group is called Dress Your Manager. Associates pay to dress their manager in something silly for the day. The manager can either wear the outfit at work all day or buy their way out. Still another idea is called a Dignity U Wear Shop Night. Select customers are invited to a Stein Mart store on a special evening, often a Sunday when the store would otherwise be closed. Those customers pay for the right to shop that evening only and enjoy gift baskets, giveaways, refreshments and a discount. Some of the focus group ideas are simple like fundraising through Christmas gift-wrapping; others are more complicated like inviting a local celebrity to a store to raffle off a personal item. All help raise money for Dignity U Wear.

There are even plans to publish a catalog, available online and in Stein Mart stores, to sell things like the Dignity/Stein Mart polo shirt, or a Dignity U Wear tote bag, coffee mug or umbrella, even this book you're reading. The hope is that eventually Stein Mart customers will help support Dignity too. In the end though, the key is that all these rollout and fundraising ideas are easily integrated into a store's existing structure without becoming too disruptive for customers or shareholders.

After the focus group meeting, Julia and key representatives from Stein Mart's Organizational Development and Training Department took the group's ideas and created something called a Partnership Pack, one for store managers and another for agenda consultants. The packs are actually big boxes containing the rollout ideas, a videotape explaining the mission and history of Dignity U Wear, a copy of Gift of Life, Dignity U Wear logo pins for each associate, and a handout with four pages of inspirational quotes on giving. Most importantly, there is also a Partnership Guide for managers and agenda consultants explaining exactly how to choose a charity recipient in their city. The Partnership Packs were sent to every manager and every agenda consultant in every Stein Mart store nationwide.

Managers and agenda consultants are free to use the rollout ideas in the Pack or come up with ideas of their own. For instance, one store manager in Portage, Michigan, near Kalamazoo, was so excited to receive her Partnership Pack and learn about Dignity U Wear she wasted no time rolling us out to her associates in her own creative way. She stopped at a thrift store on her way into work one morning and picked up an assortment of the cruddiest old clothes she could lay her hands on, tee shirts with stains, socks with holes and pants in impossible sizes. Then she gathered her associates in a meeting and handed each of them an article of thrift store clothing. "How do you feel about this gift I'm giving you?" she asked. There wasn't much reaction. Then, she handed each associate one article of new clothing. "How do you like this gift?" she asked. Of course everyone was much happier. "That's what Dignity U Wear is all about," she told the associates. "New clothes that help others help themselves."

****

When Stein Mart took us under its wing, we knew the partnership would be win-win, but no one realized just how beneficial it would be for Stein Mart. The Stein Mart associates, it turns out, had been eager for a "hands on" project. Dignity U Wear provided them with the opportunity to personally be involved in a program benefiting their community. Adopting Dignity U Wear's mission made Stein Mart associates even prouder of their positions and created stronger store teams.

****

As I often say, my children are a source of great pride for me, not just because of who they are, but also because of what they do. These days, Gary, Greg and Lisa are all in the charity world. It's something I never asked them or told them to do; it's something they just came by naturally. I've helped them get started through the Fanny Landwirth Foundation, which gives seed money to start-up foundations that will help children, but my participation ends there.

Gary started a foundation called A Gift For Teaching, which has many, many wonderful programs. At its core, A Gift For Teaching collects school supplies for teachers from unlikely sources. Gary may get boxes of old letterhead from a company that closed, or boxes of pencils from a company that changed its name. He gathers all these supplies together, and believe me, there are a lot of them. The supplies are amassed in a store called The Free Store, where teachers who work in disadvantaged schools can pick them up for free. Teachers say they love it because they no longer have to use their own money, often amounting to several hundred dollars, to buy things for needy students.

A Gift For Teaching also started a very popular and growing program called A Gift For Music. It teaches disadvantaged elementary and middle school children from some of Orlando's poorest neighborhoods how to play violins, violas and cellos. Many of these kids have never seen a stringed instrument when they start the program, but thanks to a generous grant from Disney, they get free instruments and group instruction from music education majors at the University of Central Florida. It's a wonderful sight to see these children play their instrument in a concert. You realize they've learned much more than just how to play a violin, viola or cello; they've learned discipline, teamwork and self-esteem.

A Gift For Teaching has yet another program called Bikes for Kids, where children in disadvantaged schools can earn a shiny, new bicycle as a reward for good behavior, good schoolwork and good attendance. If they earn 200 points in a semester, they will march across stage to receive a bike, with their family and friends cheering them on.

Greg is collaborating with Gary and has opened a foundation of his own called A Gift For Teaching Tampa Bay. He set-up his Free Store in a distribution park, with the store up front and a warehouse in the back to keep supplies handy. Greg says there's a great need to help teachers and students in Hillsborough County because it's the 11th largest school district in the nation. Just one year after opening, Greg distributed $300,000 in school supplies to 28 schools, 1,500 teachers and 15,000 students.

Greg has partnered with Publix Supermarkets, as well as local television and radio stations to help raise money and supplies for his foundation. Some of the fundraisers are unique. For instance, when listeners donated money to their local public radio station, some of that money was matched by a local labor union and went to A Gift For Teaching Tampa Bay. Greg says he really liked the idea of the community radio station helping the community Free Store. Above all, he likes improving education in Florida by helping students and teachers.

In addition to her duties as President of the Fanny Landwirth Foundation, Lisa is also busy with a foundation of her own. She, along with her cousin Lori, has started Art With a Heart For Children. With help from art students at the University of North Florida in Jacksonville, Lisa, Lori and the UNF students take turns pushing an art cart around the halls of Wolfson Children's Hospital in Jacksonville. They bring watercolors, pastels and paper to these children and help them paint and draw. Lisa and Lori are careful to say it's not art therapy. Rather, they're helping children improve their quality of life and relieve the boredom of a long hospital stay by creating art.

So, do I sound like a proud Papa? I hope so, because what could be better than knowing I have three children who will carry on the legacy of my charitable work.

****

In 2001 I did something I thought I'd never do again: I returned to Poland. I went back with my twin sister, Margot, my children, Linda, and a film crew from Hollywood that was making a movie about letting go of the past called "Borrowing Time." The film's accomplished director and assistant producer Robert Black, decided to make the film after we'd been introduced by mutual friends a year earlier.

The producer, David Haspel, spared no expense on this documentary. Robert and his crew followed me to Florida, North Carolina, Washington, D.C., Hawaii, and eventually The Czech Republic and Poland.

I thought I could do it, return to Auschwitz where my name is written in a big registry book, and return to other places, too, like our former apartment in what was then the Krakow Ghetto. A lot of my memory of that time is gone, replaced with a numbness that's become my way of coping. Robert wanted to see if I could free myself of the past by revisiting it and confronting the memories head on.

It didn't work. I still have the numbness. Margot and I are both forever haunted by our past, each in our own way.

The film also includes our work at Give Kids the World and shows

253

how that sunny Village is a reflection of the dark days of my childhood. It's been well-received at film festivals both here and abroad.

Two days after we wrapped shooting in Poland, I woke in the middle of the night in a hotel room in Rome to go to the bathroom. My entire body felt like it was going haywire. The room was spinning uncontrollably and I could not see. I was having a stroke. Luckily, Linda was with me and saved my life by getting me to a hospital where I made a full recovery. We'll never know if revisiting my past brought on the stroke, or if I was genetically predisposed to have a stroke at that point in time. I can tell you this though: I'll never go back to Poland again.

****

There are moments in life when many of us reflect on where we've been and how far we've come and shake our heads in amazement at the journey. For me, one of those moments came in 1997 at the University of Cincinnati when, thanks to John Glenn, I was awarded a Doctorate in Humane Letters for my work with children. As a kid who only attended school through the sixth grade, I never expected to attain such a high degree. I wore a cap and a gown and John introduced me at the graduation ceremony.

Another amazing moment came in 2003 when I was awarded The Ellis Island Medal of Honor. It's presented annually to a diverse group of citizens who've made outstanding professional and patriotic contributions to America. In 2003, there were more than one hundred of us, and we all gathered on Ellis Island for the ceremony. For me, the medal represented not just my contributions to my country, but the hope and freedom that America offers all refugees. During the ceremony, as I stood in the shadow of the Statue of Liberty, I thought of that poem called "Give Me Your Tired Your Poor." In the last line Lady Liberty says: "I lift my lamp beside the golden door." Indeed she does. I walked through that golden door some fifty years ago and it was the best thing I ever did. I'd like to thank you Lady Liberty. I never dreamed my 57 years on borrowed time would be so rewarding in this great country of ours that I love with all my heart!

Afterword

by Senator John Glenn

Civilization, that which sets us apart from animal-like, kill or be killed behavior, can sometimes have an exceptionally thin veneer, a facade which covers meaner and baser conduct than we would believe possible. Whatever we call it – mass murder, annihilation, the final solution, or genocide – words on paper cannot convey the suffering and tragedy that occur when the veneer is suddenly cut away, as it was during the Holocaust.

Historians, academicians and sociologists will continue to analyze the hows and whys of that time of terror. They will study the ethnic, religious and social pressures that were misguided into impassioned hatreds, resulting in millions of unnecessary deaths. We'd like to think that justice has been done, meted out, that all the perpetrators have received their due, but we know by the sheer number of participants that is not the case. A majority of the leaders have probably been dealt with. But it is a sobering thought to realize, that hands that turned on the gas valves in the extermination chambers and stoked the crematorium fires of hell with human cordwood, still live today.

The amazing and inspirational part of the Holocaust is not those who perpetrated the crimes, but those who endured, survived and rose to great accomplishments despite their circumstances.

This book is the story of one such remarkable person, Henri Landwirth.

As you have read this book, did you mentally put yourself in Henri's position? Did you wonder what you would do? Did you wonder what your reaction would have been if your family was split up at gunpoint, some never to be seen again? *Your* family, *your* mother and father or children, *your* aunts or uncles or friends? Could you come back from that? Many did not. But as you have seen, this book is a recounting of one man's tragedy breeding triumph, of a life begun in misery rising past the need for vengeance to a place filled with caring and unselfish love for others.

I have known Henri as one of my closest friends for almost 38 years. It was many years before he would talk, even to me, about some of his wartime experiences.

For a long time, I have urged him to do what he has started in this book. I hope there will be a sequel that expands on personal vignettes of what it was like day in, day out, on a personal basis, inside the concentration camps. I do not believe the story has been exhausted, in spite of movies and other books. Henri has just started it here.

Henri invited my wife Annie and me to accompany he and his sister on their first trip to the Holocaust Museum in Washington. It was a memorable experience. If I had taken a tape recorder along, I could almost do the sequel for him.

As we walked through the actual car brought to the museum from one of the old concentration camps, Margot and Henri talked softly, mostly to each other.

"Remember what it was like in the boxcars?"

"Remember what it meant to get a piece of bread?"

"Remember the hunger?"

Always references to hunger. Never a full meal, for years on end.

There was a story about a girl huddled in the corner of a crowded boxcar. It was night. She started singing softly. The guard's reaction was surprising. He stepped into the car and tossed the child part of a loaf of bread. A small touch of compassion in the midst of hell.

And again the hunger, memories of that particular suffering never too far away. There could be another meaningful book. I hope there will be.

No one is a prouder American than naturalized citizen, Henri Landwirth. He has little sympathy for the super critics of our nation. Many, many times through the years when something good happened to Henri, he has used one of his favorite expressions, "What a country!" I can't recount how many times he has said, "John, this couldn't happen to someone like me anywhere else in the world!"

He's right, but Henri is also a thankful, humble man. He believes it is everyone's responsibility to give something back to others. This compassion has led to Give Kids The World. This is not just another project. Give Kids The World is Henri's passion. He knew suffering in a childhood cut short, it is his mission to help other children and their families over the rough spots.

I think you will agree that this remarkable book provides a good pattern for all of us. Tragedy and adversity can be overcome. Success does not stand alone. It brings with it responsibility to give something back to others.

We all live in this great nation and on planet Earth together. At some point in our life, each and every one of us has needed a helping hand. I hope Henri's journey inspires each person who reads this book to look outward and to see how they can make a difference in the life of someone less fortunate.

Our lives are made better by reaching out to others. Henri Landwirth reaches out every day. He is making a difference at Give Kids The World.

So can we.

– Senator John Glenn
October, 1996

Sponsors

For it is in the giving that we receive.
−St. Francis of Assisi [1220]

Give Kids the World thankfully acknowledges its corporate participants

Albertsons
American Airlines and AMR Corporation
American Automobile Association
American Gladiators Orlando Live
AMC Theaters/Pleasure Island
Arabian Nights
Ariel's Restaurant at Disney Beach Club
Arnold Palmer Hospital for Children and Women
Ascent Entertainment, Incorporated
Big Time Amusements
Bell South Mobility
BluBlocker Corporation
Boatwright's Dining Hall at Disney's Dixie Landing Resort
Bonfamille's Cafe at Disney's Port Orleans
Boyle Engineering
Browning-Ferris Industries
*Budget Rent a Car Corporation
Busch Gardens Tampa
Canteen Corporation
Carlson Travel Group
Cascades Restaurant at Hyatt Grand Cypress Resort
Central Florida Hotel and Motel Association
Centex Rooney
Citrus World, Incorporated
Coca Cola
Concourse Steak House at Disney's Contemporary Resort
Continental Airlines
Cypress Gardens
Davidson Hotels
DCC Constructors, Inc.
De Efteling
Discovery Island
*Eastman Kodak Company

ECOLAB
Fishbones and Flager's Restaurants at Disney's Grand Floridian Resort
Florida Hospital
Florida Lumber and Building Material Dealers Association
Foundation for Hospice and Home Care
Friendlys Ice Cream Corporation
Gayfers Department Stores
Gayfers/Mercantile South
Gatorland
General Cinema
Green Meadows Farm
General Electric Company
Hard Rock Cafe
Hilton Inn Gateway
*Holiday Inn Worldwide
House+Med and Medi+Clinic
Hyatt Regency Grand Cypress
Hyatt Regency Orlando International Airport
Hyatt Regency Orlando
IBM
IDEAS, Inc.
International Association of Amusement Parks and Attractions
ITEC Productions
i. wanna distributors, inc.
JC Penney Portrait Studios
Jungle Jim's Restaurant
Jungleland
Kaleidoscope Magic
Kmart Corporation
Key W. Kool's
King Henry's Feast
Kraft Foods Inc./Oscar Mayer Division
Landscape Maintenance Association
Landscape Nursery
Lake Buena Vista Engineering
M&M/Mars Candies
M&R Sales and Services
*Mears Transportation Group

Medieval Times
Meeting Planners International
Middle Georgia Textiles and Furnishings Company
Mystery Fun House
National Speakers Association
National Uniform Service
The Nestle Company
Nickelodeon Studios
Northern Telecom, Inc.
Ohana's Restaurant at Disney's Polynesian Resort
Olivia's Cafe at Disney's Old Key West Resort
Orange Lake Country Club
*Orlando Entertains
Orlando Renaissance Resort
Pacino's Restaurant
 Panama Jack Resort Services & Sports
Panorama Press
Payroll One
The Peabody Orlando
Perkins Family Restaurant
Phillips Consumer Electronics Corporation
Pirate Island Golf
The Procter & Gamble Company
Publix Super Markets
Rank Leisure USA, Inc.
Red Lobster, Kissimmee
Rollpak
Russ Berrie and Company
*Sea World of Florida
Sheraton Lakeside
Sony Corporation of America
Sprint Corporation
Storyline Concepts, Incorporated
T.G.I Friday's, Kissimmee & Lake Buena Vista
Tony Roma's
Travelodge Hotel
Tiffany & Co.
Universal Studios Florida

Variety Clubs International-Textile Division
Vekoma
Verona Restaurant
Village Marketplace
Vistana Resort
Vista-United Telecommunications
*Walt Disney World Company
Walt Disney World Horticulture
WCPX Channel 6, a CBS Affiliate
Welbro Constructors, Inc.
*Wet 'n Wild
Wild Jack's Steaks and BBQ
WM. B. Dodson, Inc.
Wometco Food Services, Inc.
Yachtsman Steakhouse at Disney's Yacht Club Resort

(* Founders)

A C K N O W L E D G E M E N T S

The authors express their sincere gratitude to the more than one hundred people who allowed themselves to be interviewed for this book. Our special thanks to the wonderfully talented artists at Storyline Concepts, Inc. who created the cover painting. In addition, we gratefully acknowledge the editorial support provided by Ellen Kanner and the layout and design work of Art By Chris Design Studio.